Marriage and Sexuality in Islam

Bahram Gur and one of his wives seated under a blue cupola.
Bibliotèque Nationale, Paris

Marriage and Sexuality in Islam

A Translation of al-Ghazālī's Book on the Etiquette of Marriage from the *Iḥyā'*

Madelain Farah

UNIVERSITY OF UTAH PRESS — 1984 — SALT LAKE CITY, UTAH

Library of Congress Cataloging in Publication Data

Ghazzālī. 1058–1111.
Marriage and sexuality in Islam.

Translation of the twelfth book of the author's
Iḥyā' ᶜulūm al-dīn.
Bibliography: p.
Includes index.
1. Marriage–Religious aspects–Islam–Early works
to 1800. I. Farah, Madelain. II. Title.
HQ525.I8G5513 1984 297'.19783581 83-27365
ISBN 0-87480-231-8

To LEILA, who had to learn at a tender age
the world of books; and
To CAESAR, my intellectual beam

Contents

Preface

by
Madelain Farah

Al-Ghazālī's *Book on the Etiquette of Marriage (Kitāb Adāb al-Nikaḥ)* is the twelfth book of his larger work, *Iḥyā' 'Ulūm al-Dīn,* or *Revival of the Religious Sciences.* The *Iḥyā'* is a compendium of al-Ghazālī's whole system of thought comprising forty books divided into four categories: "Cultural Practices," "Social Customs," "The Causes of Perdition," and "The Means to Salvation." For each category there are ten books dealing with its subject. The *Iḥyā'* has been studied by Arabic, English, French, and German scholars. Until this work, *Marriage and Sexuality in Islam,* only twelve of the forty books have been translated: seven into English, one into French, and five into German.[1] A number of articles in various languages have also been written on this great work from the eleventh century.

The *Book on the Etiquette of Marriage* describes the facets and ramifications of marriage and sexual ethics within the institution of marriage, and within Islam, as visualized in al-Ghazālī's time. This includes a general description of marriage from the matrix of canon law, social customs and proprieties, with its foundation in religion. To spare the reader confusion, numerous other subjects touched upon in the work have been excluded for this translation. The book relies heavily on fiqh and hadith, and peruses Islamic moral and ethical codes of behavior, including Sufi viewpoints, the status of women, and marriage with all its ramifications: the marriage contract, sexual relations, childbirth, divorce, virginity, adultery, and so forth. The Islamic marital code as described by al-Ghazālī brings into focus the roles of man and woman that were practiced but which had not been totally delineated.

The physical format of the Arabic text presented problems in translating: There is little punctuation, sentences are lengthy and complicated, there are few titles, and even fewer subtitles. There are no explanatory notes. ᶜIrāqī, one of the great imams and Koranic scholars of the fourteenth century, added footnotes to the text, but only those pertaining to hadith. At times, he reiterated the transmittal as it was stated in the main text, thereby continuing the chain of authority. Because this chain is useful, in some instances I have translated *in toto* ᶜIrāqī's footnotes. In other instances, I have summarized the footnote to avoid redundancy or irrelevant information, especially where no basis can be found for the chain of authority or where the transmittal might be unreliable. Credit is given to ᶜIrāqī in the notes by placing his name after the hadith statements. Where possible, I have verified his research on hadith by tracing the quotation to its original sources and supplementing it with other traditions.

Koranic quotations have been documented, thus helping the reader trace them to the original text. I have used mainly Pickthall's 1954 translation of the Koran; where I found the translations by ᶜAlī or Arberry clearer, I have so indicated.

Further comments are included in the notes to aid the reader in understanding the text. A major problem arose in identifying or in giving biographical sketches for all the individuals al-Ghazālī mentions since, in many instances, he gives only one name—first, last, or "Abū" so-and-so—which made identification extremely difficult. Consequently, some names are unidentifiable and do not have explanatory notes.

Added titles and subtitles, to facilitate reading, are placed in brackets. Sentence divisions and punctuation are altered in the hope of aiding comprehension. The dates after personal names are given first in the Hijra year, followed by a slash and the Christian year.

Even though it meant duplication of material, I have quoted in the Introduction many passages from the translation to facilitate a discussion of al-Ghazālī and his work and to elucidate the subject under discussion.

The Library of Congress method of alphabetizing Arabic names in use in the Bibliography. The transliteration system adopted is similar to the one used by the Library of Congress: An apostrophe (') represents the glottal stop (hamzah) and (ᶜ) represents the voiced pharyngeal fricative (ayn); the definite article is represented by "al-." I have also used the popular spelling of "Koran" rather than "Qur'an." Authors' names and book titles are cited as they appear on the title pages, even though the transliteration system may vary. Anglicized Arabic terms such as hadith, alim, ulema, sunna, sura, and fiqh are used in their common spellings and are not italicized. A glossary of selected terms to which the reader can refer is Appendix B. The glossary mirrors, in general, existing standard definitions and is a synthesis of the works by Farah, Guillaume, Jabre, Lane, Ibn al-Nadīm, and Schacht.

Although there are many manuscripts and printed editions in Arabic of the *Iḥyā',* I have relied principally, but not exclusively, on the 1967 Ḥalabī edition, volume 2. It was collated with those printed by al-Tijārīyah (n.d.), and al-Azharīyah of 1884–85. Where major discrepancies arose in reference to wording, grammatical differences, and deletions in the three editions, the meaning that best completed the thought was incorporated in the text.

Notes include the author's last name, shortened title, and page(s) only. For a detailed entry, see the Bibliography at the end of the book.

The translation, with an introduction, of the *Book on the Etiquette of Marriage* was submitted as a doctoral dissertation at the University of Utah. My graduate study was made possible by a National Defense Foreign Language Grant at the University of Utah, as well as an American-Iranian Cultural Exchange Grant to the University of Tehran for one summer.

My special thanks to Dr. Khosrow Mostofi, Director of the Middle East Center, University of Utah, for grant recommendations and general support; to Dr. Zaki N. Abdel-Malek; and to Dr. Caesar E. Farah, who carefully compared the translation with the original. While fully acknowledging my indebtedness for the comments and criticism of these scholars, I take full responsibility for the English translation and for any defects therein.

I wish to acknowledge use of the facilities at the University of Tehran, the Majlis Library, the University of Minnesota, Portland State University, and the Aziz S. Atiya Arabic Collection of the University of Utah. My thanks and appreciation to their staffs for their assistance and kindnesses extended to me over the years. Special thanks and gratitude go to my daughter, Leila, my mother, family and friends for their support and continuous encouragement.

PART I

Introduction

By

Madelain Farah

There is nothing more technical or sensitive to discuss than sexual matters. In Islam, this is certainly the case, for the subject of sexual intimacies is rarely discussed since this impinges upon personal privacy. Very few authors have had the courage to write about this subject before or after Abū Ḥāmid al-Ghazālī. He is one of those few authors who have shed light on some of these issues and who have delineated at length the concepts of sexuality within the precepts of orthodox Islam. In his *Book on the Etiquette of Marriage* and also in his twenty-third book, *Book on the Evils of the Two Appetites: The Stomach's and the Genitals'*, the second part of which deals with carnal lust, al-Ghazālī had the courage to expound on such a delicate subject. Through his voluminous works, he stressed the Aristotelian mean in all appetites. These works became the Masters and Johnson of the Islamic world with one difference: They are not based on society's mercurial values, but on the more permanent standards of religious ethics.

Although the importance of the Middle East in the world's economic and political affairs has increased dramatically in the last two decades, the information and analytical data relevant to social and cultural change are much less abundant. This transitional period is characterized by values, attitudes and life styles changing gradually in contrast to the rapid transformation of technological and economical change. The social changes reflect an attempt to cope with and adapt to the powerful influence of industrialization and urbanization. However, social and cultural values imported from the West through communications media and Western-style education gnaw at the fiber of Islamic institutions, most importantly that of marriage, with unknown social and psychological effects. Not until this increase of Western influence and feminist movements during the last two decades did pressure build for a better understanding of sexuality in men and women within the matrix of Islam. Muslim authors have started to address the social and cultural issues, as well as the changes associated with human sexuality. However, they discuss only those subjects that have been discussed since early Islam: the rights of women and of men, divorce, dowry, choosing a mate, and so forth—the same issues that al-Ghazālī addressed in the eleventh century—but not sexuality. Few modern authors explain the biological functions of the body and still fewer include illustrative material. Moreover, they rely heavily on English and French sources. There are, nevertheless, a few isolated studies on fertility among Muslim women, birth control and population growth. On the other hand, there is much apologetic literature discussing the status and role of a true Muslim woman. This literature has increased to counter stereotypes and fantasies held about Arab women due to Hollywood's version of the harem and veil and its interpretation of Omar Khayyam's themes of wine, women and song.

Furthermore, the role of the Muslim wife has changed little over the centuries. Arabic lore that "the woman rocks the cradle with her left hand and her kingdom with her right" still applies. She is the mistress within her home as man is master in the outer domain. Stress on the honor of the male and purity of the female renders man vulnerable not only through his wife, but through his mother, daughter, sister and female relatives. This lore is as relevant today as it was in ancient Arabia in upholding the values and virtues of the members of the society within the context of Islam.

The main approach to the role of women in Islam focuses basically on their status within the institutions of family and marriage. Historically, Muslim theologians and fundamentalists showed considerable interest in spelling out the details meticulously. From them we learn that the role of Muslim women centers around childbearing and child rearing, educating children and inculcating them with Muslim precepts. These, we observe, are rooted in the Koran, traditions (hadith), and the practice (sunna) of the Prophet as revealed, carefully defined, and shaped eventually into Fundamental Law of Islam (Shari^{c}a) which since then has been expounded in jurisprudence (fiqh).

Law in Islam is not a systematic code, but rather a living, growing organism. It is the result of a continuous process of development during its fourteen centuries of existence. Since every utterance and act of the Prophet is purported to be divinely inspired, the socioreligious implication is one of permanence and finality, thereby setting limits to notions of progress and reform. These laws become inviolable and immutable. Consequently, there is a widespread dissatisfaction today with this authoritative socioreligious system established in the seventh century. For it ignores the potential power of its own elements and the need for change. Change in degree rather than in kind is imminent because the various Muslim countries accept the authority of Islam to determine the bounds of social progress. It is imperative to reconcile the old with the new way of life, to fuse the priceless values of the old heritage with the rich possibilities of the new freedoms. In the final analysis, all social reforms and advances must be carefully justified on grounds of being in harmony with the letter and spirit of the Koran. Therein lies the key!

Al-Ghazālī's book is as relevant today as it was in the eleventh century for it synthesizes preexisting views. Like no other author or theologian, al-Ghazālī restated and summarized the prevailing views from the advent of Islam up to his time. He also delineated Islamic perception of marriage and sexuality, which still stands as a basis for an important part of the Muslim's way of life. He addressed himself in depth to those issues which twentieth-century authors have generally reiterated while juxtaposing Western views with their interpretations. The question regarding the lack of information could be attributable either to issues considered sensitive or to the fact that modern Muslim authors have not been able to reconcile the forces without with those within themselves that inhibit them from applying the teachings of Islam to twentieth-century notions of sexuality and to social research dealing with changing values and mores. Therefore, the main authority on marriage and especially on sexuality in the twentieth century is the same as that of the eleventh century, namely, al-Ghazālī, a towering intellectual giant who dared to be different and bend others to his intellectual will. He was and is still widely read and cited as an unquestioned authority on Muslim sexuality. As poignantly stated by Field, "Islam has never outgrown him, has never fully understood him. In the renaissance of Islam which is now rising to view, his time will come, and the new life will proceed from a renewal study of his works."[1]

AL-GHAZĀLĪ: THE MAN

It is essential to sketch here the life of al-Ghazālī in order to understand fully the dimensions of this giant in Arabic literature and his role in synthesizing the divergent views in Islam. His full name was Abū Ḥāmid Muḥammad Ibn Muḥammad al-Ṭūsī al-Shāfiᶜī al-Ghazālī. He was commonly known as "al-Ghazālī," "al-Ghazzālī" and "Algazel." The name "al-Ghazzālī" is derived either from the profession of his father, who was a poor spinner and vendor of wool (*ghazzāl*), or from an uncle or granduncle, who was distinguished as a scholar and was called simply "al-Ghazālī." He also had a brother named Aḥmad, who was renowned as a Sufi, a Muslim mystic. He is referred to by his *kunya* (father's name) of Abū Ḥāmid, although his own name was Muḥammad.[2]

Al-Ghazālī is described as an outstanding religious reformer, theologian, original thinker, jurist, and mystic, and as "the second Shāfiᶜī" by Imām Muḥammad b. Yaḥya. He was born in Ṭūs in 450/1058. Educated at Nishapur, he ceased accepting religious dogma or truth on authority (*taqlīd*) at a young age. He was a student of Imām al-Ḥaramayn al-Juwayni, who was a leader of the Ashᶜarite or accepted school of thought, and of Abū al-Maᶜāli ᶜAbd al-Mālik, who was the leading Shafiᶜite theologian of the day. Al-Ghazālī studied science, philosophy, logic, dialectics, canon law, theology, and the doctrines and practices of the Sufis.

About 473/1080, al-Ghazālī entered the Niẓāmīyah school at Nishapur which had been entrusted by Niẓām al-Mulk, the great Seljuq vizier, to the direction of al-Juwayni. He served for a while in the court of Niẓām al-Mulk, where a retinue of canonists and theologians had been formed. Later, in 484/1091, he was appointed to teach in the Niẓāmīyah school of Baghdad. During this time, he became a skeptic, not only as to the certainty of knowledge, but also as to religion. When intellectualism failed him, he turned to Sufism. In the throes of conversion, however, he suffered a spiritual crisis and a nervous breakdown in 488/1095.[3] He fled from Baghdad as an itinerant dervish, giving himself to the ascetic and contemplative life in order to seek inner peace and certainty of mind. He spent two years in strict retirement in Syria, then went to Jerusalem, and finally made a pilgrimage to Mecca at the end of 490/1097. His monumental *Iḥyā'* and other works, such as the *Jawāhir al-Qur'ān* and *Kimiyā' al-Saᶜādah,* were written during the period of seclusion, 488/1096 to 499/1106. He began writing the *Iḥyā'* in Jerusalem and finished it in Damascus. This period was followed by nine years of retreat in different places, from which he returned now and then to his family and the world.

In 499/1106, he taught at the Niẓāmīyah school at Nishapur, but was so drawn to the silent and contemplative life that he returned to Ṭūs, where he lived in retirement with some personal disciples. There he was in charge of a school (*madrasah*) and a Sufi monastery (*khānaqah*), and there he died on the fourteenth of Jumada II, 505/December 19, 1111.

It was his compendium, *Iḥyā',* that immortalized his name and earned for him the illustrious title of Imām Ḥujjat al-Islām (*Imām,* the Proof of Islam),[4] and caused Muslims to place him on the level of the four great imams or orthodox caliphs: Abū Bakr, ᶜUmar, ᶜUthmān and ᶜAlī.

MARRIAGE AND SEXUALITY IN PRE-ISLAMIC ARABIA

It is important to understand the pre-Islamic society in order to better comprehend the relevancies of change made by Muhammad and the synthesis of all these views by al-Ghazālī. Prior to Islam, the bedouin and the sedentary population were influenced by the Arabian tribal system. This system had no legal protection for the individual outside his tribe. The tribe was responsible for the acts of its members that resulted in blood feuds. Women were also under the protection of their tribe.

The bedouin's character was greatly influenced by nature, specifically the desert, which left an indelible mark of survivorship. The climate was inhospitable and water scarce, and hardship dominated the means for obtaining food. For millennia, the bedouin had roamed the desert in search of water and pasturage. Thus the spirit of independence and freedom was reinforced in the nomad. He was a free gentleman of blood and lineage, a warrior and a knight-errant, the hero of his own romances, the desert song-master. He had developed characteristics stemming from what his environment had imposed upon him: hospitality, one of his great virtues, to counteract his inhospitable surrounding; courage and bravery to cope with physical hardships of all kinds; and pride in his lineage, that is, the tribe. The latter conjured up a fierce pride that decreed an attack on one as an attack on the whole. The result was the Arab's master passion, the vendetta. Consequently, the Arabian sands were drenched with blood by tribal wars and strife. Outside of war, life consisted mainly of his tent, camels, horses, the hunt for gazelle, and above all, his women.

Women—along with wine, war, and the virtues of hospitality—fortitude and manliness played a central role in the literature of pre-Islamic Arabia's poets. The bedouin's duties, pastimes and joys are immortalized by the song-master Ṭarafa's *Muᶜallaqa:*

> Canst thou make me immortal, O thou that blamest me so
> For haunting the battle and loving the pleasures that fly?
> If thou hast not the power to ward me from Death, let me go
> To meet him and scatter the wealth in my hand, ere I die.
>
> Save only for three things in which noble youth take delight,
> I care not how soon rises o'er me the coronach loud:
> Wine that foams when the water is poured on it, ruddy, not bright,
> Dark wine that I quaff stol'n away from the cavilling crowd;
>
> And then my fierce charge to the rescue on back of a mare
> Wide-stepping as wolf I have startled where thirsty he cowers;

And third, the day-long with a lass in her tent of goat's hair
To hear the wild rain and beguile of the slowness the hours.[5]

The theme in the verses was basically the same: a woman loved, then lost and finally mourned with the most passionate longing. This form of expression exhibited much interdependence. Man and woman drew closer because of the immense isolation imposed by the desert. The bedouin poets romanticized and idealized women in general and spoke of the unobtainable, the chaste and the unrequited loves. The poetry and proverbs idealized the Arab woman as an embodiment of modesty, fortitude, virtue and beauty. Men honored and respected her.

Conversely, women were devoted to their men. In times of warfare, the women went along on a campaign to motivate the men. Mounted on camels, they would sing and shout to them during combat. It is evident from the story of Imru' al-Qays that men must have valued more than a woman's physical attributes. Imru' al-Qays was called the Don Juan of pre-Islamic society, being handsome and witty and of noble Arab blood. When he disgraced the family with too much dalliance and neglect of responsibilities, he was expelled by his father from the family's territory. The banished youth took a vow not to marry until he found a woman who could resolve a riddle he had devised, namely, "What are two and four and eight?" The answer generally given was "fourteen." On his journeys, he would repeatedly ask this question, but to no avail. While traveling on a road in Nejd, he encountered a *shaykh* and his daughter. The latter retorted when the riddle was posed: "The two breasts of a woman, the four milking-teats of a she-camel, and the eight dugs of a she-wolf." She became his wife.

On the other hand, a bleak picture of the status of a pre-Islamic woman was given: She was, in youth, the goods and chattel of her father; after marriage, she belonged to her husband and after his death, she was appropriated as mere property by the husband's heirs if so desired. Her status is further portrayed by general promiscuity, loose unions and divorce, especially in the cities. Female infanticide (*wa'd*) was a common practice everywhere. This portrayal was perhaps overdrawn to establish a case for criticizing the social structure. In reality, the relations of the sexes were characterized not so much by polygamy, which certainly existed, as by the frequency of divorce. The loose unions and promiscuity made it difficult to draw a line between marriage and prostitution, slavery and concubinage.

As stated, the desert dweller, the bedouin, who inhabited most of Arabia, was not like the city dweller. The bedouin was basically monotheistic, while idolatry reigned in the cities; he lacked the fears of the supernatural, while the dweller in houses trembled at the thought of darkness and the jinns. The bedouin was accustomed to darkness since he slept during the day to escape the sweltering heat of the desert. The bedouin had notably higher moral standards than his neighboring city dwellers, for his rule of conduct was based on personal and tribal honor. The virtues he admired were courage, generosity, hospitality, protection of the weak, and self-sacrifice for the tribe's sake in peacetime.

Bedouin women were essentially freeborn, enjoying the right of choice before marriage and of departure from marriage if dissatisfied. They were not slaves or chattels—as were contemporary European women. They were venerated by bedouin men as indicated in the poetry of the bedouin song-master and enjoyed a better social position than did their European counterparts. Since women accompanied their men in battle, one has to conclude that they were as courageous as the men. Consequently, a whole scheme of chivalry emerged from the bedouin's way of life, their respect and idealization of women, and their gallantry and courage towards women and warfare, which later became imitated and developed more intensively in Europe.

With the advent of Islam, the Prophet was inspired by the ideals of the existing tribes to improve social conditions without violating the prevailing concept of masculine superiority. His teachings embodied reforms of existing social practices and injunctions for the abolition of infanticide, for protection of widows and orphans, and for the limitation of polygamy. The marriage contract included rights and obligations for both husband and wife, granted a marriage dowry to the woman, and contained inheritance rights for the woman. Pleasure-loving desert song-masters who sang the praises of lawless love and wine were out of harmony with the austere thoughts of Islam.

Marriage was and today remains not only a fulfillment of carnal desires and passions, but as stated in the Koran (2:187): "They (your wives) are an apparel for you and you are an apparel for them." This depicts mutual protection, mutual comfort, mutual support, as well as mutual service and companionship. The stress is not on the erotic factors in terms of sexual release, but on the spiritual union of two into one flesh. The ties binding the couple are the home, the children, the social and economic factors. Jāḥiẓ eloquently described woman's status in marriage when he wrote, "Women are superior to men in certain respects: It is they that are asked in marriage, desired, loved and courted, and they that inspire self-sacrifice and require protection."[6] Change with the advent of Islam regarding the views of marriage and sexuality was inevitable because social structure and family patterns shifted and the insularity of the bedouin was gone.

THE MUSLIM CONCEPT OF MARRIAGE

Marriage in Islam is regarded as a contract because it is based on the mutual consent of both man and woman and because it is dissoluble when the rights and duties, which are fixed by law, are not met. In contrast, marriage in Christianity is generally regarded as a sacrament and indissoluble. Some scholars assert that an Islamic marriage is also like a sacrament insofar that in this world it is an "act of worship," according to al-Ghazālī, for it preserves mankind from going astray. It is an institution ordained for the protection of society in order that human beings may guard themselves against promiscuity and unchastity. The aim of the marriage institution is procreation. This is generally the argument given by al-Ghazālī, although he does not liken it to the Christian "sacrament."

One cannot say that marriage is *merely* a contract in Islam since the Koran defines its premises and the Prophet Muhammad laid its foundation for the true believer. Here the foundation is delineated in the revealed *Surat al-Nisā'* in which polygamy was sanctioned and other important ordinances were introduced, making provision for the maintenance and protection of women and children. This important ordinance in Islam limits polygamy: "And if you fear that you cannot act equitably toward orphans, then marry such women as seem good to you, two, three, or four, but if you fear you will not do justice (between them) then marry only one or what your right hand possesses" (Kor. 4:3). With this sura, a precedent for community obligations toward widows and children was set. However, the injunction of dealing "justly and equitably with all" promotes monogamy. The term the Prophet uses is *ᶜadl,* which implies not only equality of treatment in the matter of basic needs such as food and clothing, but equality in affection and esteem as well.

Polygamy reigned in pre-Islamic Arabia; Muhammad tolerated it, but at the same time attempted to set limitations on it, allowing only four wives protected by an equitable clause in the contract which enjoined monogamy. He regulated it by saying that a man may marry more than one woman if he is able to assure the rights of each wife and treat all of them with equal consideration. Before another wife can be taken, permission must be sought from the existing wife. According to hadith literature, if the wife is chronically ill or not able to produce children or if extreme hardships prevail, the husband is permitted to take another. This latter qualifier opens the door for sanctioning *mutᶜah,* or a temporary marriage, which is still practiced today especially among the Shiᶜites.[7]

Islam introduced the first legislation which proclaimed the principle that a woman has as many rights as obligations in marriage following a just measure as embodied in Islamic law. This is generally accepted by the four juridical schools which state that marriage may be either valid (*ṣaḥīḥ*), void (*bāṭil*), or irregular (*fāsid*). A valid marriage is one that conforms in all respects to the legal requirements. A marriage is valid when there is a matrimonial guardian, a dowry (*mahr*) is established, and two irreproachable witnesses are present at the marriage.

In a valid marriage, the rights and duties of both husband and wife are as follows:

1. Sexual intercourse becomes lawful and children born of the union are legitimate.

2. The wife becomes entitled to her dowry in accordance with the stipulations of the contract.

3. The wife becomes entitled to maintenance.

4. The husband is entitled to restrain the wife's movements in a reasonable manner and to exercise marital authority.

5. Mutual rights of inheritance are established.

6. *ᶜIddah* (prescribed waiting period)[8] is observed upon the death of the husband or upon dissolution of the marriage.

7. Prenuptial agreements and stipulations are to be enforced.

8. A woman cannot be forced to change the juridical rite to which she belongs unless she so chooses in order to expedite the marriage to a man who belongs to another rite.

9. Neither party acquires an interest in the property of the other by reason of marriage.

In void and irregular marriages, there are prohibitions affecting both parties. Generally, the prohibitions are either perpetual or temporary. A void marriage is one that has the semblance of marriage but is forbidden. This pertains to union with blood relatives, affinity, and fosterage, marriage with the wife of another, and remarriage with a divorced wife when the legal bar of the prescribed waiting period still exists. Such illegal unions result in no mutual rights and obligations between the parties, and no right of dowry; the death of one of the parties does not entitle the other to inheritance. The prohibitions of consanguinity are based on the Koran (4:23): "Ye are forbidden to marry your mothers, and your daughters, and your sisters and your aunts, both on the father's and the mother's side, and your brother's daughters and your sister's daughters."

An irregular marriage, according to al-Ghazālī, stems from one of the following irregularities: a marriage without witnesses; marrying a woman undergoing *ᶜiddah;* marrying a woman of different religion—not applicable to a *kitābīyah,* that is, follower of a Scripture—marrying two sisters simultaneously, and a marriage with a fifth wife.

In regard to marrying a nonfreed person, the Islamic marital code asserts certain stipulations: A woman cannot marry a slave unless she emancipates him first and he consents to the union; while a man may marry a slave provided that he is unmarried and does not already possess a woman slave as his concubine, that he is too poor to afford a dowry for a free woman, and that he is exposed to the danger of unchastity if he remains unmarried.

Nikāḥ is the legal term for marriage, the literal meaning of the word being sexual intercourse. The legal meaning is given by the jurists as an agreement resulting in the lawful enjoyment of a woman (*mulk al-mutᶜah*). *Mutᶜah* means enjoyment, while *mulk* connotes either (a) an exclusive relationship, that is, a devoted relationship between the wife and the husband—an interpretation which has been ascribed to al-Shāfiᶜī—or (b) ownership. The general interpretation is "ownership of the right of enjoyment of the woman."[9] As mentioned earlier, *mutᶜah* is also a temporary marriage for a fixed period with a certain reward to be paid the woman. This practice was fairly common in Arabia, both before and at the time of the Prophet. Although the Prophet first permitted temporary marriages, later he forbade them.[10] Although the Koran sanctions and regulates temporary marriage (4:24), it is forbidden by all sunni Islamic juridical schools, but not by the Shiᶜites. The Shiᶜi argument for temporary marriage rests on the Koranic decree of 4:24 in that Ibn ᶜAbbās and other "readers" said this verse should be read: "and insofar as you have derived pleasure from these women *for a stipulated time,* give them their rewards as agreed upon." Consequently, the Shiᶜi commentators insist that this verse is a sufficiently explicit recognition of the institution of temporary marriage and that it would require more than a possible tradition or the opinion of the caliph, ᶜUmar, to annul it.

An important stipulation of the marriage contract is the dowry or *mahr.* It is an antenuptial settlement of a sum of money or other property to which the woman becomes entitled by marriage. In pre-Islamic times it was given to the girl's guardian, but Muhammad stipulated that it go to the woman. The dowry is stipulated in the contract of marriage, and if the contract does not indicate the amount or states that there shall be none, the woman is still entitled to the proper and customary dowry depending upon the birth, rank, wealth and accomplishments of the bride.[11]

The dowry may be payable immediately, on dissolution of the marriage by the death of the husband or by divorce, or the contract may stipulate a combination of the two.

Through his teachings, Muhammad upheld the authority of the husband over the wife, laying down strict rules with regard to the manner in which wives, children and orphans were to be provided for and treated. Through his revelations, especially in *Sūrat al-Nisā'*, Muhammad placed the burden of provisioning and caring for the family on the man, instead of on the woman and her family, as had been the case in pre-Islamic times. Thus, matrilineal institutions gave way to patrilineal ones in the society in which a new set of codes for moral and ethical relationships between husband and wife, parents and children altered the existing views regarding male and female offspring. Far greater emphasis was placed on codes of moral and ethical obligations rather than on the interrelationships that had existed in pre-Islamic times between a man and his tribe. Furthermore, honor and virtue in a woman were now maintained by the husband rather than by tribe.

Contrary to the ill-defined marital practices in pre-Islamic times, the Prophet's teachings regarding marriage were explicit. He sought to replace these ill-defined practices, which provided no protection for the woman and no legitimacy of paternity for the children, with a well-defined legal institution. According to al-Ghazālī's Introduction, the Prophet "glorified the matter of lineage, ascribed to it great importance, and forbade on its account illegitimacy and strongly denounced it through restrictions and reprimands." The institution of marriage was centered around the production of children and the caring for, protecting and providing for wives and children. Hence, procreation rather than sensual pleasure was the prime factor in marriage.

An important precept for the validation of the contract, as laid down by the Prophet, was consent of the woman for such a union whether she was a virgin or previously married (*thayyib*)[12] even if it was consent implied by silence. Abū Hurayrah narrated the Prophet's teaching that a matron should be given in marriage only after consulting her, and a virgin after getting her permission. Since the virgin was usually shy, her silence indicated her permission. However, if the father gave her in marriage in spite of her objection, such a marriage was invalid. In the event of a guardianship, the consent of the guardian was necessary. Each party was encouraged to reflect before giving his or her consent and to look at the other for qualities such as morality, piety, honesty and virtue, which were, and still are, very important for a happy conjugal life.

Marrying a virgin was stressed as a principal factor in attaining a happy conjugal life. Consequently, there is much hadith literature on this subject for chastity was considered a virtue, and a premium was placed on virginity. Of the Prophet's twelve wives,[13] only ᶜĀ'ishah was a virgin at the time of their marriage. The Prophet married her when she was six years old and consummated the marriage when she was nine. His attachment to her was evident: When he was dying, even though he had three other wives, he kept asking as to when was ᶜĀ'ishah's "turn." He died in her arms. The hadith regarding virginity was transmitted by ᶜĀ'ishah in an analogy: "[I asked,] 'Suppose you landed in a valley where there is a tree of which something has been eaten and then you found trees of which nothing had been eaten, of which tree would you let your camel graze?' He [the Prophet] said, 'of the one of which nothing has been eaten before.' "[14]

Al-Ghazālī summarized the arguments for monogamy and stressed the advantages of marrying a virgin: "It engenders a greater measure of his love for her, as it is a man's nature to be somewhat repelled by a woman who has been touched by another husband. . . . The surest love is that which is engendered with the first loved one." The argument he set forth for marrying a virgin was that it will draw the couple closer, since it would be the woman's first intimate contact and she would not have had another with whom to compare her husband. She would not be able to compare his characteristics or virtues to another. As for the man, he further stated that certain natures find it quite repulsive to touch a woman who had belonged to another. The ultimate aim in marrying a virgin was to influence favorably the conjugal attachment.

Adultery

One would expect that adultery might be discussed in a book on marriage. This is not the case in al-Ghazālī's *Book on the Etiquette of Marriage* although he approaches the subject indirectly under the headings of "Jealousy" and "Disadvantages of Marriage." As pertains to jealousy, al-Ghazālī restates the hadith regarding "unjustifiable jealousy," when there is no motive for suspicion, since certain types of suspicion are considered sinful. The other point he stresses is that of fornication by the eye, that is, looking lustfully at a woman, which can lead to an abomination (*fāḥishah*). He used the term *fāḥishah* frequently when implying fornication, or tendencies leading to adultery, or commission of a sin as such. Here al-Ghazālī stresses the Prophet's sunna, "Every eye is an adulterer."[15]

Since al-Ghazālī follows the line of orthodox Islam, he upholds the main doctrine of Islamic law, that of *al-walad lil-firāsh* —the child belongs to the bed in which he is conceived. This doctrine corresponds to the Roman maxim of *pater est quem nuptiae demonstrant*; it strengthens the code of chastity while adultery "creates an impediment to marriage," a concept derived from the canon law of the Eastern churches.[16] This concept is reinforced in the Koran (17:32 [ᶜAlī]): "And come not near unto adultery, surely it is a foul and an evil way."

There is much hadith literature stating that adultery is punishable by death by stoning,[17] which is derived from Jewish law. This penalty, however, is not indicated in the Koran, which sets flagellation only as punishment for adultery: "flog each one of them with a hundred stripes—and let a party of the believers witness their punishment" (24:2 [ᶜAlī]). On the other hand, a slave woman suffers half the punishment by the decree in the Koran (4:25): "A slave woman should suffer half the punishment for adultery which was allotted to the freed woman." The term first used in the Koran regarding an adulteress is *al-zāniyah* (17:32). However, in another sura, it is stated, "turn them not out of their houses, nor should they *themselves* leave unless they commit an act which is manifestly foul (*fāḥishah*) (65:1 [ᶜAlī]).

The Koran stipulates punishment for unjust accusation stemming from jealousy, suspicion or other causes by enjoining,

"And those who calumniate chaste women but bring not four witnesses, flog them with eighty stripes, and never admit their evidence thereafter, and it is they that are the transgressors" (24:4 [ᶜAlī]). In bringing forth charges of adultery, the man can testify by swearing in the name of Allah as decreed in the Koran (24:6): "As for those who accuse their wives but have not witnesses except themselves; let the testimony of one of them be four testimonies (swearing) by Allah that he is of those who speak the truth." However, unless there is clear evidence of adultery attested by four witnesses whose testimony should not differ or appear doubtful, the slanderer himself is punished for defaming the wife unless he can effectively prove his allegation. Such punishment then acts as a deterrent against slander. If there is no proof for accusations, the legal procedure for divorce can then be initiated by either party through *liᶜān* (mutual imprecation), whereby the partners allege infidelity without witnesses. On the other hand, the husband may slay his wife, without adjudication, if he finds her in the act with her lover. It is further decreed, "The adulterer shall not marry save an adulteress or an idolatress, and the adulteress none shall marry save an adulterer or an idolater. All that is forbidden unto believers" (Kor. 24:3).

Divorce

The relationship of the sexes in pre-Islamic society was characterized by loose unions, promiscuity and frequent divorce, which made it difficult to draw a line between marriage and legalized prostitution. The statement of divorce was simply pronounced three times and was irrevocable. Remarriage between the parties required the wife to go through a temporary marriage (*mutᶜah*) with another man who divorced her after having sexual intercourse with her. This practice was called *ḥalālah,* literally, making a thing (that is, the wife) lawful. The temporary husband was referred to as *muḥallil* (literally meaning "one who unties"). Without this process, it was not lawful for the divorced pair to return to marital relations.

It was lawful in pre-Islamic society for divorced and widowed women to remarry immediately without any regard to their physical condition. The prevalence of divorce and immediate remarriage "led to many cases of contested paternity in pre-Islamic Arab society and even during the first century of Islam."[18] Contested paternity was checked by the decree in the Koran of a legally prescribed waiting period for divorced and widowed women. It was not unlawful, however, for a man to propose marriage to a woman during this period and to have the marriage take place after the waiting period. An important consideration was that the man was required by Islamic law and Koranic injunction to provide maintenance for the woman throughout this period. During repudiation and the waiting period, there could be no sexual contact between the parties since such contact would nullify the divorce proceedings and would restore full marital rights between husband and wife.

The dissolution of marriage under Islamic law is either revocable or irrevocable and is classified under three categories: by the husband, with no court intervention; by mutual consent of husband and wife, with no court intervention; and by a judicial decree on the application of either the husband or the wife.

The following are the generally accepted legal classifications in the dissolution of marriage:[19]

1. *Ṭalāq* (repudiation). *Ṭalāq* ensues after three statements of "I divorce thee" uttered either at separate intervals or at one time. There are two approved forms of *ṭalāq: aḥsan* (most approved) and *ḥasan* (approved). The *aḥsan* consists of the three pronouncements during the woman's period of menstrual purity (*ṭuhr*), that is, when she is not menstruating, followed by abstinence from sexual intercourse during the legally prescribed waiting period. The pronouncement is revocable during the three-month period or, if the woman is pregnant, until delivery. Revocation may be by express words or by resumption of conjugal intercourse. Islam does not allow divorce during the wife's menstrual period.

The *ḥasan* form is when the husband repudiates his wife by three successive pronouncements of *ṭalāq* during three consecutive periods of purity. He can revoke this first *ṭalāq* by cohabiting with her during this period. If no intercourse has taken place in the second period of purity, he can pronounce the second *ṭalāq*. This can also be revoked; if not, a third period of purity is entered into when the husband can pronounce for the third time the formula of *ṭalāq*. This then becomes irrevocable, dissolving the marriage; *ᶜiddah* becomes incumbent upon the wife, during which sexual intercourse is unlawful. Remarriage to her becomes unlawful until she marries another man, called *muḥallil,* who lawfully divorces her after consummation of marriage. The *ḥasan* tends to treat the wife as a chattel and is the form which the Prophet regarded as "a barbarous pre-Islamic practice," one which he tried to end.[20] One of the Koranic injunctions is, "Then, when they have reached their term, take them back in kindness or part from them in kindness" (65:2); while another states, "and whoso transgresseth Allah's limits, he verily wrongeth his soul" (65:1).

2. *Īlā'* (vow of continence). Here there is a temporary cessation of marital relations and a vow is made to abstain from sexual intercourse for at least four months.

3. *Ẓihār* (injurious comparison). It is considered an insult to compare the wife to any of the husband's female relatives within the prohibited degrees, such as saying, for example, "You are to me like the back (*ẓahr*) of my mother." *Ẓiḥār* merely renders coitus unlawful, until the comparison is withdrawn and expiation is made by fasting for two consecutive months, by freeing a slave, or by feeding sixty needy ones (Kor. 33:4; 58:3–4).

4. *Ṭalāq al-tafwīd* is an antenuptial agreement which stipulates that the woman can pronounce divorce upon herself if the husband does not abide by the contract of maintenance or marries a second wife without her consent.

5. *Khulᶜ* (redemption). The wife may make some compensation to the husband or give up part of her dowry, but the latter is not absolutely necessary.

6. *Mubāra'a* is a mutual freeing, which stems from mutual aversion, and consent.

7. *Liᶜān* (mutual imprecation). Here the wife is charged with adultery, which she denies; both parties support their assertions by invoking divine wrath (*liᶜān*) upon each other.

8. *Faskh* is judicial recision, or annulment.

9. *Ridda* (apostasy). Abandonment or change of the Islamic faith by either of the parties is grounds for dissolution of the marriage, which takes effect ipso facto.

The above classifications do not take into consideration the automatic dissolution of marriage by the death of one of the spouses.

A woman can seek divorce if her husband fails to observe general marital obligations. Acts of cruelty; beatings without cause; desertion; neither cohabiting nor providing food, shelter or clothing, forcing her to beg for her living are grounds for divorce by a woman. She can also divorce her husband if he is impotent.

Among the nomads, divorce was often for reasons of disagreements or sterility, which was generally assumed to be the woman's fault.[21] Another custom that was evidently a carry-over from pre-Islamic times was when a bedouin wanted to get rid of his wife, he took three stones and threw them in front of her, one after the other, saying each time: "I divorce you, go to your parents." The woman could do the same thing, saying each time: "Go your way, you have had your share, you are no longer wanted." In pre-Islamic times, the most commonly pronounced utterance by the husband was "Thou art to me as the back of my mother."[22]

The *aḥsan* form of divorce was approved by the Prophet as the proper orthodox form and was endorsed by al-Ghazālī in his *Book on the Etiquette of Marriage.* Maintaining the orthodox line in Islam, al-Ghazālī upholds that divorce is permissible, but of "all permissible things, it is the most detestable to Almighty God."[23] In harmony with etiquette, he brings in an element of compassion, sympathy and understanding, which he enjoins the husband to exercise toward the wife. Dissolution of marriage is to be sought only under exceptional circumstances. If differences should arise, however, every effort should be made to achieve reconciliation, by appointing a judge for each party to mediate their differences. If reconciliation is not thereby effected, then divorce can take place according to Koranic decrees (2:228–32, 236–37; 4:20, 35, 127–30; 33:49; 65:1, 2, 5). It is preferable in such circumstances that divorce be uttered twice, that is, that two public pronouncements be made and only during the menstrual purity of the woman. Once the divorce has been announced, the woman enters the legally prescribed period of waiting (*ʿiddah*), which varies depending on how long it takes to determine pregnancy. A widow generally has to wait four months and ten days to make certain whether she is pregnant; a woman already pregnant must wait until the child is delivered; and the divorced woman has to wait until three menstrual periods have elapsed (Kor. 2:228, 234–35; 33:49; 65:4, 6).

In general, al-Ghazālī emphasized four points on the matter of divorce: One, that divorce should take place during the woman's menstrual purity. Two, that the man should restrict himself to one utterance of repudiation and not pronounce all three consecutively, for then the divorce will become irrevocable unless a *muḥallil* makes the woman lawful again; but having a *muḥallil* will engender adverse or repulsive effects in the woman. Moreover, this practice was discouraged by the Prophet. Three, that the man should have a pretext for divorcing the woman which avoids stern censure and belittlement and that he should make provision for her. Four, that he should not reveal her confidences while divorced from or married to her. His major points are steeped in moral ethics, compassion and basic etiquette. Here al-Ghazālī brings out an important point regarding marital confidences by quoting Abū Saᶜīd, who reiterated the words of the Prophet: "The greatest betrayal in the opinion of God on the Day of Judgment is for the man to reveal everything to the woman and vice versa, then reveal her secret." Another interesting anecdote related by al-Ghazālī which best illustrates the etiquette of discretion toward the woman when divorcing her was: "It is related that a virtuous man wanted to divorce his wife and he was asked, 'What grievance have you against her?' And he replied, 'A wise man does not reveal the secrets of his wife.' After divorcing her he was asked, 'Why did you divorce her?' And he replied, 'The affairs of someone else's wife are not my concern.' "

THE *IḤYĀ'* AND AL-GHAZĀLĪ'S SUFISTIC APPROACH TO MARRIAGE

In the *Iḥyā'* al-Ghazālī not only expounded the precepts of Islam in general and Sufism in particular, he also reconciled Sufism to and assimilated it within the body of orthodox Islamic sciences. This is best summarized by Gibb, who, in referring to the *Iḥyā'*, states that al-Ghazālī "demonstrated the truly Islamic foundation of Sufism, and reconciled both by the argument that orthodoxy without the revivalist leaven of Sufism was an empty profession, and Sufism without orthodoxy dangerous subjectivism."[24] Needless to say, credit for this accomplishment cannot be given solely to al-Ghazālī. He built on and quoted from previous works which had already paved the way for the reconciliation and the assimilation mentioned above. These great works include those of Abū Ṭālib al-Makkī (died 386/996), *Kitāb Qūt al-Qulūb;* Abū Bakr al-Kalabādhī (died 388/998), *Kitāb al-Taᶜarruf li-Madhhab Ahl al-Taṣawwuf;* and ᶜAlī b. ᶜUthmān al-Ḥujwīrī (died 465/1073), *Kashf al-Maḥjūb.* Al-Ghazālī, in his *Confessions,* states:

> As it was easier to learn their doctrine than to practice it [Sufism], I studied first of all those of their books which contain it: *The Nourishment of Hearts,* by Abū Ṭālib of Mecca, the works of Ḥārith al-Muḥāsibi, and the fragments which still remain of Junayd, Shibli, Abū Yazīd Bustami and other leaders.[25]

It is apparent that al-Ghazālī assimilated existing works and reconciled their precepts to Islam. In his *Counsel for Kings,* he indicates that it was a common practice of the age to quote from works of other authors without acknowledgment.[26] Furthermore, in his later writings, he used material from his earlier works without referring to them.

The *Iḥyā'* is as complicated as al-Ghazālī's personality. He has been described as having a "Protean character," that is to say, "he was pioneering, constantly exploring the applicability of fresh ideas to a variety of subjects."[27] He pioneered in this book by focusing on hitherto undelineated aspects of marriage among other things. However, to use Imām al-Ḥaramayn al-Juwayni's metaphor, al-Ghazālī's thoughts are "a vast ocean in which all but the most skilled navigators are liable to lose their way."[28]

Al-Ghazālī's conversion to Sufism and his reconciliation of it to orthodoxy had impact and consequences for Islam similar to those made on the Christian faith by St. Augustine's conversion to Christianity.[29] His influence on European thought has been recognized by scholars, in that his teachings "flowed through the *pugio fidei* of Ramon Marti, and affected first Thomas Aquinas and later Pascal."[30]

Al-Ghazālī was regarded as a mystic and had espoused mystical notions of marriage. A major controversy of the time, which had continued for several hundred years within Islam, was that of celibacy versus marriage. This stemmed from the influence of the mystics and the mixed feelings among the orthodox Muslims who favored marriage and those who did not. Islam had to meet the needs of divergent elements that were tearing at its roots. The call to meet this need elicited al-Ghazālī's response, and his works have been immortalized in the *Iḥyā'*.

The *Iḥyā'* embodies the undefined Islamic marital code, steeped as it is in jurisprudence and ethics. It is intricate and complex, woven on the whole loom of al-Ghazālī's intellectualism to produce a multipatterned tapestry. Al-Ghazālī pioneered in the area of marital ethics and sexuality by focusing on hitherto undelineated aspects of Muslim marriage and sexuality. He reconciled and assimilated divergent existing beliefs and practices, integrating in the process Sufi notions on the subject within the body of accepted orthodox Islamic sciences.

Since Islamic views on marriage are here examined through the work of al-Ghazālī, who was a Shafiᶜi,[31] greater emphasis is placed upon that rite. Although each rite has elaborate juridical precepts in regard to the institution of marriage, and since a Muslim may "pass from one into the other without ceasing to be known as an orthodox or Sunni Muslin,"[32] only major differences between the rites will be indicated.

Furthermore, because of his commitment to Sufism, the Islamic version of mysticism, al-Ghazālī consciously undertook to juxtapose the Sufi notion of marriage and sexuality with those expounded by the ulema. The Sufis confronted what was absent in the consideration of the theologians in Islam, namely, does marriage and the sexuality attending it distract from full concentration on God? Many Sufis, because of their total commitment to the process of meditating on God, sincerely believed that the commitments they would have to make in marriage would distract from their total absorption in the meditation upon God.

The meditation process in Sufism required a rigorous commitment to the Path, which required much concentration and rigorous physical and spiritual exercises.

While the subject of love received much attention in Sufi literature, the love they expounded was that of God, as best exemplified in the utterances of two famous mystics of early Islam: Rābiᶜah al-ᶜAdawīyah and Manṣūr al-Ḥallāj. The former is known for her famous prayer:

> O God, if I worship Thee for fear of Hell, burn me in Hell, and if I worship Thee in hope of Paradise, exclude me from Paradise; but if I worship Thee for Thy own sake, grudge me not Thy everlasting beauty.[33]

And by al-Ḥallāj:

> I am He whom I love, and He whom I love is I.
> We are two spirits dwelling in one body.
> When thou seest me thou seest Him,
> And when thou seest Him, thou seest us both.[34]

This love of God is the ultimate attainment; the mystic hopes in this mortal life to win a glimpse of immortality by passing away from self (*fanā'*) into the consciousness of survival in God (*baqā'*).

A major portion of the *Book on the Etiquette of Marriage* is concerned with delineating the advantages and disadvantages of marriage from a Sufistic point of view. With his being a Sufi, Sufi views naturally figured in al-Ghazālī's discussions of marriage. He had to tread lightly, however, when expounding his views on the advantages and disadvantages of marriage for the Sufi. He brought to the foreground the two divergent views: the exoteric, which advocated adherence to the word and letter of the sunna, and the esoteric, which maintained that the only path to salvation lay in devoting oneself totally to the service of God. This excluded having dependents.

Although al-Ghazālī realized that Sufism was existential, he insisted, in setting forth arguments against celibacy, that the foundation of the Sufi life was also the observance of the outward forms of activity as prescribed by the Koran, sunna and hadith, or as systematized in the Islamic sciences. He further clarified the Sufi way of life by stating its principles were not an alternative to the formal Islamic observances but presupposed them and were therefore the complement or consummation of these precepts.[35] In order to be an orthodox Muslim, the mystic had first to admit to all of the teachings of the law. This law did not embrace celibacy. Here al-Ghazālī had to contend not only with the Koranic ordinance, but also with the voluminous hadith literature directed against asceticism, the primary hadith being, "There is no monasticism in Islam (*la rahbanīyah fi al-Islam*)—the monasticism of my community is the Jihad," which bears the "obvious stamp of anti-Christian polemic";[36] and the Prophet's saying, "I fast and I eat, I keep vigil and I sleep, and I am married. And whoever is not willing to follow my Sunna does not belong to me."[37] Abū Dā'ūd, an uncompromising opponent of the Sufi teachings, reiterates in hadith literature the words of the Prophet: "There is no monasticism" or celibacy in Islam.[38] In the Koran, monasticism is condemned as being an innovation introduced by the Christians themselves and not by divine decree (57:27). In a well-known tradition, the Prophet had asked ᶜAkkāf al-Hilāli if he was married and he said that he was not, to which the Prophet replied, "Then you are one of the followers of Satan, or one of the Christian monks. If so, go to them; but if you are one of us, then do as we do, for our sunna includes marriage. The most wicked among you are your celibates and the most ignoble among your dead are your celibates."[39] Nevertheless, in the early part of the third century, it appears that the Muslim ascetic was not easily distinguished from the Christian.[40]

The arguments against celibacy according to Ḥujwīrī are two: neglect of the sunna; and the fostering of "lust in the heart and the danger of falling into unlawful ways."[41] Al-Ghazālī quotes well-known mystics of the eighth and ninth century such as Ḥasan of Basra, Bishr b. al-Ḥārith, Rābiᶜah al-ᶜAdawīyah, Abū Sulaymān al-Dārānī, Ibrāhīm Ibn Adham, Muᶜādh Ibn Jabal, Junayd, Abū al-Ḥasan Aḥmad b. al-Hawwārī and others to bring forth existing arguments among the Sufis regarding celibacy versus marriage.

To argue the case for celibacy, the account in Sufi literature which best exemplifies the strong rejection of marriage and the views of those mystics who wish to remain celibate and pursue the One unhindered by marriage is that of Rābiᶜah al-ᶜAdawīyah. She received many offers of marriage but rejected them all, feeling that only in the celibate life could she pursue her quest unhindered. One of her suitors was ᶜAbd al-Waḥīd b. Zayd (died 177/793), founder of the first monastic communities near Basra, who was renowned for his asceticism and sanctity of life. To him is attributed an important Sufi belief:

> The Ways are various and the Way to the Truth is one; those who travel on the way of Truth are many but they do not know nor are their aims correct. They proceed slowly seeking their goal and people are ignorant of what is desired therefrom. Most of them are asleep or oblivious of the Way to the Truth.[42]

In answer to another proposal, from the wealthy ᶜAbbāsid Amir of Basra, Muḥammad b. Sulaymān al-Hāshimī (died 172/788–89), Rābiᶜah responded by saying:

> Renunciation of this world means peace, while desire for it brings sorrow. Curb your desires and control yourself and do not let others control you, but let them share your wealth and the anxiety of the time. . . . but as for me, God can give me all you offer and can more than double it. It would not please me to be distracted from Him for a single moment.[43]

In another account, a proposal came from the ascetic, Ḥasan of Basra (died 110/728), to which Rābiᶜah replied:

> The contract of marriage is for those who have a phenomenal existence (that is, who are concerned with the affairs of this material world). Here (that is, in my case) existence has ceased, since I have ceased to exist and have passed out of Self. My existence is in Him, and I am altogether His. I am in the shadow of His command. The marriage contract must be asked for from Him, not from me.[44]

Some other general views that reflect the attitude of the celibates were: "Preoccupation with celibacy is better than preoccupation with women";[45] Ibrāhīm Ibn Adham said, "He who gets used to the thighs of women will not succeed, and no doubt the woman calls for luxuries which will prevent full preoccupation with God";[46] al-Ghazālī reiterated, in his twenty-third book of the *Iḥyā',* what Abū Sulaymān al-Dārānī had said: "I have not seen any one of our companions who got married and remained on His Path."[47]

Generally, the Sufi views against marriage are based on the notion that whoever marries inclines toward the temporal or phenomenal world. However, only by showing contempt for the world, abhorring its snares and attractions, and desiring to escape from it and its fetters can a man or a woman be free to pursue without hindrance the unitive life. Since retirement from the affairs of the world for all those who sought to follow the mystic path became the ideal of the Sufi because it freed him from responsibilities and distractions, celibacy figured prominently in Sufi exhortations. Al-Qushayrī emphasized the value of retirement and solitude for the seeker after God by saying: "To go into retreat is fitting for God's elect, and retirement is essential for those who seek Union."[48] Bishr b. al-Ḥārith answers to the responsibilities of marriage by saying, "Were I to care for a chicken, I would fear becoming a butcher on the bridge"; and "I have a greater need of divorcing my Self than of marrying a wife."[49] Even the Prophet stated that the man with a "light-back" (that is, with no responsibilities) is the one who has "no wife or children."[50] However, Abū Ṭālib al-Makkī states that celibacy was favored after the second century of the Hijra (after A.D. 800).[51] Real separation is defined as being free from property outwardly and from all that is unreal inwardly, and requires that one's actions should all be in relation to God. To the Sufis, separation from the unreal, or purification, is then the true "virginity" which will "end in the attainment of the goal, the power to see God and be united with Him. This is the true spiritual marriage in which the soul cleaves to the immortal Bridegroom, and its fruition is the True Wisdom, that is, God."[52]

Al-Ghazālī, in his lengthy discussion of the advantages and disadvantages of marriage, tries to reconcile these two divergent views, which in essence embody his own: "The asceticism of an ascetic is not complete until he marries" for the ascetic's heart cannot overpower desire except through marriage and true asceticism cannot be reached unless the heart is empty. He further asserts: "Whoever marries safeguards half of his religion; let him fear God for the second half."

The Sufi *shaykh*s generally argue that marriage is desirable as a means of quelling lust and of sustenance because it frees the mind from anxiety.

Another major view is that, although the object of marriage is procreation, if the child dies before his father or parents, he will intercede for them before God on the Day of Judgment; if a parent dies first, then the child will remain to pray for him. The implication is that a Sufi should marry if he cannot curb his sexual desires, care for his house, or do without family associations and if he can gain a livelihood.

When a Sufi finds it necessary to marry, the selection of the proper wife becomes all-important. The Prophet stated: "women are married for four things: wealth, nobility, beauty, and religion. Do take one that is religious, for, after Islam, there is nothing that profits a man so much as a believing and obedient wife who gladdens him whenever he looks on her."[53] However, the singularly most important quality for a Sufi to seek in a woman is religious devotion for the devout wife will aid him in remaining on the Path and in attaining unitive life with God. Al-Ghazālī states that the woman should be superior to the man in four things: beauty, education, fear of God and morality.[54] The proof of a sincere Sufi is that he marry a poor and religious woman, not a rich one. Marrying a rich woman has five "inconveniences": excessive dowry, delayed celebration of marriage, lack of service on the part of the woman, and great expenditure.[55] Should he want to divorce her, he would not be able to do so for fear of losing her fortune. Marriage with a poor woman does not have these drawbacks. Hence, the best are the poor and virtuous women, and the "virtuous wife is a man's best treasure."[56] As the Prophet said, "A virtuous wife is better than the world and all that it contains."[57] Luqmān describes the virtuous wife as being "like a crown on the head of a king; and a wicked wife is like a heavy burden on the back of an old man."[58]

The general overview of self by the Sufis is that the lower soul, or carnal self, is the main source of evil and temptation and must therefore be subdued if the higher soul, the spirit, is to be set free to pursue its upward flight to God. A further argument for this stand is that true self-discipline and real abstinence were not of the body and bodily things, but of the soul. Margaret Smith concludes:

> It was not the cleansing of the body from its defilements and its desires —though this was a necessary preliminary—which was all-important, but the cleansing of the soul from its impurities and from all the desires which might lead it to seek its own will, rather than the will of God, and which might, in any respect, distract it from its preoccupation with God Himself.[59]

Ḥujwīrī, on the other hand, states that Sufism was "founded on celibacy; the introduction of marriage brought about a change."[60] It is this change that al-Ghazālī reconciles by giving the option to the Sufi novice to decide after weighing all the advantages and disadvantages, evils and benefits, needs and desires of his station in order to attain to gnosis (of God). This attainment can only be achieved by conquering the carnal self through the force of a rival love, that is, the love of God, which will then dominate the whole body and its senses.

INTIMATE RELATIONS

Sexual Intercourse

There is no separate code of ethics in Islam apart from that which is contained in the Koran. This branch of theological thought is not developed independently or apart from canon law, as it is with the Roman Catholics. The divine law, or the Shariᶜa, encompasses what is termed "law mixed with ritual, morals, and good manners."[61] Consequently, all the ramifications of physical intimacies are included in the Shariᶜa, or the sunna and hadith, and the Koran. From this matrix, al-Ghazālī argues against masturbation, sodomy, coitus interruptus, and having intercourse with a menstruating woman.

Sexual intercourse forms, then, a part of religious ethics in Islam. Its prohibition outside of marriage is a Koranic ordinance (2:223): "Your women are a tilth for you (to cultivate) so go to your tilth as ye will, and send (good deeds) before you for your souls, and fear Allah, and know that ye will (one day) meet Him." This makes sexual intercourse lawful along with: "He created for you helpmeets from yourselves that ye might find rest in them, and He ordained between you love and mercy" (33:21). Hadith firmly supports the proposition that the work of the flesh itself is agreeable in the eyes of God and the satisfaction derived from it is well looked upon, for the sexual drive is a natural instinct which God has ordained within the sanctity of marriage. For the harmonious marriage there are guidelines that govern coitus with the rights of both the husband and the wife explicitly expressed. Coitus should take place at least once in every three days, or four if the man has four wives. In the case of multiple wives, he has to apportion his time equitably. However, if the man marries another wife who is a virgin, he should reserve seven successive nights for her; and if she is not a virgin, then three successive nights. Although marriage can be contracted with a girl nine years of age or younger, intercourse cannot take place until she has attained puberty. If, as it can happen on rare occasions, the man has coitus with his wife and tears her vagina, which in turn impairs the fulfillment of her conjugal obligations, the man must keep her and is thereafter responsible for her for life.

There are prohibitions governing sexual intercourse. It is not permitted during the pilgrimage to Mecca, as this is a time for prayer and supplication. On a voyage, coitus is always prohibited in the presence of other wives, unless, according to some juridical schools, her nudity is covered. It is forbidden during menstruation and with secret concubines or idolaters. Thus the act is sanctioned only when it is honorable and within the context of marriage or legal concubinage. However, not all types of physical relations are permitted, even with the lawful wife.

The etiquette of sexual intercourse encompasses bathing before and after coitus. The hadith discusses this concept extensively. The man has to perform ablution and recite a prescribed prayer before the sex act. Several acts necessitate bathing. Clothes worn during intercourse may be worn during the prayer (*salāṭ*) without being washed.

The etiquette of coitus includes prayer. Foreplay should include words, kisses and caresses, and the heads of the couple should not be in the direction of Mecca at the time of coitus. At the moment of coitus, one pronounces the formula, "*Bismallah*" (In the name of Allah), followed by another formula such as, "O Allah, ward off the Devil from that which Thou grantest us." The end result of coitus is to beget children, so the prayers are intended to ward off any harm that might befall the child upon conception. At the moment of orgasm one recites to oneself, "And We have sent thee (O Muhammad) only as a bearer of good tidings and a warner" (Kor. 25:56). Passing urine after completion of the union is necessary because it is believed that it prevents weakening of the nerves.

There is a controversy among the four juridical schools regarding the degrees of nudity permissible in marriage, for there are slight variations of prescribed modesty stipulated by the different rites. According to the Malikis, the husband may see the whole body of his wife and of his concubine, and vice versa. The Shafiᶜi is permitted the same with one exception, which is not to see the private parts of either one unless there is consent. The latter view is one subscribed to by al-Ghazālī. Again, this is in emulation of the Prophet's preference when he said, as transmitted by ᶜAbd al-Raḥmān b. Abū Saᶜīd al-Khuḍarī from his father, "No woman shall look at the genitals of another woman, and no man shall look at the genitals of another man."[62] There is another hadith from ᶜĀ'ishah in which she states, "I did not look at, nor did I see, the genitals of the Prophet."[63] In general, the degree of sanctioned nudity in Islamic ethics is dictated by the customs of the different juridical schools.

Al-Ghazālī has a lengthy discussion on the etiquette of coitus, laden with valuable moral and ethical instruction. He stresses the importance of being patient with the wife; the woman's satisfaction should come before the man's, and he should not come unto her like "an onager." Upon reading his instructions, it is difficult to believe that it was written in the eleventh century and not by a present-day psychologist. One would have to assert that the sex act itself is also based on religious precepts, for al-Ghazālī states in his *Book on the Etiquette of Marriage:*

> It is desirable that it [coitus] should commence in the name of God and with the recitation: "Say: 'He is God, the One and Only'; then he should glorify and exalt His name saying: 'In the name of God, Most High, Most Great; O God cause it to be a good progeny if You cause it to issue forth from my loins.' "

The gratification of sexual urges is regarded as a means for averting fornication. It is related that the Prophet said: "When a woman approaches, she approaches in the image of the devil; so if any of you sees a woman who appeals to him, let him approach his wife because she has what that woman has."[64] In supporting this assertion, al-Ghazālī quotes a hadith, that in time of hardship it is better for the celibate to marry and have coitus with a bondmaid, even if it means enslaving the child that might issue forth, rather than to choose the evil course of masturbation or committing the worst sin of all, fornication. The logical conclusion drawn here by al-Ghazālī is that marriage should precede coitus, patience is enjoined until emission takes place, and the sperm is presumably implanted in the uterus. All of these steps follow a sequential order carefully observed.

In conclusion, the sexual drive is a natural instinct that God has ordained. Islam has placed sanctions on this drive in order to avert transgressions, especially that of fornication. Both the penal code and the ethical view regulate the manner in which this instinct is satisfied. In most cases, infraction, that is, fornication after marriage, is punishable by death. All this ideological construction relative to fornication is for the purpose of assuring strict observance of the divine law, which clearly spells out how one avoids an infraction. The provisions in the Shari^{c}a, that is, the Koran and hadith, emphasize the purposefulness of the sex act, which points clearly to the begetting of progeny. Moreover, it has to be preceded and accompanied by certain prayers that emphasize the reverential nature with which the act is approached.

Menstruation

Islamic law puts menstruation in a legal realm that has no counterpart in the West: A woman cannot be divorced when she is menstruating because divorced women "shall wait, keeping themselves apart three (monthly) courses" (Kor. 2:228) to establish that there is no pregnancy.[65] When ^{c}Abdullah b. ^{c}Umar divorced his wife during her period, the Prophet made him take her back until she was pure, which requires the observance of the waiting period (*^{c}iddah*). As previously stated, a man is forbidden intercourse with his wife during the waiting period; to do so would render null and void the intention of divorce since intercourse is lawful only by reason of marriage or legal possession.[66] The Koranic injunction states (4:25 [ᶜAlī]): "And whoso of you cannot afford to marry free, believing women, let him marry what your right hands possess, namely, your believing handmaids."

As decreed in the Koran, intercourse during menstruation is considered a harmful thing (2:222): "It is an illness, so let women alone at such times and go not in unto them till they are cleansed." As a consequence of these Koranic injunctions, hadith literature is profuse in discussing all the ramifications of menstruation.

Al-Ghazālī is explicit in his guidelines to the husband on this matter. He is told that intercourse during menstruation is not allowable, and why it is incumbent upon him to instruct his wife regarding prayers during this time. These guidelines also include the husband's role during the wife's menstrual period, particularly enjoining him not to avoid her, and outline the proper etiquette of cohabitation and intimacies during this time. What is permissible to the husband, according to all four juridical schools, is that he may enjoy the woman's upper body while the lower part is covered.

The general accepted view as transmitted by ᶜĀ'ishah is that it is incumbent upon the menstruating woman to fast but not to pray. The reason for this is that the prayers are many and repetitive, whereas fasting is ordained once a year and the period of menstruation is only a matter of days.[67] The custom had been for the menstruating woman to remain in the house and not pray or fast until the end of her menstrual period. However, ᶜĀ'ishah complained to the Prophet about these restrictions when approaching Mecca on a *hajj* because she was menstruating. So he told her, "Do what the pilgrim does," which was explained by al-Shāfiᶜī to mean, "Do what the pilgrims do but not circumambulate the Kaaba until purified."[68] In another tradition of the Prophet, it was stated that whoever performed the pilgrimage, let the last contact be with the Kaaba except for the one who is menstruating; but later he gave women permission to set aside this prohibition.[69] An interesting contradictory point lies in the hadith of the Prophet which states: "Whoever has intercourse with a menstruating woman, let him offer a *ṣadāqah.*"[70] Ibn ᶜAbbās went so far as to say, "If the blood is red, offer a dinar; and if the blood is yellow, half a dinar."[71] The generally accepted norm subsequently is, "If it is blasphemous to have intercourse with a menstruating woman, it was not decreed by God to be blasphemy."[72] Another interesting point is that the hadith on menstruation is transmitted mainly by women: ᶜĀ'ishah, Umm Ḥabībah, Umm Salamah, and Ṣafiyyah, all wives of the Prophet. Al-Bukhārī indicates that women, however, look generally to ᶜĀ'ishah for explanations and elucidations.[73] In dealing with this subject, al-Ghazālī took into consideration the fact that the principles and the scientific explanations of precepts governing the rules of conduct during menstruation are lengthy and many-faceted.

Coitus Interruptus

Coitus interruptus, or withdrawal prior to ejaculation in the hope that there will be no sperm present to fertilize an ovum, was a practice of the ancient Arabs and continued to be practiced even after the revelation of the Koran. The Prophet sanctioned it, stating that there is not a soul whose existence God has decreed but who will exist. On the other hand, if it was licit, the Koran would have defended it in a formal manner. The hadith indicates that coitus interruptus was practiced in times of war, with women who were taken captive, or when a man had intercourse with a servant. (According to some juridical schools, an offspring born of a slave was also enslaved.) In marriage, however, coitus interruptus may be practiced only with the permission of the wife.

The Jews claimed that coitus interruptus was the "lesser degree of burying children alive," to which the Prophet retorted, "The Jews lied"; that "If God willed the existence of a creature, he [the servant] cannot prevent it."[74] In the hadith of Ibn Jābir, it is stated: "We used to have coitus interruptus while the Koran was being revealed."[75] The other main point raised in the hadith and related by Mālik b. Anas: "A free woman is to be consulted[76] for coitus interruptus, and the bondmaid is not."[77] Another tradition, resting on the authority of the caliph, ᶜUmar, through Abū Hurayrah, reasserts the former injunction without mentioning the second part.[78] Thus a group of ulema and companions of the Prophet permitted coitus interruptus.[79]

The issue of coitus interruptus relies on the authority and transmittals of Ibn Jābir, Mālik b. Anas, and Abī Saᶜīd al-Khuḍarī without further discussion or elucidation. Al-Ghazālī, on the other hand, brings forth these traditions and expounds at length on the ethical and moral issues concerning its practice. He argues from a moral point of view that even though it is not forbidden (*ḥarām*), it is not recommended since the institution of marriage is to appease sexual appetites and to have an offspring who will pray for parents after their death and who will be an intercessor with God for them. Coitus interruptus will break the chain of life.

Al-Ghazālī discusses at length the pros and cons of coitus interruptus, and it is difficult at times to ascertain his stand. However, one can conclude that, while he does not find it reprehensible, he seems to oppose it for the intention of the act and tends to place it in the same category as refraining from marriage. He divides all the arguments regarding coitus interruptus into four categories which point in differing directions: unconditional permissiveness under all circumstances, prohibition in all circumstances, permissible with the woman's consent, permissible with the bondmaid but not with the free woman.

Masturbation

Masturbation also has its place in theological ethics. The Koranic reference to it is in the verse, "And those who guard their private parts—except from their wives and from those whom their right hands possess—such indeed are not to blame; but those who seek to go beyond that, it is these who are transgressors" (70:29–31). Al-Ghazālī condones masturbation at the hands of the woman. He discusses this in the context of the menstruating woman and the legitimacy of the husband being near the wife during this time and enjoying what is concealed by the loincloth short of coitus. In marriage, masturbation is allowable, while in celibacy it is forbidden. A tradition of the Prophet states that "God, at the Day of Judgment, will not throw a glance at the one who masturbates; he will be the first to enter Hell, unless he repents."[80] Al-Ghazālī quotes another hadith by Ibn ᶜAbbās, who was asked by a young man about masturbation. He replied that it was a disgusting act and that marrying a bondmaid was better than masturbation. Nevertheless, it was better than committing fornication. Al-Ghazālī's conclusion, however, is that overcoming the evils of masturbation by marrying a bondmaid cannot be construed as unrestricted permissiveness or as an absolute virtue.

Homosexuality and Sodomy

Since homosexuality existed in pre-Islamic society, the Koran addressed the subject of sodomy. It is a reference in over seventy Koranic verses which deal with the social structure of the time. These verses dwell on the background of homosexuality, including Lot and his people and their refusal to heed the warnings of the prophets before Muhammad. The injunction by the Prophet, "Lo! Ye commit lewdness such as no creature did before you," received the response, "Bring Allah's doom upon us if thou art a truth-teller!" (Kor. 29:28–29). However, only Lot and his family, desiring to change their ways, repented and asked for forgiveness. Allah forgave Lot and his family, except for an old woman, thereby saving them and destroying the rest of the tribe.

Homosexuality, *al-lawāṭah* in Arabic, is not discussed apart from *lūṭ*, or sodomy. Verses in the Koran refer to the sodomites, or the people of Lot, and condemn their acts of homosexuality. The Prophet states the revelation, "Lo! Ye come with lust unto men instead of women. Nay, but ye are wanton folk" (Kor. 7:81). The other verses dealing with homosexuality are basically the same injunctions. The Koran stipulates strict punishment for the act (4:16): "And as for the two of you who are guilty thereof, punish them both. And if they repent and improve, then let them be."

The hadith, which elucidates the practice of the Prophet as embodied in the Koran, is lengthy on the topic of sodomy, and there are many transmitters who dwelt on this subject. The main transmittal regarding sodomy comes from Ibn ᶜAbbās, quoting the Prophet: "Whoever is found conducting himself in the manner of the people of Lot,[81] kill the doer and the receiver."[82] This is also transmitted by the five well-known relators of hadith, although not by al-Nisā'ī.[83] On the other hand, Ibn Isḥāq said, "Cursed are the ones who do the deeds of the people of Lot," without mentioning "kill."[84]

The ulema had different opinions regarding the judgment of one who commits sodomy. Some said that the "person should be stoned, whether he refrains or not."[85] Mālik b. Anas and al-Shāfiᶜī agreed with them; so did such followers of fiqh as Ḥasan al-Baṣrī and ᶜAta' b. Abī Rabbah and others who believed that the judgment passed on one who commits sodomy should be the same as that passed on one who commits adultery. This was also the belief of al-Thawrī and the people of Jufa. Another hadith similar to Ibn ᶜAbbās's and related from the Prophet by Ibn Mājah: "The thing I fear most about my people is that they should conduct themselves in the manner of Lot."[86] Ibn Mājah further states in relating the hadith of Ibn ᶜAbbās, "Whoever comes upon a forbidden being, kill him, and whoever comes upon an animal, kill him and the animal."[87]

The hadith mentioned repeatedly that sodomy and homosexuality, including lesbianism, were forbidden by the Prophet. That is, he forbade sexual intercourse between man and man, and intimate relations between woman and woman.[88] There was no exposition on this point, other than that found in an injunction relayed with slight variations from the hadith forbidding intercourse between two undressed male or female partners; neither should one male or female come upon a partner of the same sex in "one garment."[89] The limitations regarding the latter are difficult to ascertain, unless impersonation of the other sex is what is implied. This is the core of hadith regarding sodomy and related lewd acts that are contrary to the Koran's teachings. Islamic law is explicit on the question of sodomy and marriage, for the male sodomite would also be prohibited from marrying female relatives of the boy or man with whom he committed sodomy—mother, sister and daughter.

Al-Ghazālī's only reference to homosexuality is that it is shameful for a man to look at the face of the beardless boy when it may result in evil. The other allusion to the subject by al-Ghazālī is in connection with intercourse during menstruation. He states that while intercourse during menstruation is forbidden because it is harmful, sodomy will cause permanent harm. For that reason, sodomy is more strongly prohibited than intimate relations during menstruation.

AL-GHAZĀLĪ'S VIEW IN PERSPECTIVE

Al-Ghazālī's views in general, and those on marriage and sexuality in particular, form an intricate mosaic. The complexity of its colors is rivaled by the profundity of his thinking on various topics. Ibn Ṭufayl (died 581/1185) suggested that al-Ghazālī "wrote differently for ordinary men and for the elite, or, in other words, he had esoteric views which were not divulged to everyone."[90] In summing up the advantages and the disadvantages of marriage, al-Ghazālī unifies the divergent views by stating that if a man has inherent, refined traits, or if these good traits are enhanced as a result of self-discipline which he developed on the Sufi path, thereby attaining knowledge and revelation, he has no need for marriage; he is beyond dependence on physical needs and gratifications. The levels that Sufis refer to here are the body, the soul, and the spirit, with the highest of these the spirit. As Nasr states.

> What remains of man, namely the soul or *anima,* is precisely the subject of the spiritual world. This is the lead that must be transmuted into gold, the moon that must become wed to the sun, and at the same time the dragon that must be slain in order that the hero may reach the treasure.[91]

When a Sufi attains this higher state, he is no longer dependent on physical needs.

Another interesting point that al-Ghazālī stresses in reference to the marital code lies in his definition of endurance:

> Endurance is a form of self-discipline, an appeasement of anger, and an improvement of character. A person who secludes himself or who associates himself with someone of a refined character does not reflect on the evils of his inner self, nor are his hidden faults revealed. It is, therefore, the duty of one who walks the path of the hereafter to tempt himself by being exposed to the like of such agitations, and to become accustomed to enduring them so that his character should be set straight, his soul should be calm, and he should be purified of the base qualities hidden within him.

Enduring family and dependents "is an act of worship." On the other hand, al-Ghazālī states that if the act of worship is the mere act of providing for the family, "seeking knowledge is better than that because it, too, is a form of work but its benefits are more numerous and more encompassing than the benefit of providing for dependents."

Although at first one might conclude that the articulation of al-Ghazālī's advantages and disadvantages of marriage appears to be a circular argument, what he is saying in essence is that if one is beyond the physical level and does not need to fulfill those desires, one would do best to follow the internal plane of seeking ultimate truths and knowledge by becoming one with God. If marrying and providing for dependents is one form of serving God, then one should marry; combining the two is better. Hence, one must keep the goal of serving and being one with God in mind, which will check the reins of his behavior and thus govern the means of fulfilling those objectives by adhering to His laws as manifested to the Prophet and as embodied in his sunna.

The weakest aspect of the *Book on the Etiquette of Marriage* is al-Ghazālī's quoting a hadith that was not deemed reliable, or quoting reliable traditions along with the unreliable to bolster his arguments for or against marriage. This appears to fall short of sound logic. A lesser problem is the fact that al-Ghazālī perused only some aspects of marriage and their ramifications, as he could not have made an in-depth study when he covered so many subjects. The strength of the book lies in the fact that it tries to establish hitherto known concepts, written and unwritten, both in the Koran and the traditions, as guidelines of etiquette for Islamic society to follow. The crux of his discourses lies in his use of the term "etiquette," which neither entails nor reflects sufficiently persuasive logical arguments. Etiquette falls far short of legal requirements, so perhaps weak hadith is not so serious.

Throughout the book, al-Ghazālī weaves together threads of etiquette and Islamic law. In chapter 2 he dwells on the specific negative types of women to be wary of, as well as the good qualities to look for in a woman, and in chapter 3 he concentrates on specific actions. He stresses always the "virtuous and religious woman" and, conversely, enjoins against a woman who is a hypochondriac, an upbraider, a yearner, a coveter, a narcissist, a prattler, or one who is too preoccupied with makeup, jewelry and flashy things.

Al-Ghazālī fully maintains the Christian marital affirmation for the woman "to honor and obey." He stresses this throughout by emphasizing that a woman should not feed anyone, unless the food is about to spoil, without the permission of her husband; that she should not go out of the house or to the mosque for prayer without his permission; that she should be discreet in dress and manner, and careful about to whom she speaks when on the streets or in the markets; that she should not emphasize the obvious, that is, as al-Ghazālī puts it, in case she be beautiful and her husband ugly; and that she should be conservative in spending and not wasteful of the husband's money.

In al-Ghazālī's *Book of Counsel for Kings,* he devotes chapter 7 to "Describing Women and Their Good and Bad Points," wherein he states:

> A wife will become dear to her husband and gain his affection, firstly by honouring him; secondly by obeying him when they are alone together; and (further) by bearing in mind his advantages and disadvantages, adorning herself (for him only), keeping herself concealed (from other men) and secluding herself in the house; by coming to him tidy and pleasantly perfumed, having meals ready (for him) at the (proper) times and cheerfully preparing whatever he desires; by not making impossible demands, not nagging; keeping her nakedness covered at bedtime, and keeping her husband's secrets during his absence and in his presence.[92]

Teaching a woman proper etiquette, correct behavior, and good manners is the responsibility of her parents, and specifically, her mother. The moral and ethical upbringing of the son is the father's duty. Historically the tradition exceeds the boundaries of Islam and can be seen in Polonius's instruction of his son upon his departure to a foreign land, or Kai Kaus Ibn Iskandar's *Qābūs-nāma,* a book of moral and practical instruction of a prince for his son, Gilanshah, written in A.D. 1032–83. Nothing, however, is more eloquent in epitomizing the basic role of a woman in the Muslim world than the advice of Asmā' to her daughter upon the latter's marriage, as related by al-Ghazālī.

> You have left a nest in which you grew up and proceeded to a bed which you know not and a mate with whom you have not associated; be an earth for him, and he will be your sky; be a resting place for him, and he will

> be your pillar; be his bondmaid, and he will be your slave; do not make excessive demands, for he will then desert you; do not become too distant from him, for he will then forget you; should he draw near, then draw close to him; should he become distant, stay away from him. Shield his nose, his hearing and his eye so he will smell nothing from you but that which is sweet, hear nothing but that which is good, and look at nothing but that which is beautiful.

This advice does not reflect a role of docility, but one of fortitude and strength in which the mates share responsibilities and obligations, giving and taking in a manner insuring a stable relationship. The woman is placed at the center of the wheel from which the activities and strengths of the household radiate, appealing to and satisfying the husband's senses. The priorities of responsibilities for a woman include being with her husband, her children; attending to her household; and performing her prayers and fasting. These exemplify complete fulfillment in her realm. Al-Ghazālī emphasizes that since women are "wards" of the guardian or "prisoners" in the hands of men, men should have forbearance for them and protect them. In essence, the Islamic code of behavior, for men and women, stems from the religious matrix as stipulated in the Koran that their actions should be steadfast and upright at all times and be pleasing unto God, thus earning merits with their Lord for the Hereafter (33:35–36).

Finally, in elucidating the myriad conventions accepted by society regarding marriage along with its many ramifications, a heavy intellectual burden is placed on the reader. Hopefully, some light may have been shed in this chapter on al-Ghazālī's synthesis of existing views on marriage within Islam. The *Book on the Etiquette of Marriage* is germane to the delineation of the hitherto undefined Islamic code on sex and marriage. It is fitting to end this preliminary discussion with a prayer that al-Ghazālī attributed to the Prophet and which best epitomizes al-Ghazālī's sincerity and religious piety, as well as his intellectual endeavors:

> O God, I take refuge with Thee
> from knowledge which does not benefit,
> from the heart which does not humble itself,
> from the act which is not lifted up to God,
> and from the prayer which is not heard.[93]

PART II

Book on the Etiquette of Marriage

Being the Second Book of the Section on Customs in the Book

The Revival of the Religious Sciences

By

Abū Hāmid Al-Ghazālī

Translated By

Madelain Farah

al-Ghazālī's Introduction

In the Name of God, the Merciful and Compassionate

Praise be to God the marvels of Whose creation are not subject to the arrows of accident, for minds do not reflect on the beginnings of such wonders except in awe and bewilderment, and the favor of Whose graces continue to be bestowed upon all creatures, for they [graces] come in succession upon them [creatures] whether or not they [creatures] wish to receive them [graces]. One of His marvelous favors is creating human beings out of water [Kor. 21:30],[1] causing them to be related by lineage and marriage, and subjecting creatures to desire through which He drove them to tillage *(ḥirāthah)*[2] and thereby forcibly preserved their descendants. Then He glorified the matter of lineage, ascribed to it great importance, forbade on its account illegitimacy and strongly denounced it through restrictions and reprimands, making the commission thereof an outlandish crime and a serious matter, and encouraging marriage through desire and command.

Glory be to Him who decreed death to His creatures and humbled them thereby through destruction and annihilation, then placed seeds[3] in the soil of the wombs and raised therefrom creatures, forcibly to defeat death, calling attention to the fact that the seas of Providence flood the worlds with benefit as well as harm, prosperity as well as evil, difficulty as well as facility, and concealment as well as revelation. Prayer and peace be upon Muhammad who was sent with warning[4] and good tidings, and upon his household and his companions—prayer that knows neither bounds nor confinement, and may He grant him much peace.

Accordingly, marriage is an aid in [the fulfillment of] religion, an insult to devils, a strong fortress against the enemy of God, and a cause of increase through which the master of prophets outshines the rest of the prophets. How worthy it is, therefore, that its causes be examined and its sunna and etiquette be learned, its aims and ends be explained, and its chapters and sections be clearly specified.

The major guidelines in the *Book on the Etiquette of Marriage* may be revealed in three chapters: The first chapter deals with the advantages and disadvantages of marriage; the second chapter deals with the etiquette to be observed in the marriage contract and between the two contracting parties; and the third chapter deals with the etiquette of cohabitation after marriage and until dissolution.

Chapter One

Advantages and Disadvantages of Marriage

GENERAL BACKGROUND

Be it known that the ulema[1] have disagreed over the virtue of marriage: Some stressed it to the point of claiming that it is preferable to seclusion for the worship of God. Others have admitted its virtue but subordinated it to seclusion for the worship of God, regardless of how much the soul yearns for marriage to a degree that disturbs one's state [of mind] and causes him to succumb to temptation. Others have said: It is preferable to abstain from marriage in this our age; but formerly it was a preferable virtue whereby the means of earning a livelihood was not illicit and the character of women was not censurable.[2] The truth about it cannot be revealed except by first presenting what has been transmitted in the *akhbār*[3] and the *āthār*[4] regarding encouragement and discouragement of marriage, and by explaining its benefits and shortcomings, thereby elucidating the virtues or disadvantages of marriage as pertains to everyone who has or has not been spared its calamities.

[Koranic Verses on Marriage]

Among the Koranic verses: God has said, "And marry such of you" [24:32]; this is a command. He also said, "Place not difficulties in the way of their marrying their husbands" [2:232].[5] This prevented abstinence and enjoined against it. God has said in describing and praising messengers: "And, indeed, We sent Messengers before thee, and We gave them wives and children"

[13:38 (ᶜAlī)]. Thus he said this in the context of praise and in pointing out excellence. He also praised his saints for requesting it in supplication saying: "And those who say, 'Our Lord, grant us of our wives and children the delight of our eyes, and make us a model for the righteous." It is said of the prophets that God has not mentioned in His book any but those who have families. Thus it was said that [St.] John*[6] married but did not cohabit. It is said that he did that to gain virtue and honor, thereby upholding the sunna. Others said that it was to avert the eye. As for Jesus,* he will marry should he come down to earth and will have children.

[Traditions of the Prophet]

As for the *akhbār,* we have his [the Prophet's] sayings: "Marriage is of my sunna; whoever refrains from my sunna refrains from me"; and he* also said: "Marriage is of my sunna; whoever likes my *fiṭrah* (natural disposition),[7] let him follow my sunna."[8]

He* also said: "Marry and multiply for I will boast about you over other nations on the day of resurrection, even about the least among you."[9]

And he* also said, "Whoever refrains from my sunna, he is not of me, and marriage is part of my sunna; whoever loves me, let him follow my sunna."[10]

And he* also said, "Whoever refrains from getting married for fear of having a family, is not of us."[11] This is perhaps a reprimand [directed] against abstinence and not a reason for abstinence.

He* also said, "Whoever has the means, let him get married,"[12] for it will avert the eyes[13] and assure more relief and virtuousness; and who does not, "let him fast for fasting to him is [a form of] castration (*wijā'*)."[14] This indicates that the reason for the encouragement of marriage is fear that the eye might become corrupted,[15] as well as relief.[16] *Wijā'* is a form of castration of the male [organs] so that his manhood is removed; it [the term] is used metaphorically for sexual impotence during the fast.

And he* also said, "If someone whose religion and trustworthiness you approve should come to you, then get him married;

if you do not, you will cause discord on earth and great corruption."[17] This also explains encouragement [to marry] out of fear of corruption.

He* also said, "Whoever marries or gives in marriage, for the sake of God, deserves the friendship (*wilāya*)[18] of God."[19] And he* also said, "Whoever marries safeguards half of his faith; let him fear God for the second half."[20] This is also an indication that its virtue is in safeguarding against disobedience, and fortifying against corruption. For the corrupting factor in a man's religion lies for the most part both in his sexual organs (*farj*)[21] and stomach;[22] he can satisfy one of them by marriage.

He* also said, "All acts by the son of Adam shall cease except the third: a righteous son making invocation for him," etc.[23] He cannot attain this except through marriage.

As for the *āthār*, ᶜUmar[24] has said, "Nothing should prevent marriage except incapacity or adultery (*fujūr*)."[25] He thus asserted that religion does not prohibit marriage, and he limited its prevention to two disparate factors.

[Traditions of the Companions]

Ibn ᶜAbbās*[26] said, "The asceticism of an ascetic is not complete until he marries." It is possible that he considered marriage an act of devotion which renders asceticism perfect; but it seems that he meant to say thereby that the heart would not be safe from being overcome by desire except through marriage, and that asceticism is not perfect without emptying (*farāgh*)[27] the heart [of all preoccupations]. For that reason he would gather his young bondsmen (*ghilmān*), ᶜAkramah and Kurayb[28] and others reaching adulthood, and would say, "If you wish to get married, I will get you married; for when a slave commits adultery, he removes faith from his heart."

Ibn Masᶜūd*[29] used to say, "Were there but ten days left of my life, I would be inclined to get married so as not to meet God a celibate."

Two of Muᶜādh Ibn Jabal's*[30] wives died from the plague, and he, too, was afflicted with the plague; so he said, "Get me married, for I would not like to meet God a celibate." And this coming from both of them indicates that they considered marriage a virtue rather than a defense against the excessiveness of desire.

ᶜUmar* used to marry frequently and would say, "I only marry for the sake of having offspring."

One[31] of the companions attached himself to the Messenger* of God serving him and staying with him in case he needed to have something done; so the Prophet* said to him, "Won't you get married?" He answered, "O Messenger of God, I am a poor man possessing nothing and would be compelled to abandon your service." The Prophet said nothing, then repeated [the question], and he [the companion] repeated the answer. Then the companion reflected and said, "By God, the Messenger* of God knows better than I what is best for me in my earthly life and in my hereafter and what draws me near to God, and if he should tell me a third time, I will do it." and he [the Prophet] told him a third time: "Won't you get married?" The companion said: "O Messenger of God, get me married." He [the Prophet] said, "Go to such a family[32] and say that the Messenger* of God commands you to give your daughter in marriage to me." He [the companion] said, "O Messenger* of God I have nothing." So he [the Prophet] said to his companions, "Gather for your brother the weight of a date-pit in gold," and they did. Thus they took him to those people and got him married; so he said to [them], "Make a feast"; and they obtained for him from the companions a ewe for the feast."[33] This repetition indicates a virtue in marriage itself. It is possible that he [the Prophet] recognized in him [the companion] a need for marriage.

[Later Transmittals]

It has been related that a certain devotee in olden times excelled his contemporaries in devotion. The goodness of his devotion was brought up to the Prophet of his time. His reply was, "It is so," although he had forsaken somewhat the tradition [of worship]. It grieved the worshiper to hear that, so he asked the Prophet about it, and the Prophet said, "Have you forsaken marriage?" And he said, "I don't consider it forbidden, but I am poor and a burden to people."[34] The Prophet said, "I will give you my daughter in marriage," and he* gave him his daughter in marriage.

Bishr b. al-Ḥārith[35] said, "Aḥmad b. Ḥanbal[36] was preferred over me on three accounts: for seeking what is lawful for himself and others, while I seek it for myself only; for his ability to get married in contrast to my inability; and for being appointed an imam for the common people."

It is said that Aḥmad* married the second day following the death of the mother of his son, ᶜAbdullah, and said, "I detest spending the night as a celibate." As for Bishr, when it was said to him, "People have been talking about you because you have refrained from marriage, saying, 'He has forsaken the sunna,' " he replied, "Tell them that religious duties preoccupy him, leaving no time for the sunna." He was blamed on another occasion, so he replied, "Nothing keeps me from marrying except the words of the Almighty [Kor. 2:228 (ᶜAlī)]: 'And they (the women) have rights similar to those (of men) over them in equity.' " That was mentioned to Aḥmad, who declared, "And where is the like of Bishr?" His position is likened unto the point of a spearhead (*ḥadd al-sinān*).[37]

In spite of that, it has been related that he was seen in a dream and was asked, "What has God done to you?" He replied, "My stages (*manāzilī*) in Paradise have been elevated and I was placed close to the stations (*maqāmāt*)[38] of the prophets in rank, but I have not attained the stages of those with families." And in one account he told me, "I would not have wanted you to encounter[39] me as a celibate"; so we asked him, "What did Abū Naṣr al-Tammār do?" He said, "He was placed seventy steps (*darajah*) above me." We asked, "For what reason? We used to see you above him." He replied, "Because of his patience with his daughters and dependents."

Sufyān b. ᶜAyyīnah said, "Having numerous wives is not [indicative of love] of the world because ᶜAlī* was the most ascetic of the companions of the Prophet* and yet he had four wives and seventeen concubines." Thus marriage is an ancient sunna and one of the traits of the prophets.

A man said to Ibrāhīm b. Adham,*[40] "Blessed art thou, for thou hast dedicated thyself to worship through celibacy."[41] He replied, "Indeed your concern for dependents is preferable to all that which I now enjoy." He [the man] replied, "And what prevents you from marriage?" He said, "I have no need for a woman. I do not wish to misrepresent myself to a woman."

It has been said, "A married man is preferred over the celibate in the same way that the *mujāhid*[42] is preferred over the non-*mujāhid*; and one bow (*rakᶜah*)[43] [in worship] of the married man is preferable to seventy bows of one who is celibate."

[Sufi Views on Marriage]

As for what has been related concerning the disadvantages of marriage, the Prophet* said, "The best of all people outside the two hundred[44] is a man light of back who has neither wife nor child."[45] The Prophet* also said, "There will come a time upon people when a man's destruction shall be at the hands of his wife, his parents, and his children; they shall taunt him for poverty and demand of him beyond his means. He will enter paths wherein he will lose his religion and perish."[46]

And there is a *khabar,* according to which, "One of the two sources of comfortable living is having fewer children, while one of the two sources of poverty is having many of them."[47]

Abū Sulaymān al-Dārānī[48] was asked about marriage, and he said, "To abstain is better than to endure them [women], and to endure them is better than to suffer hellfire." He also said, "The single man will find in the pleasures of work and in the emptiness (*farāgh*) of the heart that which the family man cannot find." He once said, "I have not seen any of our companions who married and was able to retain firmly his first rank (*martabah*)."[49] He also said, "He who seeks the following three is inclined toward the world: he who seeks a living, or who marries a woman, or who transcribes a hadith."[50]

Ḥasan* [al-Baṣrī] has said, "When God wishes the servant well, he does not preoccupy him with a family or with possessions." Ibn Abū al-Ḥawwārī[51] once said, "A group exchanged views over this hadith and came to the conclusion that it did not mean that a man [in this case] could not have both, but that he could have both and they would not preoccupy him." This is a reference to the saying of Abū Sulaymān al-Dārānī, "Whatever diverts you from God—whether wife, possession, or children—is a curse upon you."

In general, none has been quoted as discouraging marriage unconditionally. As for encouragement to marriage, it has been related both unconditionally and conditionally. Let us, therefore, remove the veil from this subject by delineating the advantages and disadvantages thereof.

[ADVANTAGES OF MARRIAGE]

There are five advantages to marriage: procreation, satisfying sexual desire, ordering the household, providing companionship, and disciplining the self in striving to sustain them.

[Procreation]

The first advantage—that is, procreation—is the prime cause, and on its account marriage was instituted. The aim is to sustain lineage so that the world would not want for humankind. As for sexual desire, it was created as an ingrained urge: like an overseer unto the male. In the male it is, as it were, an overseer to produce the sperm; in the female it serves to facilitate cultivations so as to produce children out of coitus.[52] It is like luring the bird by spreading about the seed which it likes in order to lead it to the net.

The eternal powers of the Almighty were not incapable of creating beings from the beginning without tilling (*ḥirāthah*) or coupling. But wisdom decreed the ordering of causes and effects together with the lack of need to demonstrate the power of God to complete the wonders of creation and to fulfill what the Divine Will decreed beforehand; thereby the Word was fulfilled as decreed by the pen [Kor. 96:4].

To bring forth a child[53] is a four-faceted intimacy which is the original reason for encouraging it even after being safeguarded against excessive desire, so that no one wants to meet God as a celibate. The first: to conform to the love of God by seeking to produce the child in order to perpetuate mankind. The second: to earn the love of the Prophet* of God by increasing those in whom he can be glorified.[54] The third: to seek the blessing of the righteous child's invocation after him.[55] The fourth: to seek intercession[56] through the death of the young child should he precede his [father's] death.

As for the first facet: It is the most delicate of all the facets, the most removed from the understanding of the common folk, and the most meritorious as well as the strongest in the eyes of those with keen insight into the wonders of the Almighty's creation and into the course of His wisdom. It may be illustrated thus: if the master should give seed and cultivating tools to his slave, and prepare for him the soil to cultivate; if the servant is able to cultivate; if he [the master] should appoint someone to supervise him [the servant]; and if he [the servant], nevertheless, is lazy or does not use the ploughing instruments and neglects the seed until it rots, and he rids himself of the supervisor through some trickery, then he [the servant] would deserve contempt and reprimand from his lord.

God Almighty has created the pair; He has created the male organ and the two ovaries, as well as the sperm in the sheath; He has prepared for it [the sperm] in the ovaries, arteries and ducts, and created the womb as a depository for the sperm; He has endowed both the male and the female with desire. These deeds and instruments bear eloquent testimony to the design of their creator and declare their purpose unto those imbued with wisdom. This would be the case [even] if the Creator had not revealed the design through His Prophet* in the statement "Marry and multiply"; how [much more] if He had openly declared the matter and revealed the secret! Everyone who refrains from marriage neglects tilling, wastes away the seed, does not use the prepared instruments which God has created, and is a violator of the aim of nature as well as the wisdom implied in the evidences of creation foreordained upon these organs by divine writ, unexpressed in letters or voices—writ which can be read by every [person] who has divine insight to understand the intricacies of everlasting wisdom. For that reason, divine legislation exceedingly made the killing of children and the burying [of girls] alive[57] an abomination, for they [such acts] were forbidden for the fulfillment of existence. To this alluded the one who said, "coitus interruptus (*ᶜazl*) is one of the two burials."[58]

The one who marries is seeking to complete what God has desired, and the one who abstains, wastes away what God detests to have wasted. Because of God's desire that mankind should survive, He made feeding [the hungry] a decree, encouraged it, and referred to it by the term "loan" when He said, "Who is it that will lend unto Allah a goodly loan?" [Kor. 2:245].[59]

Should you say: your statement, that sustenance of the species and of self is desirable, on the assumption that their passing away is detestable to God, which is the difference between life and death, not to mention the will of God Almighty, it being known that all is by the will of God and that God is not in need of creation, then what can the distinction be with Him between their life, or survival (*baqā'uhum*), and their extinction (*fanā'uhum*)? Know then that this word is a truth from which an untruth was sought, for what we have mentioned does not invalidate the relation of all things—good and bad, beneficial and detrimental—to the will of God. Love and abomination (*karāhīyah*) contradict each other but they do not oppose the will [of God]; for many a desired aim is hated and many a detested aim is loved; acts of defiance are detestable and they, in spite of being hated, are desired; acts of obedience are desired and they, along with being desired, are loved and pleasing. As for apostasy and evil, we cannot say that they are pleasing and loved but, nevertheless, they are desired. For the Lord has said, "And He is not pleased with ingratitude in His servants."[60]

How then could the extinction of man, or the hatred thereof, with respect to the love for God, be the same as his subsistence? For the Almighty has said, "I have never hesitated over anything as I hesitate in taking the soul of my Muslim servant. He detests death and I detest harming him, but there is no escape for him from death."[61] His saying, "There is no escape from death for him" is a reference to predetermination and to the decree stated in His words, "We have ordained death for *all* of you" [Kor. 56:60]; and in His saying, "Who hath created life and death."[62] There is no contradiction between the Almighty's words, "We have ordained death for *all* of you," and His saying "and I detest harming him."

However, elucidating the truth therein requires defining the meaning of will, love, and hatred; it also requires revealing their essences, because preliminary to understanding them are matters which suit the desire of created beings, their love and their hatred. How preposterous! For between the traits of Almighty God and those of created beings, there is as much distance as between His beloved essence and theirs. The essence of creations is substance and form, while that of God is hallowed beyond theirs; and just as that which is not essence and form cannot be the same as that which is essence and form, likewise His traits are not the same as the traits of creation. These facts lie within the realm of that which could be disclosed. Beyond them lies the mystery of divine decree, the disclosure of which has been prohibited. So let us stop short of mentioning it and let us confine ourselves to that about which we have been told concerning the difference between undertaking and refraining from marriage. For one of the two would cause the loss of lineage, perpetuating its existence from Adam,* generation upon generation, thus ending with him [Adam]. Therefore, he who refrains from marriage cuts off continuous being from himself [back] to Adam* and dies childless with no descendants.

If, however, the inducement to marriage is simply warding off desire, Muᶜādh would not have said when he contracted the plague, "Get me married, I will not meet my Lord celibate." Should you say, "But Muᶜādh could not expect to have children at that time, so why was he interested in it [marriage]?" I would reply, "Children result from coitus,[63] which is a consequence of desire." That is a matter which does not fall in the realm of choice; what is dependent upon the servant's choice is providing the motivation for desire. That is expected in any event. Thus, whoever contracts [marriage], fulfills his obligation and what is incumbent upon him. The rest is beyond his choice. For that reason marriage is desirable also for the impotent; for the urges of desire are veiled and cannot be seen. Even the eunuch who cannot be expected to have an offspring still desires it, in the same manner that a bald man desires to have the blade pass over his head in emulation of others and in keeping with the precedent of the righteous progenitors, and in the same manner that trotting (*al-ramal*) [while performing the circuit around the Kaaba] and cloaking (*al-idṭibāᶜ*) oneself over the left shoulder during the pilgrimage today are desirable.[64] The purpose at first was to indicate [physical] endurance to the infidels. The emulation[65] of those who manifested endurance has become a religious duty for those who succeeded them.

This desire is weak when compared to the desire of one who is capable of tilling. Perhaps it is even weaker when compared with the undesirability of impairing the woman [that is, not using her] with regard to the gratification of desire, for this is not free of danger. Such an interpretation explains the great disapproval [by the righteous] of eschewing marriage in spite of languid sexual desire.

The second facet: striving to attain the love of the Messenger* of God and to please him by increasing that which he can boast of, inasmuch as Messenger of God has openly declared it. Concern for procreation is indicated by what has been related concerning ᶜUmar*: that he used to marry often and used to say, "I marry for [the sake of producing] children." It was related in the *akhbār* that the Prophet* said regarding the deprecation of the barren woman, "A straw mat in the corner of the house is preferable to a barren woman."[66] He also said, "The best of your women are the affectionate childbearers."[67] He also said, "A black childbearer is better than a beauty that cannot give birth."[68] This indicates that seeking children has been considered a greater virtue in marriage than satisfying the demands of sexual desire, seeing that a beautiful woman is more suitable for fortification [against desire], in averting the eye, and curtailing desire.

The third facet: that he should be survived by a righteous child who would invoke blessings upon him, as related in one *khabar* that all the works of the son of Adam will cease except for three, and he mentioned [among them] a righteous child, and in another that "invocations are offered to the dead on platters of light." The saying that "the son might not be virtuous," would not make any difference for he is a believer. Virtue predominates in the offspring of religious parents, particularly if it is resolved to bring him up in and direct him along the path of virtue. By and large, the invocation of the believer for his parents is beneficial be he pious or wicked. He [the believer] is rewarded for his invocations and good deeds, for he has earned them, and he is not rebuked for his ill deeds; for the sin of a sinner is not superimposed upon another. For that reason the Almighty declared, "We cause their progenies to join them, and We deprive them of naught of their (life's) work" [Kor. 52:21]; that is, we do not take away from their deeds and we make their children an addition to their good deeds.

The fourth facet: that the child should die before him [the parent] and thus he has an intercessor. It has been related concerning the Prophet* of God that he said, "The child drags his parents into heaven."[69] In some *akhbār,* it is related that "the child takes him [the parent] by the garment the same [way] as I now take you by the garment."[70] He* also said, "the progeny is told to enter paradise, but he stands at the gate of paradise in rage and anger saying, 'I will not enter paradise except in the company of my parents.' Then it is said, 'Let his parents enter paradise with him.' "[71]

In another tradition, it is stated that "the children gather at the place of resurrection when created beings are brought to judgement, and it will be said to the angels, 'Take these [the children] to paradise,' but they will stand at the gate of paradise and it will be said to them, 'Welcome to the progeny of the Muslims. Enter! There is no reckoning for you.' They will say, 'Where are our fathers and mothers?' The keepers will reply, 'Your fathers and mothers are not like you, for they have committed sins and ill deeds and they are now rendering account and are making amends for them.' He [the Prophet] said, 'They shout and scream in unison at the gates of paradise.' The Lord Almighty who knows more about them says, 'What is this noise?' They [the keepers] will reply, 'Lord, the children of the Muslims say "We shall not enter paradise except in the company of our parents." Almighty God will say, 'Go through the crowds, take the parents by their hands, and lead them into paradise.' "[72] The Prophet* said, "Whoever has lost two of his children will be shielded from the fire."[73] He* also said, "Whoever has lost three that did not attain puberty, God will make him enter paradise by virtue of His mercy for the children's sake." The Prophet was asked, "O Messenger of God, what about two?" And he replied, "Even two."[74]

It is related that marriage was propounded to one of the righteous men, but he hesitated for a while. The Prophet said, "One day he [the righteous man] awoke from his sleep and said, 'Get me married, get me married!' So they got him married. He was asked concerning that matter, to which he replied: 'God may grant me a child, and then receive him unto Himself; thus he would serve as a prelude for my afterlife.' Then he said, 'I saw in a dream that resurrection had come to pass and myself among the created beings there. I was suffering from mortal thirst; the other created beings were also suffering from intense thirst and distress. While we were in that state, behold a group of children[75] filtered through the crowds covered with veils of light, carrying silver pitchers and golden goblets in their hands and offering drink to one [person] then to another; they filtered through the crowd yet bypassed most of the people. I stretched out my hand to one of them and said, "Give me water to drink, for I am extremely thirsty." But he [the child] replied, "You do not have a child amongst us; we only offer our fathers water to drink." So I said, "And who are you?" They replied, "We are the deceased infant children of the Muslims." ' "[76] One of the meanings incorporated in his statement, which is mentioned in the Almighty's saying, "so go to your tilth as ye will, and prepare beforehand for your souls" [Kor. 2:223], is children for the hereafter. Thus it has become clear from these four facets that the greatest virtue of marriage lies in its being the means of having children.

[Satisfying Sexual Desire]

The second advantage: fortification against the devil, curbing lust, warding off the excesses of desire, averting the eye, and safeguarding relief. To this the Prophet* referred when he declared, "He who marries fortifies half of his religion, so let him fear God for the second half." To this he also referred when he stated, "You are enjoined to establish homes. He who cannot do it should fast, for fasting is a [form] of castration." Most of what we have quoted from the *āthār* and the *akhbār* points to this interpretation; and this purpose is inferior to the former one because desire is a charge to produce children. Marriage is sufficient for bringing this about, a reason for causing it to be, and a safeguard against the evil of it becoming dominant. One who obeys his master in order to please him is not like one who obeys in order to be freed from a heavy obligation. Sexual desire and children are foreordained and between them exists a tie. It is not appropriate to say that the aim is pleasure and the child is a necessary result, just as elimination is a necessary result of eating, not an aim in itself. Rather, the child is the aim by instinct and decree, and sexual desire is merely an inducement thereto. I cannot conceive of any purpose for sexual desire except procreation. The pleasure which accompanies it—pleasure which would be unrivaled were it to last—is a harbinger of the promised pleasures in paradise. For to encourage pleasure which one cannot enjoy is pointless. Thus were an impotent male encouraged to seek enjoyment of coitus, or were a young boy encouraged to seek rule and power, encouragement would be to no avail. One virtue of the world's pleasures is that people wish to see them [pleasures] continue in paradise; thus they are an inducement to the worship of God.

Behold the wisdom, the mercy, and the divine fulfillment (*al-ta^cbiyah al-ilāhīyah*):[77] how two lives, one external (*ẓāhirah*) and one internal (*bāṭinah*), were fused together by one desire.[78] The exoteric life is the perpetuation of the individual through the preservation of his lineage, which is a form of the perpetuation of existence. The esoteric life is the life in the hereafter, "so if this pleasure, diminished by the speedy passage of time, activates the desire for [attaining] pleasure by becoming everlasting, then it encourages the kind of worship which leads to it [pleasure]." Consequently the servant [of God] benefits by becoming so desirous of it and gains the ability to persist in that which leads him to the blissfulness of paradise.

There is not an atom in the body of man, internal or external in the Kingdom of Heaven and Earth, within which one would not discover a measure of wisdom and wonder that baffles the mind. Nevertheless, it can be revealed only to a pure heart in proportion to its purity and to the extent that it resists the world's pleasures, its enticements, and its snares. Thus, marriage for the sake of curbing excessive desire is important in religion to all who do not suffer from impotence—these happen to constitute the majority of created beings. For if sexual desire prevails and encounters no resistance from the force of piety, it will lead to the commission of an abomination (*fāḥishah*).

To this the Prophet* referred when conveying the word of the Almighty, "If ye do not so, there will be confusion in the land, and great corruption."[79] If it [sexual desire] is bridled with the bridle of piety, and the purpose [of marriage] is to curtail the limbs [of the body] (*jawāriḥ*)[80] from responding to desire, then marriage would avert the eye and preserve relief by guarding the heart as well as the mind against temptation. For that is not a matter of one's choice, rather the self will continue to entice him and tempt him to have coitus, and the tempting devil will not abandon him most of the time. That could occur during prayer; thus he may envision such details of coitus which, were he to confess them to the lowliest of creatures, they would blush. Yet God knows [the secrets of] his heart because the heart is to God as the tongue is to man. For the chief preoccupation of the novice (*murīd*)[81] who wants to pursue the path of the hereafter is his heart.[82] [Moreover], persistence in fasting does not eliminate the element of temptation as pertains to most people, unless it is coupled with weakness of the body and disturbance of the temperament. For that reason Ibn ᶜAbbās* declared, "The asceticism of the ascetics cannot be complete without marriage."[83] This is a universal ordeal from which few can be delivered.

Qatādah[84] said, in interpreting the words of the Almighty, "Impose not on us that which we have not the strength to bear":[85] that is, lust. It is said that ᶜAkramah[86] and Mujāhid[87] interpreted the Almighty's words "for man was created weak" [Kor. 4:28] by saying, "He cannot refrain from women." Fayyāḍ b. Najīḥ said that "When the male experiences an erection, he loses two-thirds of his mind"; others say "He loses a third of his religion." One of the rare interpretations rendered by Ibn ᶜAbbās* of the verse "From the evil of the darkness when it is intense" [Kor. 113:3][88] is to the male erection, which is an overpowering catastrophe should it rage, as no mind or religion can resist it; for, although it can become an impetus for the two lives as was mentioned earlier, it is the devil's strongest instrument against the sons of Adam. To this he* referred in these words: "Among those who are deficient in intelligence and religion, I have never seen any who are more successful than you [women] in prevailing over those [men] of intelligence."[89] And that is because of the rage of desire. The Prophet said in his invocation, "O God! I seek refuge in Thee from the evils of my hearing, my seeing, my heart, and the evils of my semen."[90] He also said, "I ask you to purify my heart and safeguard my genitals";[91] so how can there be laxity for others wherefrom the Messenger* of God seeks refuge.

A righteous man used to marry frequently; he never had less than two or three [women]. Some Sufis criticized him, to which he replied, "Has any of you presented himself before God or stood (*waqafa*) before Him[92] and experienced sexual desire?" They replied, "This thing occurs frequently." He retorted, "Were I to accept throughout my life such a state as you have experienced once, I would not have married; but never did a distracting thought occur to me which I did not carry through, thereby relieving and enabling myself to return to my work. And for forty years, no transgression has befallen me." Some people criticized the status of the Sufis, to which a man of religion replied, "What is it you blame them for?" He [one of the people] replied, "They eat a lot." To this he retorted, "And you, also, if you hungered as they do, would eat as they do." He [one of the people] said, "They marry often." To which he replied, "If you should safeguard your eye and genitals as they do, you, too, would marry as they do." Junayd used to say, "I am as much in need of coitus as I am of food, so the wife is definitely nourishment and a means for the purification of the heart."

For that reason the Messenger* of God commanded that everyone who sees a woman and is attracted to her should have intercourse with his wife,[93] for that would ward off temptation from his soul.[94] Jābir* related that the Prophet* of God saw a woman, so he had intercourse with Zaynab [his wife], fulfilled his desire, and departed. The Prophet* declared: "When a woman approaches, she approaches in the image of the devil; so should a man see a woman who appeals to him, let him approach his wife because she has what that woman has."[95]

The Prophet* said, "Do not have intercourse with a woman whose husband is absent[96] because the devil flows through your veins as does the blood." So we said, "And your veins?" He replied, "And mine; but God has fortified me against it and therefore I am safe."[97] Sufyān b. ᶜAyyīnah said, " 'safe' means delivered from it [temptation]. That is its meaning because the devil does not deliver."

It was also related that the son of ᶜUmar*, one of the ascetics among the companions, also of the ulema among them, used to break the fast by coitus before eating. It is probable that he had intercourse before the evening prayer, after which he would perform absolution and pray, all for the purpose of emptying the heart to enable it to concentrate on the worship of God and to remove from it the implements of the devil. It has been related that he [son of ᶜUmar] had coitus with three of his concubines during the month of Ramadan before the last evening prayer.

Ibn ᶜAbbās has declared, "The best of this nation is mostly women";[98] and since sexual desire was a predominant force in the temperament of the Arabs, the frequency of marriage among their righteous men was more common.

It was for the purpose of freeing the heart that marriage with the bondmaid was permitted when there was fear of hardship, even though it results in enslaving the son,[99] which is a kind of attrition; such marriage is forbidden to anyone who can obtain a free woman. However, the enslaving of a son is preferable to destroying the faith, for enslavement affects temporarily the life of the child, while committing an abomination results in losing the hereafter; in comparison to one of its days the longest life is insignificant.[100]

It has been related that one day some people departed from a gathering with Ibn ᶜAbbās, except for one young man who did not leave. Ibn ᶜAbbās asked him, "Do you have something to ask?" He said, "Yes, I wish to ask you a question, but I was ashamed [to ask] in front of the people. Now I stand in awe out of respect for you." "An alim[101] takes the place of the father," said Ibn ᶜAbbās, "so what you would have divulged to your father, disclose to me." He said, "I am a young man with no wife. On occasion I have feared distress for myself, and thus sought relief in masturbation. Is there an act of transgression in it?" So Ibn ᶜAbbās turned away from him, then said, "How disgusting! Marrying a bondmaid is better than that, yet it is better than committing fornication."

This is an indication that a youthful bachelor is torn among three evils: The least of these is marrying a bondmaid, which would lead to enslavement of the offspring; worse than that is masturbation; and the most abominable of the three is fornication. Ibn ᶜAbbās did not permit the commission of either because both [the first two] are forewarned against and should be resorted to only to prevent committing a greater evil, in the same manner as one would eat carrion to avoid self-destruction. Preponderance over the lesser of two evils cannot be construed as unrestricted permissiveness or as absolute virtue; cutting off a malignant arm is not a good act even though it is permissible when death is impending. Therefore marriage is meritorious in this respect, but this does not apply to all [people], only to most. Many a person's desire cools off on account of old age, illness, or the like, and therefore this factor would not apply to him; and what has already been mentioned concerning procreation remains intact. This is general except in the case of the eunuch, which is rare.

It is preferable for a person with temperament so overcome by desire that one woman cannot curb it to have more than one woman, up to four. For God will grant him love and mercy, and will appease his heart by them [women]; if not, replacing them is recommended. Seven nights after the death of Fāṭimah,* ᶜAlī* got married. It is said that al-Ḥasan, the son of ᶜAlī, was a great lover having married more than two hundred women. Perhaps he would marry four at a time, and perhaps he would divorce four at a time replacing them with others. The Prophet* said to al-Ḥasan, "You resemble me in appearance and in character.[102] He* also said, "Ḥasan takes after me and Ḥusayn takes after ᶜAlī."[103] It was said that his indulgence in marriage is one of the characteristics in which he resembled the Messenger* of

God as well as al-Mughīrah Ibn Shuᶜbah who married eighty women.[104] Among the companions were those who had three and four [wives] while those who had two cannot be counted.

No matter how well known the inducement, the cure should be in proportion to the ailment; for the aim is tranquilizing one's self, and therefore this must be taken into consideration in deciding how many wives one should have.

[Companionship]

The third advantage: comfort and relaxation for the soul through companionship; seeing and dallying comfort the heart and strengthen it for the performance of the obligatory rituals. For the self grows weary and has the tendency to shun work because that is contrary to its nature. If compelled to adhere to what disagrees with its nature, it becomes recalcitrant and defiant. If it finds an outlet for itself periodically, it becomes stronger and more energetic. The companionship of women provides relaxation which relieves distress and soothes the heart. It is incumbent upon the pious to acquire such comfort by permissible means. For that reason Almighty God declared, "that he might take rest in her" [Kor. 7:189] and ᶜAlī said, "Relax the heart an hour, for if it is compelled it is blinded." A *khabar* states, "A wise man should divide his time three ways: one for meditating, one for self-examination, and one for eating and drinking. In this [latter] time, there is help for the other period."[105] The same is stated in another expression: "The wise man is desirous[106] only of three things: provisioning himself for a return journey (*maᶜād*),[107] seeking a livelihood (*marammah*), or [seeking] pleasure in something not forbidden."[108] The Prophet* states, "For every desire (*irādah*)[109] there is a *shirrah* (eagerness), and for each *shirrah* there is a *fiṭrah* (natural disposition).[110] He whose *fiṭrah* leads to my sunna is guided."[111] *Shirrah* is the striving and the enduring which come about in the beginning when exercising the will, while *fiṭrah* means stopping for rest. Abū al-Dardā' used to say, "I find relaxation for myself with a little diversion (*lahū*), thereby gaining strength to walk in uprightness thereafter."

In some *akhbār* pertaining to the Prophet,* he said, "I complained to Gabriel* of my inability to have coitus, and he suggested [I eat] *harīsah*."[112] If this be true, it can be interpreted only as a preparation for relaxation and cannot be interpreted to imply warding off desire; for it is rather a kindling of desire, and whoever is deprived of sexual desire is denied most of this intimacy.

The Prophet* also said, "Three things of your world have been made desirable to me: perfume (*ṭīb*), women, and my delight (*qurrat al-ᶜaynī*) in prayer."[113] This, too, is a benefit that cannot be denied by one who has experienced the weariness of thoughts and remembrances (*dhikr*)[114] and different types of work, which lie outside the two previously mentioned benefits. Indeed, it extends even to the eunuch and to the one who has no sexual desire. As a matter of fact, this advantage renders marriage meritorious if it is concluded with such an intent, but rare are those who marry for this end.

As for the aim of having an offspring as well as that of warding off desire and the like, they are prevalent. Besides, many a person finds pleasure in looking at flowing water, greenery, and the like and is not in need of relieving himself by conversing and dallying with women. Thus this [aim] varies with circumstances and individuals; so let it be taken into consideration.

[Ordering the Household]

The fourth advantage: being free from the concerns of household duties, as well as of preoccupation with cooking, sweeping, making beds, cleaning utensils, and means for obtaining support. If a human being had no desire (*shahwah*) for coitus, it would still be difficult for him to live in his house alone; because if he were saddled with all the work of attending the house, he would waste most of his time and have very little of it left for learning and working.

The virtuous woman who takes care of the house abets religiousness in this manner, and any disturbance of these preoccupations would perturb the heart and impede life. For that reason Abū Sulaymān al-Dārānī* declared, "The virtuous wife is not of this world, for she liberates you for the hereafter. Her contribution to freeing [the man] is by both taking care of the house and by satisfying sexual desire." Muḥammad b. Kaᶜb al-Qarazī said in interpreting God's words, "O Lord! Give unto us in the world that which is good" [Kor. 2:201]; he meant a virtuous woman. The Prophet said, "Let each among you have a grateful heart; a tongue which invokes [the name of God]; and a faithful, virtuous wife who assists you toward the hereafter."[115] Behold how he has equated her with invocation and thanksgiving.[116] In a commentary regarding the Almighty's word, it is stated: "him verily We shall quicken with good life" [Kor. 16:97]; he meant a virtuous wife.

ᶜUmar b. al-Khaṭṭāb* used to say, "Next to faith in God, the best gift which has been given to man is a virtuous woman. There are some women that are priceless and others that are yokes from whom one cannot be redeemed"; by priceless is meant that she [woman] cannot be replaced by any other gift.

The Prophet* also said, "I was preferred over Adam by two gifts: His wife abetted him into transgression, while my wives urge me in obedience; his devil was a blasphemer and my devil [is] a Muslim[117] who only enjoins to good."[118] Thus he [the Prophet] considered her helping him towards obedience as a virtue. This, also, is one of the virtues to which the righteous [men] aim, except that it is pertinent to some individuals who have no legal guardian or manager. It does not call for two wives, [since] plurality may render life miserable and disrupt the affairs of the home.

The aim of such an advantage is the expansion of kinfolk [through the wife] as well as gaining strength by virtue of inter-family relations. This is one of the things that is needed in warding off evil and seeking tranquility. For that reason it was said, "Abased is the one who has no protector; but he who finds someone who repels evil from him, his state is secured and his heart is freed for worship." For abasement disturbs the heart while strength in numbers wards off abasement.

[Disciplining the Self]

The fifth advantage: disciplining the self[119] and training it to be mindful, faithful, loyal, and respectful of the rights of the *ahl* (wives),[120] tolerating their manners, enduring harm from them, striving to reform them, guiding them to the path of religion, striving toward making lawful gains for their sake, and undertaking the upbringing of their children. All these are deeds of great merit, for they are an exercise in compliance [with God's injunction] and trust and loyalty; the wives and the offspring being the protected ones, and the virtue of guardianship is great. Those who avoid these responsibilities do so for fear of being unable to do justice by them, otherwise the Prophet* would not have said, "One day of just guardianship is more preferable than seventy years of worship." Then he said, "Indeed, every one of you is a shepherd, and every one of you is responsible for his flock."[121]

The one who is preoccupied with reforming himself and others is not the same as the one who is preoccupied with reforming himself only; nor is the one who endures harm like the one who seeks pleasure and comfort for himself. Bearing the burden of wives and of offspring is equivalent to jihad for the sake of God. For that reason Bishr said, "Aḥmad Ibn Ḥanbal was preferred over me on three counts, one of them being the fact that he sought what was lawful for himself and for others."[122] The Prophet* also said, "Whatever a man spends on his wife is a *ṣadāqah,*[123] and a man will be compensated for the morsel of food he offers his wife."[124]

Someone told one of the ulema, "The Lord has granted me a share of every deed!" and he mentioned the *ḥajj* (pilgrimage), jihad, and the like. So he replied to him, "Where do you stand as concerns the deeds of the substitutions (*ibdāl*)?"[125] He asked: "And what are those?" To which he retorted, "Lawful gain and spending on dependents."

Ibn al-Mubārak said while with his companions during a battle, "Do you know of anything better than what we are doing?" They said, "We know of none." He answered, "I do." They asked, "What is it?" He said, "A virtuous man." He continued, "A virtuous man rose during the night and beheld his sleeping children uncovered, and so he covered them with his garment. His deed is more virtuous than what we are doing."

The Prophet* said, "He whose prayer is good, and whose

children are many and whose possessions are few, and who does not neglect (*yaghtub*) the Muslims will be with me in paradise like these two women."[126] In another hadith it is said, "The Lord loves the poor, virtuous father of children."[127] Another hadith related, "If the sins of the believer become many, God preoccupies him with the burden of children [in order] to make restitution for them [the sins]."[128]

One of the forefathers said, "There are offenses that cannot be atoned for except through family burdens." A tradition relates that the Prophet* said, "There are certain sins that cannot be atoned for except by the burden of seeking a livelihood."[129] He also said, "Whoever has three daughters whom he supports and to whom he is kind until the Lord renders them independent of him, God will most certainly make paradise his reward —unless he commits a deed for which he cannot be forgiven."[130] Ibn ᶜAbbās would say whenever he referred to this hadith, "By God, this is one of the strangest (*gharīb*)[131] and most misleading articles of the hadith."

It has been related that a devout person used to provide well for his wife until she died. It was suggested to him that he remarry after her death, but he refrained and said, "Solitude is more soothing to my heart and allows me to concentrate better on my meditations." He continued: "I saw in a dream, a week following her death, the gates of heaven open, and men descending and marching in succession through the air. Every time one descended, he looked at me and told the one behind him, 'This is the unfortunate one.' The other would reply, 'Yes!' I refrained from asking them out of awe until the last one, who was a child, passed by me. I asked him: 'Say, who is the unfortunate one to whom you are referring?' He replied, 'You.' And I asked, 'Why so?' He replied, 'We used to exalt your deeds among those who have striven for the sake of God; but a week ago we were commanded to record your deed with those who have been inimical, and we do not know what you are guilty of.' " So he said to his brethren, "Get me married, get me married." After that, he was not without two or three [wives].

It is related in one of the *akhbār* of the prophets* that a group entered upon Jonah, the prophet, and he* was hospitable to them. He [Jonah] would enter and leave his house and be mistreated by his wife, yet remain silent. They were astonished, but he said, "Don't be; for I have beseeched Almighty God saying, 'Hasten upon me in this life whatever punishment thou hast prepared for me in the hereafter'; so He said, 'Your punishment is the daughter of so and so whom you should marry.' So I married her and am enduring from her what you see."

Such endurance is a form of self-discipline, an appeasement of anger, and an improvement of character. A person who secludes himself or who associates himself with someone of a refined character does not reflect on the evils of his inner self, nor are his hidden faults revealed. It is, therefore, the duty of one who walks the path of the hereafter to tempt himself by being exposed to the like of such agitations, and to become accustomed to enduring them so that his character should be set straight, his soul should be calm, and he should be purified of the base qualities hidden within him.

Enduring the burden of dependents, which is a form of exercise and struggle to provide for them and sustain them, is an act of worship in itself. However, only one of two types of men benefits from it: either a man who seeks striving, exercising, and character training because he is at the beginning of the Path and is therefore not unlikely to consider this a manner of striving by which his soul is exercised; or, a worshipper who does not pursue virtue through the path of the esoteric (*sayr bil-bāṭin*), mental activity, and the experiences of the heart, but whose [virtuous] deeds are physical,[132] such as prayer, performing the pilgrimage, and the like. His working to gain lawfully for his wives and children, maintaining them and bringing them up properly, is better for him than acts of worship which are imposed upon his body and whose benefits do not extend to others.

As for the man whose character is well formed either through inherent traits or through a previous effort, if he wants to succeed in obtaining an inner life and an intellectual and spiritual activity in the domain of religious and mystical sciences, then he should not marry for that reason because he has no need for exercise.[133] As for worship in the form of providing for dependents, seeking knowledge is better than that because it [seeking knowledge], too, is a form of work, but its benefits are more numerous and more encompassing than the benefit of providing for dependents. These then are the advantages of marriage, which in religion are decreed to be virtuous.

[DISADVANTAGES OF MARRIAGE]

[Inability to Seek Lawful Gain]

The disadvantages of marriage are three: one—the strongest—is the inability to seek gain lawfully.[134] For that is not available to every person, especially nowadays, because of social instability and because marriage encourages the amplification of attempts to provide [for dependents] through unlawful means. In it [marriage] is, thus, a man's destruction and the destruction of his family; a bachelor is safeguarded therefrom. As for a married man, he is most often driven into the paths of evil by following the whims of his wife and selling his hereafter for this world.

There is a *khabar* which states that "the servant (*ᶜabd*) is made to stand before the scales with good deeds that resemble mountains in weight.[135] He then is questioned concerning the care and support of his family, the source of his wealth and how he spent it, until such reckoning absorbs all his good deeds, thus not one good deed remains to his account; whereupon the angels cry out: 'Behold, here is the man whose dependents consume his good deeds in the world and is today mortgaged by his deeds.' "[136]

Is is said that those first to cling to man on the day of resurrection will be his wife and children who will cause him to stand in the presence of Almighty God and then say, "O Lord! Give us our just due from him, for he taught us not what we were ignorant of, feeding us by unlawful means and we did not know it." He [God] will punish him for their sake. One of the forefathers said, "When God wills evil to a servant, He sets upon him fangs in this world to devour him"; meaning dependents.

The Prophet said, "No one will meet God with a greater offense than one who ignores [the needs of] his dependents."[137] This is a general calamity from which few are delivered, excepting one with possessions that are inherited or gained lawfully, which he uses to redeem[138] himself and his family, provided he is content not to seek more. Such a person will be delivered from this calamity as will be a craftsman who is able to gain lawfully through permissible means, such as gathering firewood, hunting, or engaging in a craft that is not dependent upon rulers, and thereby is able to deal with virtuous people; also, the one who manifests blamelessness and most of whose possessions are lawfully gained [will be delivered by God].

Ibn Sālim said when asked about marriage: "It [marriage] is more desirable in this time of ours for someone who is overcome by lust: like the male donkey who sees a female donkey and can neither be dissuaded from her by beating nor can he control himself; should he control himself, it is preferable to leave him alone."

[Failure to Uphold Wives' Rights]

The second disadvantage: the failure to uphold their [wives'] rights, to tolerate their manners, or to endure harm from them. This is less prevalent than the previous [disadvantage], inasmuch as it is easier to overcome the latter than the former. Improving one's manners with women and upholding their rights are easier than seeking lawful gain. There is also danger in this because he [the husband] is a shepherd and is responsible for his flock. The Prophet* said, "It is sin (*ithm*) enough for a man to destroy those for whom he provides."[139]

It has been related that one who deserts his family is like a runaway slave in that his prayer and his fasting are not acceptable until he returns to them. Whoever fails to uphold his wives' rights, even though he might be present, is like a fugitive. The Lord has said, "Ward off from yourselves and your families a [hell]Fire" [Kor. 66:6]. He commanded us to safeguard them from the Fire as we would safeguard ourselves.

A person might fail to uphold his own right, and were he to get married this obligation would be compounded, and to his self another person be added. Self is an impellent to evil; if self is increased, the incitement to evil usually increases. For that reason, a certain man declined to get married and said, "I am afflicted with my [own] self; how can I add another self to it?"[140] As has been said, "The mouse hole would not be large enough to contain it [the mouse] if a broom was tied to its tail."

Ibrāhīm Ibn Adham*[141] also declined [to get married] by saying, "I will not attach a woman unto me, nor do I have need for women; that is to say, I am unable to care for them, protect them, and provide for them since I lack the means." Likewise Bishr declined saying, "I am prevented from marriage by the Almighty's words, 'And they (women) have rights similar to those (of men).' "[142] He used to say, "Were I to care for a chicken, I would fear becoming a butcher on the bridge."[143]

Sufyān b. ᶜAyyīnah* was seen at the gate of the sultan and was told: "This is not your place!" He replied, "Have you seen a man with a family who is more successful?" Sufyān used to say, "I yearn for celibacy, the key,[144] and a place of dwelling which the wind can penetrate and where no commotion or shouting [exists]."

This [the second disadvantage] is, too, a common evil—though less prevalent than the first—from which only an intelligent, wise man can be delivered: A man possessing good character and insight into the ways of women, is tolerant of their tongues, is not driven by their desires, is careful to fulfill his obligations towards them, can overlook their mistakes, and is cognizant of their manners. Most people are given to impudence, boorishness, irascibility, frivolity, bad manners, and injustice while seeking full justice. Inevitably, such men through marriage become more corrupt in this respect. Hence celibacy is safer for them.

[Distractions from God]

The third disadvantage—which is less [of an evil] than the first and the second—[lies in the possibility] that the wife and the offspring could distract him from Almighty God, luring him to pursue the world and indulge in providing a comfortable life for his children through gathering wealth and hoarding it for them, and enticing him to seek exaltation and multiplication through them. Whatever distracts [one's attention] from God—whether wife, wealth, or offspring—brings misfortune upon the possessor. I do not imply by this that it would lead to forbidden deeds, for that [whatever leads to forbidden deeds] has already been listed under the first and second disadvantages, but rather that it would entice him to indulge in the enjoyment of what is permissible, leading into excesses in dallying, flirting, and excessive enjoyment of them [women]. From marriage arise various types of such distractions that engross the heart; thus night and day would pass and the person would not have time to think about the hereafter or prepare for it. For that reason Ibrāhīm Ibn Adham* said, "No good can come out of one who becomes accustomed to the thighs of women." Abū Sulaymān* said, "Whoever marries attaches himself to the world." That is to say, he is lured to depend on the world.

[CONCLUSIONS]

This is the sum total of disadvantages and advantages. To judge that a person is absolutely better off [by] being married or single falls short of taking into consideration all these matters. Rather, such advantages and disadvantages can be considered a precept and a criterion against which the novice should measure himself. If the disadvantages [of marriage] are nonexistent in his case and the benefits are all present, that is, if he has lawfully gained possessions, good character, and earnest pursuit of religion, marriage would not distract him from God; if he [the novice] is, nevertheless, a young man in need of appeasing his sexual desire, if he is a bachelor in need of someone to take care of his house, and if he needs fortification through family associations, then marriage is unquestionably better for him even though its [primary] aim is to produce offspring. If the advantages are refuted and the disadvantages are brought together, being celibate is preferable for him; but if the two are equal, which is most likely, it is necessary to weigh on just scales the extent to which the advantages contribute to the promotion of his religion and the extent to which the disadvantages detract from it. If it appears that one group outweighs the other, it should be acted upon. For the most obvious advantages are procreation and appeasing desire, while the most obvious disadvantages are the need for unlawful gain and distraction from

God. Let us assume that these matters are comparable in importance: We would then conclude that if a man is not troubled by sexual desire, if the benefit of his marriage lies in the endeavor to obtain an offspring, and if the evils of his marriage lie in the necessity to gain unlawfully and to be distracted from God—then celibacy is preferable. There is no advantage in whatever distracts one from God or in earning unlawful gain.

The matter of offspring cannot compensate for the absence of these two considerations, [because] marriage for the purpose of obtaining an offspring is illusory and this constitutes a consummate deficiency in religion. To preserve his own life and to guard it from destruction is more important than seeking to produce an offspring; that is a gain, and religion is an investment. For in the corruption of religion lies the loss of the hereafter and the dissipation of the investment. Such a benefit cannot counteract either of those two disadvantages. However, if to the matter of the offspring is added the need to appease desire, which results from one's yearning for marriage, then one might consider marriage. If the reins of righteousness are not strengthened in his mind, and if he fears committing fornication, then marriage is preferable for him because he is hesitant between committing fornication and attaining unlawful gain; earning unlawful gain is the lesser of the two disadvantages. If he trusts himself not to commit fornication, and is unable at the same time to avert the eye from what is unlawful, then abstaining from marriage is preferable. For, to look [lustfully] is unlawful and to earn gain in an improper way is unlawful. Seeking gain takes place continually and in it lies his [ultimate] ruin and the ruin of his family, while looking takes place occasionally and this pertains to him [and does not involve his relations] and passes away quickly. Looking constitutes adultery by the eyes but, if not rectified by relief, is easier to forgive than eating forbidden fruit, unless it is feared that looking should end in the defiance of relief, thus entailing the threat of affliction.

If this be the case, then we are confronted with the third situation: that is, to have the strength to avert the eyes but not to ward off thoughts distracting the heart; here it is preferable to abstain from marriage because the [evil] deeds of the heart are easier to forgive. Emptying the heart for the sake of worship is desirable; [besides] the act of worship is precluded by unlawful gain, consuming it [gain], and feeding it to others. Thus it is necessary to weigh these disadvantages against the advantages and to judge accordingly. Whoever becomes aware of this will not find it difficult to comprehend what we have transmitted from the righteous forefathers, namely encouragement of marriage in certain situations and in others discouragement therefrom inasmuch as this is dependent upon circumstances.

If you should ask, "Which is better for someone who is safeguarded from the disadvantages [of marriage], seclusion for the worship of God or marriage?" I would reply: Combine the two, because marriage is a contract and does not preclude seclusion for the worship of God; rather, it pertains to the need for lawful gain. If he is able to earn lawful gain, then marriage is also better, because it is feasible for him during the night and the rest [that is, the unoccupied portion] of the day to be in seclusion for worship; persistence in worship without relaxation is not feasible. If it be assumed that earning a livelihood preoccupies his whole time to the extent that he has none left other than that prescribed—sleeping, eating, and performing the necessaries—and if he is one of those who do not pursue the hereafter except through the supererogatory prayer, pilgrimage, or similar physical activities, then marriage is better for him. For earning lawful gain, supporting a family, seeking to obtain offspring, and tolerating the manners of women constitute forms of worship whose merits do not fall short of supererogatory acts of worship. If he should worship by means of knowledge, meditation, and the path of esotericism, and should lawful gain complicate that, then abstaining from marriage is preferable.

Should you ask, "Why then did Jesus* abstain from marriage in spite of its virtue? And if it is preferable to free oneself for the worship of God, why then did our Prophet* take on numerous wives?" Know ye, then, that it is preferable to combine the two in the case of one who is able, whose desire is strong, and whose ambition is high, because no preoccupation can distract him from God.

Our Messenger* armed himself with strength and combined the virtue of worship and that of marriage. In spite of his nine women,[145] he still dedicated himself to God. For him, the satisfaction of the sexual need was not an obstacle. At the same time, those who are preoccupied with worldly needs are not constrained in their affairs by the fulfilling of natural needs; outwardly, they perform that which is necessary, but their hearts are preoccupied with solitude not unmindful of their important duties. The Messenger* of God, because of his elevated status, was not deterred by the dictates of this world from the presence of the heart with God. He used to receive revelation (*waḥy*) while he was in his wife's bed.[146] If this is true in the case of someone else, it is not inconceivable that irrigation canals can be altered by what cannot alter the mighty ocean; in other words, one cannot compare others unto him [that is, the Prophet].[147] As for Jesus,* he armed himself with resolutions and not strength; he took precautions, for perhaps his state was such that preoccupation with a family could have affected it, or made it difficult to seek lawful gain, or made marriage and seclusion for worship irreconcilable. Thus he preferred to devote himself to worship. For they [prophets] are more aware [than others] of the secrets of their states, of the precepts of their times regarding virtuous gain, of the manners of women, of the calamities of marriage upon the marrier, and of the benefits he [that is, the marrier] has therein. No matter how different the circumstances are, in some cases it is preferable to marry and in others to abstain. We should deem the deeds of the prophets as preferable in all cases —and God knows best.

Chapter Two

As Concerns Marriage: Conditions of the Woman and Stipulations of the Marriage Contract

[MARRIAGE CONTRACT]

As for the marriage contract (*ᶜaqd*), it has four conditions that facilitate its establishment and dissolution:

1. Permission of the guardian; if not, then [that of] the ruler.[1]

2. Consent of the woman if she is a nonvirgin adult (*thayyib bāligh*) or a virgin adult given away in marriage by someone other than her father or grandfather.

3. The presence of two witnesses openly known for fairness. If both enjoy a blameless record, then the establishment of the contract is decreed.

4. A declaration (*ījāb*) and a related acceptance (*qabūl*) encompassing the term "marry," "give in marriage," or some similar term, pronounced by two individuals charged with the responsibility, neither of whom is a woman; but [they] could include the husband, the guardian [of the woman], or the representative [of either party].

[ETIQUETTE OF MARRIAGE]

Concerning the etiquette of marriage: The engagement should be arranged with a guardian, not during the legally prescribed waiting period (*ᶜiddah*) of the woman, but rather after its termination if the woman is observing such a period, and provided that she is not already engaged to another, since an engagement while another is pending is forbidden.[2] Proper etiquette requires an engagement [period] prior to marriage, and associating the expression of praise [to God] with the declaration and the acceptance; thus the one giving the woman in marriage says, "Praise be to God and blessings upon the Messenger of God. I give you my daughter, so and so, in marriage"; and the husband replies, "Praise be to God and blessings upon the Messenger of God. I accept her in marriage upon this dowry (*ṣadāq*)." Let the dowry be fixed and small. It is also desirable to pronounce the words "Praise be to God" before the engagement. Its etiquette includes that the affairs of the husband be revealed to the wife; if she is a virgin, this is more appropriate and more conducive to congeniality between them. For that reason it is desirable that he should look at her before marriage, as it is more likely to lead to enrichment of their relationship.

Its etiquette also calls for the presence of a group of righteous people in addition to the two witnesses who are required to establish the validity [of the contract]. The etiquette also specifies that the intent of marriage should be upholding the sunna, averting the eye, bearing children, and the rest of the aforementioned advantages; thus the purpose of marriage will not be merely for pleasure and enjoyment, which would render such an act a worldly endeavor. This does not preclude such intentions, for many a virtue coincides with passion. ᶜUmar b. ᶜAbd al-ᶜAzīz*[3] declared: "If virtue coincides with passion, it is like 'butter with dates' " (*al-zubadu bil-nirsiyān*).[4] It is not impossible that one should be motivated by his desires and the dictates of religion simultaneously. It is desirable that the marriage be contracted in the mosque and during the month of Shawwal.[5] ᶜĀ'ishah*[6] said, "The Prophet* married me in Shawwal, and consumated the marriage in Shawwal."[7]

[REQUISITE QUALITIES FOR THE WOMAN]

A woman given in marriage is either one who is taken as a lawful wife, or one who is taken for enjoyment and the attainment of certain purposes.

[Legal Disabilities to or Restrictions on Marriage]

The first type: The woman taken as a lawful wife should be

free from that which would prohibit her marriage. There are nineteen restrictions.[8]

1. That she be married to another.

2. That she be in a legally prescribed waiting period [which precedes marriage] to another [person], regardless of whether that period is due to [the husband's] death, to divorce, to suspicion [of adultery], or is being cleared from suspicion aroused by [her] owner [that is, being a concubine-slave of the owner].

3. That she be an apostate for having uttered an expression of unbelief.

4. That she be a Magian.[9]

5. That she be an idolator or freethinker (*zindīq*) who follows neither a prophet nor a book. Women in this category include those who follow the doctrine of libertinism—marrying them is not lawful; also [included in this category is] every female subscribing to a false doctrine whose believer is deemed an infidel.

6. [If] she is a follower of a revealed religion (*kitābīyah*)[10] which she adopted after conversion or after the Prophet's mission [as Messenger of God], and who furthermore is not a descendant from the Children of Israel, unless both conditions apply, marrying her is not permissible; but if she lacks genealogy only, then [among the jurisprudents] there is no consensus.

7. That she be a slave and the marrier a free man who is capable of marrying a free woman or who fears committing fornication (*ʿanat*).[11]

8. That she be totally or partially a slave of the marrier.

9. That she be related to the [man] either by descent from his progenitors (*uṣūl*) or collaterals (*fuṣūl*), or of the collaterals of his first progenitors, or from the first collateral of every progenitor after a progenitor. By *uṣūl,* I mean mothers and grandmothers; and by his *fuṣūl,* [male] children and grandchildren; and by *fuṣūl awwal fuṣūl,* brothers and their children; and by *awwal faṣl* from every *aṣl* [singular of *uṣūl*] after it, the progenitor of maternal and paternal aunts, not their children.

10. That she be unlawful [for marriage] through nursing;[12] and among those prohibited by reason of nursing are the relations prohibited in terms of the *uṣūl* and *fuṣūl* discussed above.

However, those forbidden are the ones who have been nursed five times, not the ones nursed fewer times.

11. That she be forbidden because of marriage ties; that is, (a) if the marrier were already married to her daughter or granddaughter,[13] or (b) if he previously possessed them [as slaves either] by direct contract or semicontract, or (c) if he had had sexual relations with them in a quasi-contract [common marriage], or (d) had sexual intercourse with her mother or one of her grandmothers in a marital contract or quasi-contract; for the mere contract of marriage with a woman renders her maternal female ascendants unlawful. Her collateral relatives are forbidden only on account of coitus, or if his [the marrier's] father or son had married her before.

12. That the woman be the fifth,[14] that is, that the marrier already has four [wives] acquired either by marriage or by virtue of [the fact that at least one of his wives is in] the state of the legally prescribed waiting period pending remarriage (*ᶜiddat al-rajᶜah*) to him. But if her divorce is final and she is in another prescribed waiting period (*ᶜiddat baynūnah*),[15] then marrying the fifth is not unlawful.

13. That the marrier be married to her sister, her maternal aunt, or her paternal aunt; that is, through marriage he would bring both of them together [as wives]. Marriage is not permissible between a related pair if one is male and the other a female, and thus they cannot be brought together [in marriage].

14. That she be divorced three times by the marrier and thus be unlawful to him unless another husband [*muḥallil*] has sexual intercourse with her in a lawful marriage.[16]

15. That the marrier has exchanged curses with her; in this case, after the oath of condemnation (*liᶜān*),[17] she is forever unlawful to him.

16. That she be in a state of ritual consecration of the major (*ḥajj*) or lesser (*ᶜumra*) pilgrimage, or that the husband be in the same state; marriage then cannot take place until the completion of the period of sanctification.

17. That she should be a deflowered young woman;[18] marrying her is then not permissible until she has reached puberty.

18. That she be an orphan, in which case marrying her is not permissible until she reaches the age of puberty.

19. That she be one of the widowed wives of the Messenger* of God or one with whom he has mated, for they are regarded as mothers of the believers; that [restriction] is not applicable in our [al-Ghazālī's] time. These are the prohibitive hindrances.

[QUALITIES CONDUCIVE TO A HAPPY CONJUGAL LIFE]

There are eight qualities which render a conjugal life happy and which must be sought in the woman in order to assure the perpetuity of the marriage: piety, good character, beauty, a small dowry, ability to bear children, virginity, [good] lineage, and she should not be a close relative.

[Piety]

That she should be virtuous and religious is the most fundamental requisite, and to that end [special] care must be taken. For, if her religious principles are too weak to give her the strength to be virtuous and constant,[19] she will humiliate her husband, disgrace him among people, trouble his heart with jealousy, and thereby render his life miserable. Should he succumb to passion and jealousy, he would remain in trial and tribulation. Should he, on the other hand, follow the path of permissiveness, he would be apathetic toward his religion and honor and would be guilty of lacking zeal and pride. Also, if she is beautiful but corrupt, she will be the cause of greater tribulation; for then it becomes difficult for the husband to separate from her: Thus he is neither able to renounce her nor to endure her. His position is like that of one who came to the Prophet* and said, "O Messenger of God, I have a wife who cannot turn back a touching hand." The Prophet said, "Divorce her"; to which he replied, "I love her." The Prophet responded, "Then, keep her."[20] The Prophet commanded him to hold onto her, for if he divorces her he would yearn for her and become corrupt like her. Seeing that the man's heart was in anguish, he [the

Prophet] considered it preferable for him to continue his marriage and thus safeguard himself against corruption. If her faith be corrupted in squandering his possessions or in some other respect, he will remain in misery. [However,] if he remains silent and does not denounce [her deeds], he becomes a partaker of her transgression and a violator of the Almighty's command: "Ward off from yourselves and your families a Fire." If he, on the other hand, denies and disputes [her ways], he will be miserable throughout his life.

For that reason, the Messenger* of God took pains in encouraging people to adhere to the faith saying, "A woman may be married either for her possessions, her beauty, her reputation, or her religion; for if you do marry other than a religious woman, may your hands be rubbed with dirt [*taribat yadāk*]."[21] Another hadith states: "He who marries a woman for her possessions and beauty loses both her beauty and her possessions; [but] he who marries her for the sake of her faith will be blessed by God with her possessions and her beauty."[22] The Prophet* also said, "A woman should not be married [only] for her beauty, because her beauty may destroy her; neither for her wealth, as this may make her tyrannical; [rather] marry the woman for her religious faith."[23] He emphatically recommended religious faith, because such a woman would bolster up the [husband's] faith. If she is not pious, she will be an element of distraction and of trouble in her husband's religion.

[Good Character]

Good character is the second quality. It is an important requisite in the search for emptying the heart[24] and in the pursuit of favorable surroundings for religion. For if she is vicious, ill-tongued, ill-mannered, and ungrateful, more harm than good will come from her. Toleration of a woman's tongue would try the saints. An Arab said, "Do not marry one of the following six types of women: an *ᶜannānah* [hypochondriac], a *mannānah* [upbraider], a *ḥannānah* [yearner], a *ḥiddāqah* [coveter], a *barrāqah* (narcissist], or a *shaddāqah* [prattler]. The *ᶜannānah* is one who excessively moans, complains, and [always] wraps her head.

Marrying a constantly ill [woman] or one who feigns illness is of no avail. The *mannānah* is one who is constantly needling her husband by saying, "I did such and such for you." The *ḥannānah* is one who yearns after a previous husband or after her offspring from some other husband. This, too, is among the things to be avoided. The *ḥiddāqah* is one who looks at everything, covets it, and forces her husband to buy it. The *barrāqah* can be one of two: (a) one who spends the whole day fixing her face or making it up and beautifying it in order to give it a lustre, or (b) one who becomes angry at mealtime, thus eating only by herself and singling out her share from everything. A Yemeni expression which is appropriately used for a woman, or a child, who is not satisfied with the food given to her [or him], is *Baraqat al-mar'atu wa baraqa'l-ṣabiyyū al-ṭaᶜāma;* that is, to become angry at meal-time. *Al-shaddāqah* is one who prattles a great deal; in this context the Prophet* said, "Almighty God detests the loudmouthed prattler."[25]

It is related that the Azdi traveler,[26] during his journey, met Elias* [the prophet] who ordered him to get married and discouraged him from celibacy. He then said, "Don't marry any of the following four types: a *mukhtaliᶜāh* [divorce-minded], a *mubāriyah* [boaster], an *ᶜāhirah* [harlot], or a *nāshiz* [conceited]." *Al-mukhtaliᶜāh* is one who asks for the divorce (*khulᶜ*) every hour for no reason;[27] *al-mubāriyah* is one who boasts of the superiority of another and is proud of her worldly advantages, and *al-ᶜāhirah* is a loose woman who is known to have lovers and intimate companions. To her the Almighty referred when He said, "nor of loose conduct" [Kor. 4:25]. *Al-nāshiz* is one who adopts a haughty attitude toward her husband in deed and word: the word *nashaz*[28] designates that which is elevated above the ground.

ᶜAlī* used to say, "The worst characteristics of men constitute the best characteristics of women; namely, stinginess, pride, and cowardice. For if the woman is stingy, she will preserve her own and her husband's possessions; if she is proud, she will refrain from addressing loose and improper words to everyone; and if she is cowardly, she will dread everything and will therefore not go out of her house and will avoid compromising situations for fear of her husband. These accounts indicate the sum total of the good qualities sought in marriage.

[Beauty]

The third, beauty of face, is desired because through it fortification is attained. For [a man's] natural disposition is generally not contented with an ugly woman, [even] when good character and physical beauty are often inseparable. What we have transmitted is encouragement to look for a pious woman and not marry one for her beauty, which does not discourage the cherishing of beauty, but rather discourages marrying a woman for her beauty alone [while she be] corrupt in religion. Beauty, per se, oftentimes makes marriage desirable and detracts from the importance of religion. Indicative of the regard given to beauty is the fact that closeness and love are often realized through it. For that reason the Shari ᶜa[29] enjoined the safeguarding of the means to intimacy, and seeing [the woman] before marriage was deemed desirable.

The Prophet said, "If God should incline the heart of one of you toward a woman, let him look at her, for it will bring them closer together."[30] That is to say, it will cause them to be closer to each other like the closeness of the epidermis to the endodermis, which is the inner skin [as opposed to] the epidermis [which] is the outer skin. He mentions that only to stress the degree of closeness. The Prophet* said, "There is something in the eyes of the Anṣār;[31] therefore, if one of you wishes to marry one of their women, let him look at them."[32] It was said [in effect] that those women were "blear-eyed." It was also said, "small-eyed."

Some God-fearing men would not marry off their daughters until they are seen as a precaution against delusion. Al-Aᶜmash[33] said, "Every marriage occurring without looking ends in worry and sadness." It is obvious that looking does not reveal character, religion, or wealth; rather, it distinguishes beauty from ugliness.

It was related that during the time of ᶜUmar* a man got married. The man had colored his hair and the dyestuff had faded. The woman's family complained to ᶜUmar saying, "We thought he was a young man." ᶜUmar beat him excessively and said, "You have deceived the people." It is related that Bilāl and Ṣuhayb came to a bedouin household and asked to marry their daughters. They were asked: "Who are you?" Bilāl said, "I am Bilāl and this is my brother, Ṣuhayb. We were misguided, but God has directed us; we were enslaved, but God freed us; we were dependent [on others], but God has made us independent; if you should give us wives, then thanks be to God; and if you should turn us away, then praise be to God." They [the household] answered, "Rather, you will marry, and thanks be to God." Ṣuhayb said to Bilāl,[34] "Would that you had mentioned our association and dealings with the Messenger* of God." He replied, "Be quiet. I spoke the truth and the truth will get you married."

One may be deceived both in beauty and in character; therefore it is desirable to avoid deception in beauty by looking, and [deception] in character by description and inquiry. It is desirable that this precede marriage. A description of her character and beauty should not be sought from any but one who is keen, who is truthful, who is well versed in the apparent and the hidden [qualities], who is not predisposed toward her lest he should praise her too much, and who does not envy her lest he should not praise her enough. In stating the basis for marriage and in describing the would-be wives, the natural disposition leans toward exaggeration and excessiveness. Few are the ones who are truthful and are inclined to modesty; rather, deception and enticement often predominate. Caution, therefore, is important for one who would guard himself against longing for a woman other than his wife.

As for the man whose purpose in having a wife is mere observation of the sunna, bearing children, or caring for the house, should he renounce beauty, he would draw nearer to asceticism; because seeking beauty, in short, is a wordly interest even though in the case of some individuals [it] may be an aid to religion.

Abū Sulaymān al-Dārānī said, "Indifference (*zuhd*) [to worldly interests may be] in anything, even in women." Thus a man [might] marry an old woman because he has preferred to renounce worldly delights. Mālik b. Dīnār*[35] used to say, "Many a man among you would refrain from marrying an orphan, whose feeding and clothing would cost little and who would be easily satisfied, thus gaining merit [before God]. Rather, he would marry the daughter of so and so—meaning prominent people—who would make many demands of him saying, 'Clothe me with such and such.' " Aḥmad b. Ḥanbal preferred a one-eyed [woman] over her sister who was beautiful. For he asked: "Who is the better behaved of the two?" He was told: "The one-eyed." He replied: "Give her to me in marriage." Such is the constant endeavor of one who does not seek [mere] sensual pleasures. If someone cannot secure his faith without a source of pleasure, then let him seek beauty because enjoyment of what is lawful strengthens faith.

It has been said that if a woman is beautiful, of good character, with black eyes and hair, large eyes, white complexion, loves her husband, and has an eye to no other man, she is in the image of the houris [*ḥawar*].[36] For Almighty God has ascribed to the women of paradise this description in the verse, "the good and beautiful" [Kor. 60:70] (by "good" He meant "those enjoying good manners"); in the verse "of modest gaze" [37:48]; and in the verse "lovers (*ᶜurub*), friends" [56:37]. (By "lovers," He means someone who is in love with her husband and desirous of seducing him so as to complete her pleasure. By *al-ḥawar,* He meant whiteness; *al-ḥawrā'* is a woman with intense whiteness of the sclera, profound blackness of the eyes matching the profound blackness of the hair, and big, wide[-set] eyes.)

The Prophet* said, "The best of your women is one who pleases her husband when he looks at her, who obeys him when he commands her, and guards his memory and his possessions when he is absent."[37] Her husband will be delighted to look at her if she loves him.

[Dowry]

The fourth quality is that her dowry should be small. The Messenger* of God declared that "The best women are those whose faces are the most beautiful and whose dowries are the smallest."[38] He enjoined against excessiveness in dowries.[39] The Messenger* of God married one of his wives for a dowry of ten dirhams[40] and household furnishings that consisted of a hand mill, a jug, a pillow made of skin stuffed with palm fibers,[41] and a stone (*ᶜiliyy*);[42] in the case of another, he feasted with two measures[43] of barley;[44] and for another, with two measures of dates and two of mush (*sawīq*).[45]

ᶜUmar* [also] used to enjoin against excessive dowries and used to say, "In getting married and in marrying of his daughters, the Messenger* of God never spent more than 400 dirhams."[46] If paying excessive dowries for women were a virtue, the Messenger* of God would have been the first to do so. One of the companions of the Messenger* of God was married for a date-pit of gold equal to five dirhams.[47] Sa ᶜīd b. al-Musayyab married his daughter to Abū Hurayrah* for two dirhams. He then took her personally to him by night, let her in through the door, then departed. Seven days later, he came back and greeted her. Even if he [Sa ᶜīd] had married for ten dirhams to be different from the rest of the ulema, there would be nothing wrong with his act.

A *khabar* states that "a woman's blessing is in marrying and in bearing children quickly,"[48] and "in the reasonableness of her dowry."[49] He also said, "The most blessed among them are the ones with the smallest dowries."[50]

Just as it is undesirable for the woman's dowry to be excessive, it is undesirable for the man to ask about the possessions of the woman. Marriage should never be motivated by avidity for wealth. Al-Thawrī[51] said, "Should one marry and ask 'What does the woman possess?' know ye that he is a thief; and should a person give them a present, it should not be with the purpose of forcing them to reciprocate with more; likewise, should they give him a present, the expectation of receiving more [than they gave] is immoral. Exchanging gifts is desirable, and results in friendship." The Prophet* said, "If you exchange gifts, you will love each other."[52] As pertains to seeking more, it is included in the words of the Almighty: "And show not favor, seeking worldly gain" [Kor. 74:6], that is to say, give [not] in order to receive more; also in the Almighty's words: "That which ye give in usury in order that it may increase on (other) people's property" [30:39], for usurious interest is the increase, and that [giving a gift] is an attempt to increase the principal, though it is not usurious. All such attempts are detested and are regarded as heretical in marriage. For they resemble trading and gambling, and their aim corrupts marriage.

[Childbearing]

The fifth quality is that the woman be able to bear children. Should she be known to be barren, then one should avoid marrying her. The Prophet* said, "Marry the loving child-bearer";[53] if she has no husband and her affairs are not known, the decision should be based on her health and her youth for, given these two qualities, she will most likely be capable of bearing children.

[Virginity]

The sixth quality is that she should be a virgin. The Prophet* said to Jābir, who had married an unwed deflowered woman, "Would that she were a virgin so you could dally with her and she with you."[54] Virginity has three advantages:

(a) First, the virgin will love the husband and feel close to him, which will favorably influence their conjugal attachment. The Prophet* said, "Marry the loving (woman)"; for the natural disposition is to be attached to the first mate with whom one has had intimate relations. On the other hand, a woman who has experienced men and life may not be satisfied with some of the qualities that differ from those she is accustomed to, and may, therefore, loathe the husband.

(b) Second, it engenders a greater measure of his love for her, as it is a man's nature to be somewhat repelled by a woman who has been touched by another husband; that would contradict [a man's] nature regardless of what might be said [to the contrary]. Certain natures find it more repulsive than others.

(c) Third, the virgin does not yearn after the first husband, because, in general, the surest[55] love is that which is engendered with the first loved one.

[Good Lineage]

The seventh quality is that the wife should be of good lineage, that is to say, she should come from a religious and righteous background, because she will bring up her daughters and sons. If she is not well bred, she will not be able to raise her children well. For that reason the Prophet* said, "Beware of the green dung (*khaḍrā' al-diman*)."[56] It was asked, "What is the green dung?" He said, "The beautiful woman with an evil origin."[57] The Prophet* said, "Exercise care in choosing [wives] for your sperm, for a hereditary quality is wont to return."[58]

[Not a Close Relative]

The eighth quality is that she should not be a close relative, as that would lessen desire. The Prophet* said, "Don't marry close relatives for then the child is born scrawny";[59] that is to say, weak; such is the weakening effect it [marrying close relatives] has on desire. For desire is excited by the deep emotions which result from sight and touch; emotions are strengthened by whatever is unfamiliar and new. On the other hand, what is familiar and seen continuously renders the faculties incapable of fully appreciating it [desire], being affected by it, or becoming aroused through it. These are the qualities desired in women.

[INQUIRY INTO THE HUSBAND'S CHARACTER]

It is incumbent upon the guardian also to examine the qualities of the husband and to look after his daughter so as not to give her in marriage to one who is ugly, ill-mannered, weak in faith, negligent in upholding her rights, or unequal to her in descent. The Prophet* has said, "Marriage is enslavement; let one, therefore, be careful in whose hands he places his daughter."[60] Exercising caution on her behalf is important, because she becomes a slave by the marriage and cannot be freed from it, while the husband is able to obtain divorce at all times. Whoever gives his daughter in marriage to a person who is unjust, licentious, heretical, or an inebriate commits a crime against his religion and exposes himself to the wrath of God for having severed his parental tie by having made a bad choice. A man said to al-Ḥasan,[61] "A number of suitors have asked for my daughter's hand in marriage; to whom should I give her?" He replied, "To the one who fears God; because if he loves her, he will be kind to her; and if he hates her, he will not wrong her." The Prophet* said, "Whoever gives his daughter in marriage to a licentious man has betrayed her womb."

CHAPTER THREE

Etiquette of Cohabitation, What Should Take Place During the Marriage, and the Obligations of Husband and Wife

FIRST PART OF THIS CHAPTER
Etiquette of Cohabitation

[OBLIGATIONS INCUMBENT UPON THE HUSBAND]

As for the husband, he is obligated to observe moderation and good manners in twelve matters: feasting, cohabitation, dallying, exercising authority, jealousy, support, teaching, apportionment, politeness at times of discord, intimate relations, producing children, and separation through divorce.

[Feasting]

The first etiquette is feasting, and that is desirable. Anas* said, "The Prophet* of God saw a trace of paleness in the face of ᶜAbd al-Raḥmān b. ᶜAwf* and said 'What is this?' To which he replied, 'I married a woman for a date-pit of gold.' The Prophet replied, 'May God bless her for you. Have a feast, even with a sheep.'[1] The Prophet of God feasted for Ṣafiyyah[2] with dates and *sawīq*."[3] The Prophet* said, "The food of the first day is an obligation; of the second, a sunna; and of the third, a [cause for good] reputation; he who spreads the news is made known by God.[4] Only Ziyād b. ᶜAbdullah mentions it as being *gharīb*.[5]

It is desirable to congratulate him [the husband]; thus one who enters [the house of] the husband should say, "May God bless you and yours and bring you together in prosperity."[6] Abū Hurayrah* recounted that the Prophet* made it a command.

The publicizing of marriage is desirable. The Prophet said, "The separator of the lawful and unlawful [in marriage] is the tambourine and the voice."[7] He also said, "Make known this marriage, perform it in the mosques, and celebrate it with the beating of tambourines."[8] It is related that al-Rubayyiᶜ, the daughter of Muᶜawwidh, said, "The Prophet* came and entered upon me the morning that my marriage was consummated. He sat on my bed while some of our young girls were beating their tambourines for us and lamenting those of my forefathers who had been killed, until one of them said, 'and among us there is a prophet who knows what the morrow holds,' to which he replied, 'Don't say this and say only what you were saying before.' "[9]

[Conjugal Harmony]

The second etiquette: good conduct with them [wives] and tolerating offense from them out of pity for their mental deficiencies. Almighty God declared, "But consort with them in kindness" [Kor. 4:19]. He also said in upholding their rights, "And they have taken a strong pledge from you" [4:21]. He [God] also said, "And what your right hands (possess)" [4:36 (ᶜAlī)].[10] Some say that [the verse] refers to women.

The last commandments that the Prophet* left were three, which he continued to utter until he stammered and his words became incomprehensible. He kept saying: "Pray, pray![11] Do not impose upon your slaves that which you could not support. Fear God; fear God as concerns your women for they are like putty in your hands, that is, captives. You have taken them as a trust from God, and intimate relations with them was made lawful through the word of God."[12]

The Prophet* also said, "If a man is tolerant of his wife's bad manners, God will grant him the same recompense that He granted Job for his affliction; whoever tolerates the bad manners of her husband, will be granted by God the same recompense[13] that was granted to Āsiyah the wife of Pharaoh."[14] Know ye that good conduct with her does not mean not harming her, but rather enduring harm from her and forbearance in the face of her fickleness and anger in emulation of the Prophet*; for his wives used to talk back to him, and on occasion one would leave him for the whole night.[15]

ᶜUmar's wife talked back to him and he said to her, "Do you talk back to me, O foolish woman?" And she said, "The wives of the Prophet talk back to him and he is better than you."[16] To which ᶜUmar retorted, "How inappropriate of Ḥafṣah[17] to talk back to him!" Then he said to Ḥafṣah, "Don't be deceived [by the conduct] of the daughter [ᶜĀ'ishah] of Ibn Abī Quḥāfah [*sic*], for she is the dearest of the Prophet's wives; and he warned her against talking back."[18]

It was also related that one wife hit the Prophet* in the chest, so her mother scolded her. The Prophet* said, "Leave her alone; they [wives] do worse than that."[19] He and ᶜĀ'ishah got into an argument to the point that Abū Bakr was called upon to arbitrate, and the Prophet took him as a witness. So the Prophet* said to her, "Are you going to talk, or shall I?" She replied, "You talk, but say only the truth." Abū Bakr struck her until her mouth bled, and said to her, "O enemy of yourself, does he utter anything but the truth?" So she took refuge with the Prophet* and sat behind him. The Prophet* then told him, "you were not called for this, nor did we desire this of you."[20] She told him once in anger, "And you are the one who claims to be the Prophet of God!" So the Prophet* smiled and bore that out of forbearance and kindness.[21] He used to say to her, "I know when you are angry and when you are pleased." To which she replied, "And how do you know it?" He said, "When you are pleased, you say 'No, by the God of Muhammad'; and when you are angry you say, 'No, by the God of Abraham.' " She said, "You are right; I leave your name out."[22] It is said that the first love that took place in Islam was the love of the Prophet* for ᶜĀ'ishah*.[23] He used to say to her, "I am to you like Abū Zarᶜ vis-à-vis Umm Zarᶜ; however, I won't divorce you."[24] He used to say to his wives, "Don't talk ill of ᶜĀ'ishah to me for, by God, I have not received revelation under the cover of any of you but [rather under] hers."[25] Anas* used to say that the Prophet* was the kindest of all people toward women and children.[26]

[Toleration of Wives]

The third: Dalliance, jesting, and playfulness add to the toleration of offense; for these delight the hearts of women. The Prophet* used to joke with them and lower himself to the level of their minds in deeds and manners, to the extent that it was related that he* used to race ᶜĀ'ishah; she won once and he won several times, so he* said, "Now we're even."[27] In a *khabar* it is related that he* was one of the merriest with his wives.[28] cĀ'ishah [once] said, "I heard the voices of some Ethiopians and others playing on the day of *cĀshūrā'*.[29] The Prophet* asked me, 'Do you wish to see them play?' I said, 'Yes.' He sent after them and they came. The Messenger* of God stood between the two doors, placed his palm on the door and extended his arm; I leaned with my chin against his arm. They began to play, and I looked on. The Prophet* kept saying, 'That's enough (*ḥasbuki*)'; and I would say, 'Be quiet,' twice or three times. Then he said, 'cĀ'ishah, that's enough!' So I said, 'Yes.' He pointed to them and they departed."[30]

The Prophet* of God said, "the most perfect of believers in faith are those who are the finest in manners and most gentle toward their wives."[31] He said, "The best among you are the most charitable toward their wives, and I am the best among you toward my wives."[32] In spite of his harshness, cUmar* said, "It is necessary that a man be like a child in his family;[33] but if they seek what he possesses, he should be found a man."[34] Luqmān* said, "A wise man should be like a child in his family, and when he is in public, he should be found a man." In a commentary on the related *khabar,* [it is stated that] "God detests the *jacẓarī al-jawwāẓ*";[35] that is, one who is harsh toward his family and who is arrogant. The same explanation has been offered for the term *cutul* used by Almighty God [Kor. 68:13]: for it has been said that *cutul* designates one who has a harsh tongue and who is cruel toward his family.

The Prophet* said to Jābir, "Would that she were a virgin, so you could dally with her and she with you."[36]

[Asserting Authority]

The Fourth: not so to indulge in dalliance, good manners, and conformity in following her whims that he would corrupt her manners and lose respect altogether in her eyes. Rather, he should observe moderation, never abandon dignity and seriousness no matter how much evil he sees, nor open the door to abetting abomination; rather, whenever he sees an act which violates divine legislation and manliness (*murū'ah*),[37] he should become resentful and angry. Al-Ḥasan said, "Verily whoever obeys the whims of his wife will be cast by God into the Fire." ᶜUmar said, "Disagree with your wives, because disagreement with them is a blessing." It was also said, "Consult them, then disagree with them."

The Prophet* said, "Miserable is he who is a slave to his wife."[38] He said so because if the husband obeys her whims, he becomes her slave and thereby miserable; for God made him possessor over the woman but if he makes her possessor of himself, he reverses the order of things, overturns the matter, and obeys Satan when he said, "and surely I will command them and they will change Allah's creation" [Kor. 4:119]. It is a man's right to be followed, not to be a follower. God has appointed men as trustees over women, and has called the husband "master"; and the Lord has said, "and they met her lord and master at the door" [Kor. 12:25]. For if the master is transformed into a slave, then he has exchanged God's grace for thanklessness.[39] The woman's behavior depends on you: If you slacken her reins a little, she will run off for a long distance; should you loosen the harness a span (*fitr*),[40] she will take a cubit (*dhirāᶜ*);[41] but if you restrain her and treat her firmly where firmness is called for, you will be her master.

Al-Shāfiᶜī* said, "There are three who will insult you if you honor them: the woman, the servant, and the Nabataean."[42] He was referring to pure kindness and not harshness mixed with compliance, or coarseness with gentleness.

Arab women used to teach their daughters [how] to test their husbands. One would say to her daughter, "Test your husband before taking a step and before showing boldness toward him. Remove the edge of his spear; should he remain quiet, hack bones with his sword; and if he should still be quiet, then put the saddle on his back and ride him, for he is your donkey." At any rate, it is with justice that the heavens and the earth are upheld; whatever exceeds its limits turns into its opposite.

For that reason it is necessary to follow the path of moderation both in disagreement and in agreement, and to follow the truth in it all, so as to be safe from their [women's] evil; because their scheming is great,[43] their evil is widespread; their predominant characteristics are bad manners and weak minds, and this cannot be set straight except through a certain amount of kindness mixed with diplomacy. The Prophet* said, "A virtuous woman amongst women is like an *aᶜṣam* among a hundred crows";[44] an *aᶜṣam* is a [rare] white-footed crow.

In the will of Luqmān to his son [it is stated]: "My son, beware of the evil woman, for she will age you before your time; and beware of the evils of women, as they do not encourage good deeds; and be very careful of the better ones among them." The Prophet* said, "Beware of the three causes of poverty,"[45] and among them he listed the "evil woman" for she is the one who ages a man before his time. In other words, "If you come to her, she will curse you; and if you are away from her, she will be unfaithful to you." The Prophet* said concerning the best of women, "If [only] you were the companions of Joseph";[46] that is, turning Abū Bakr away from prayer indicates that, on your part, you have ignored the truth and turned to pleasure. Almighty God said when they [women] revealed the secret of the Prophet,*[47] "If you two turn in repentance to Him, your hearts are indeed so inclined" [Kor. 66:4 (ᶜAlī)];[48] that is, so disposed. He [God] said that about the best of the Prophet's* wives.[49] The Prophet* said, "No people dominated by a woman can succeed."[50] ᶜUmar scolded his wife when she talked back to him saying, "You are no more than a toy in a corner of the house; if we have need of you [we take you], otherwise, you sit as you are."

Thus there is evil and weakness in them [women]; while diplomacy and harshness are a cure for evil, consolation and mercy are the cure for weakness. The skillful doctor is one who can estimate the amount of cure needed for the ailment; so let the man first know her character through experience, then let him deal with her in a manner that will set her straight in accordance with her state.

[Jealousy]

The fifth: moderation in jealousy; which means that one should not overlook preliminaries whose consequences may be undesirable, and should not go to extremes in misjudging, in acting adversely, or in spying upon concealed matters.

The Prophet* of God enjoined against seeking out the faults of women[51]—that is, against unexpectedly coming upon women. When the Prophet* returned from a journey, he said before entering [the city of] Medina, "Don't come upon your wives at night." Two men disagreed with him and went ahead [of the rest], and each saw in his home what he detested.[52] In a famous *khabar* [it is stated]: "A woman is like a rib: if you [attempt to] straighten it, you break it; leave it alone and enjoy it in spite of its crookedness."[53] This refers to rectifying her character.

The Prophet* said, "There is a type of jealousy which God detests, and that is the unjustifiable jealousy of a man over his wife when there is no justification [for suspicion]"[54] because that suspicion we have decreed against. Certain [types of] suspicion are sinful. ᶜAlī* said, "Do not indulge excessively in showing jealousy over your wife lest she be accused of evil behavior because of you."

However, jealousy in its proper place is both necessary and commendable. The Prophet* said: "Almighty God experiences jealousy, and the believer experiences jealousy as well; Almighty God's jealousy stems from the believer's perpetration of what God has enjoined against."[55] The Prophet* said, "Do you marvel at the jealousy of Sa ᶜd?[56] By God, I am more jealous than he, and God is more jealous than I."[57] Because of Almighty God's jealousy, He has prohibited abominations, whether manifest or hidden. Forgiveness is dearer to none than to God; for that reason He has sent warners and preachers. And praise is dearer to none than to God; for that reason He has promised Paradise.

The Messenger* of God said, "I saw on the night [*Miᶜrāj*] [that] I was taken through Paradise (*laylata usrīya bī fi al-jannah*) a mansion and a maid in its courtyard; I inquired, 'To whom does this mansion belong?' and I was told, 'To ᶜUmar.' I wanted to look at her, but I remembered, O ᶜUmar, your jealousy." ᶜUmar wept and said, "Would I be jealous because of you, O Messenger of God?"[58]

Al-Ḥasan used to say, "Do you call upon your wives to jostle uncouth men in the market places? May God curse those who are not jealous."

The Prophet* said, "God favors certain types of jealousy and detests others; He favors certain types of pride and detests others. As for the jealousy which God loves, it is jealousy which results from just suspicion; and the jealousy that God detests is that which results from unfounded [suspicion]. The pride which God favors is that which a man has in battle and in the face of difficulties; and the pride that God detests is pride in falsehood."[59] The Prophet* said, "I am indeed a jealous man and none is free from jealousy save one whose heart is degenerate.[60] The only way to avoid jealousy is by having no man enter upon her and by preventing her from going into the marketplaces."

The Prophet* asked his daughter Fāṭimah,* "What is best for a woman?" She replied, "That she should see no man, and that no man should see her." So he hugged her and said they were "descendants one of another" [Kor. 3:33].[61] Thus he was pleased with her answer.

The companions of the Prophet* used to close peepholes and perforations in the wall to prevent women from looking at men. Muᶜādh [b. Jabal] saw his wife looking through a peephole, and he struck her; he also saw her giving an apple to his male slave from which she had eaten, and he struck her again.

ᶜUmar* said, "Strip the women of their [beautiful] clothes and they will stay in their rooms." He said so because they [women] do not desire to go out in worn clothes. He also said, "Accustom your women to 'No!' "

The Prophet* permitted women to go to the mosques;[62] the appropriate thing now, however, is to prevent them [from doing so], except for the old [ones]. Indeed such [prevention] was deemed proper during the days of the companions; ᶜĀ'ishah* declared, "If the Prophet only knew of the misdeeds that women would bring about after his time, he would have prevented them from going out."[63] When the son of ᶜUmar quoted the words of the Prophet,* "Do not prevent the bondwomen of God from going to the mosques of God," one of his sons replied, "Yes, by God, we will prevent them." So he struck him and was irate with him, saying, "You hear me say that the Prophet of God said, 'Do not prevent [them],' and you say, 'Yes [we will]?' "[64]The dared to disagree because he knew that times had changed, and the father was angry with him for openly expressing disagreement without giving the reason. The Prophet* also permitted them [women] to go out especially during feasts;[65] but they could not go out without the approval of their husbands.

Nowadays, it is permissible for a chaste woman to go out with the permission of her husband; however, remaining [at home] is safer.[66] She should not go out except for an important purpose; going out for the sake of looking [about] and for unimportant matters detracts from virtue and may lead to corruption. If she goes out, she must avoid looking at men. We are not saying that the man's face is shameful for her to look at as is the woman's face for him. Rather, it is for her like the face of the beardless boy which a man should be prevented from seeing when sight may result in evil; when evil is not likely to result, sight should not be prevented. For men throughout the ages have had unveiled faces while women go out veiled; if their faces were shameful for women to look at, men would have been commanded to be veiled or prevented from going out except for a necessary purpose.

[Support of the Woman]

The sixth: moderation in spending. One should not be stingy toward them nor should he be extravagant; rather he should be moderate. The Almighty said, "and eat and drink but exceed not the bounds" [Kor. 7:31 (ᶜAlī)]. He also said, "And let not thy hand be chained to thy neck nor open it with a complete opening" [17:29].[67] The Messenger* of God said, "The most favored among you is the one who is most generous toward his wife."[68] The Prophet* also said, "A dinar spent for the sake of God, a dinar spent for ransoming a slave, a dinar offered [as charity] to a poor man, and a dinar spent on your wife—the one that earns you the greatest reward is the one spent on your wife."[69]

It was related that ᶜAlī* had four wives and that he used to buy every four days a dirham's worth of meat for each. Al-

Ḥasan* said, "Some men spent plenty, but when it came to furnishings and clothes they were tight." Ibn Sirīn* said, "It is desirable that a man prepare *falūdhajah* (pastry) every week for his wife; for even though sweet foods are not among the necessary things, to completely omit them is a stingy practice."

It is desirable that he should order her to offer as charity whatever food remains [after the meal] and whatever would spoil if kept. This is the least thing to do as far as charity is concerned. The wife has the right to do this as circumstances dictate without specific permission from the husband.

He should not keep to himself, to the exclusion of his family, a delectable food. Not feeding them of it would incite malice and render it difficult to have a harmonious relationship. If he decides to withhold it [from them], let him eat in seclusion so that his family does not know about it; nor should he describe to them food which he does not intend to give them.

When he eats, let the whole family sit at his table; for Sufyān* [al-Thawrī] said, "We have been told that God and His angels invoke prayers on the members of the household who eat together."

The most important thing for the husband to observe in spending is to feed the family from what is gained lawfully and not to pursue evil endeavors for their sake, as that constitutes a crime against them rather than upholding their rights. We have already mentioned the pertinent *akhabār* when talking about the disadvantages of marriage.

[Instruction Concerning Menstruation]

The seventh: that the married man should know enough about the matter of menstruation to enable him to take necessary precautions; he also should teach his wife the rules of prayer: which prayers should be performed during menstruation and which should not. He has been commanded to safeguard her against the [hell]Fire according to the words of the Almighty, "Ward off from yourselves and your families a Fire" [Kor. 66:6].

It is incumbent upon the husband to teach her the proper beliefs of the followers of the sunna, to remove from her heart every innovation should she lend an ear to it, and to make her fear God should she be lax in matters of religion.

The husband should also teach her the precepts governing menstruation and irregular menstrual flow, and the taking of precautionary measures.[70] The information on menstruation is lengthy, but what a woman must be taught concerning menstruation are the prayers she should perform.[71] If the blood stops shortly before the sunset (*maghrib*) by [the end of] one prostration, then it is incumbent upon her to perform the noon (*ẓuhr*) and the afternoon (*ᶜaṣr*) prayers; if it stops before morning by [the end of] one *rakᶜah* then she should perform the *maghrib* and *ᶜishāʾ*.[72] This is the least that the women ought to observe.

If the husband is diligent in teaching her, she will not have to go out and ask the ulema about it. If the husband's knowledge does not encompass such matters, and if he should ask on her behalf, conveying to her the information from the mufti, then there is no need for her to go out. Otherwise, she has the right to go out and ask; in fact, she is obligated to do so, and the husband would be in defiance should he prevent her. No matter how much she learns about her obligations, she should not go out to attend a *dhikr*[73] nor to receive instruction in superfluous knowledge without the consent of her husband.

Whenever a woman neglects one of the obligations imposed upon her by menstruation and irregular menstrual flow, and the husband does not teach her [concerning these matters], he, too, becomes her partner in sin.

[Equality Among Wives]

The eighth: If he has several wives, then he should deal equitably with them and not favor one over the other; should he go on a journey and desire to have one [of his wives] accompany him, he should cast lots (*aqraᶜ*) among them,[74] for such was the practice of the Messenger*. If he cheats a woman of her night, he should make up for it, for making up for it is a duty upon him. For that reason it becomes necessary for him to learn the rules of apportionment which would take a long time to explain here. The Messenger* of God said, "Whosoever has two wives and favors one over the other—that is to say, does not deal equitably between them—he comes to the Day of Judgment bent to one side."[75]

He should be equitable in giving and in cohabiting at night. As concerns love and intimate relations, these do not come under the rubric of choice. Almighty God has declared, "Ye will not be able to deal equally between (your) wives, however much ye wish (to do so)" [Kor. 4:129]; that is to say, you cannot deal equally with regard to the desires of the heart and the preferences of the soul from which stems inequality in intimate relations. The Messenger* used to be equitable to his wives in giving and cohabiting at night saying, "O Lord, this is the limit of my ability within my means, I have no access to that which You possess and I do not have,"[76] by which he meant love. He loved ᶜĀ'ishah* most,[77] and the rest of his wives knew that. During his [last] illness, he was carried every day and every night in order to spend a night with each one of his wives. He would say, "Where am I supposed to be tomorrow?" So one of his wives saw through his question and said, "He is asking for the day with ᶜĀ'ishah." So they [his wives] said, "O Messenger of God, we permit you to stay at ᶜĀ'ishah's house, because it is difficult for you to be carried every night." He replied, "Are you agreeable to that?" They replied, "Yes," so he said, "Take me then to ᶜĀ'ishah's house."[78]

Whenever one wife grants her night to another with the husband's consent, the second wife gains the right to that night. The Prophet* used to allot time among his wives. He wanted to divorce Sawdah, the daughter of Zamᶜah, when she became old, so she granted her night to ᶜĀ'ishah and asked him to keep her in order that she [Sawdah] might remain in the circle of his wives. He left her and did not apportion for her; rather, he apportioned two nights for ᶜĀ'ishah and one night each for the rest of his wives."[79]

On account of his* fair justice and virility, whenever he desired one of his wives whose turn was not due and had intercourse with her, he would then visit during the same day or night the rest of his wives. It has been related that ᶜĀ'ishah* said the Messenger* of God visited all of his wives in one night.[80] Anas also related that he* visited all nine wives in one morning.[81]

[Insubordination of the Wife]

The ninth: as pertains to discord (*nushūz*)[82] and whatever dissension takes place between them that cannot be reconciled. If it should ensue from both sides or from the husband, and the wife wants to dominate the husband, and if it is not possible for him to set her straight, then two arbitrators should be called representing each of the two families [husband's and wife's] to look into the matter and to reconcile them. "If they desire amendment [reconciliation], Allah will make them of one mind"[Kor. 4:35]. ᶜUmar sent an arbitrator to a couple, but he returned without succeeding in reconciling them; whereupon he [ᶜUmar] beat him saying, "Almighty God says, 'If they desire amendment [reconciliation], Allah will make them of one mind.' " So the man returned and with [good] intention[s] and gentleness toward them, he reconciled them.

However, if the discord is the woman's fault, it is the husband's right to chastise and induce her forcibly to obey, since men are guardians over women. Likewise, should she be remiss in performing her prayers, it is his right to force her to perform them. However, he should chastise her gradually: That is to say, first he should preach, then warn, then threaten; should he not succeed, he should turn his back to her in bed, sleep in another bed, or avoid her—while still remaining in the house—from one night up to three. Should all of this fail, then he should beat her but not excessively, that is, to the point that he would inflict only pain but without breaking a bone or causing her to bleed. He should not strike her face for that is forbidden.

The Messenger* of God was asked, "What rights can a woman claim from a man?" He replied, "To feed her when he eats, to clothe her when he is clothed, [but] not to be insolent or beat her excessively. He is to avoid her only in cohabitation [that is, desert her bed]."[83] He can be angry with her and avoid her over matters of religion up to ten or twenty [days], or up to a month; the Prophet* did so to Zaynab when he sent her a present and she returned it to him. The wife at whose house he was staying said to him, "She has insulted you by returning your presents,[84] that is to say, she has humiliated and belittled you." The Prophet* replied, "You [wives] are too despicable in the sight of God to insult me!" Whereupon he became angry with all of them for a month, then returned to them.

[Etiquette of Intimate Relations]

The tenth: on the etiquette of intimate relations. It is desirable that it should commence in the name of God and with the [following] recitation: Say, "He is God, the One and Only" [Kor. 112:1]; then he should glorify (*takbīr*) and exalt (*tahlīl*)[85] His name saying, "In the name of God, Most High, Most Great; O God, cause it to be a good progeny if you cause it to issue forth from my loins." The Prophet* said, "If one of you say when he comes upon his wife, 'O God, avert the devil from me and avert the devil from what You have granted us.' Then should a child result, the devil shall not hurt him."[86]

When you near ejaculation, say to yourself without moving your lips: "Praise be to God Who has created humans out of fluid, and made thereof relatives and in-laws, for thy Lord is omnipotent."[87] One of the men of hadith used to raise his voice in praise to the extent that the members of the household could hear his voice. Then he would turn away from the *qiblah,* and would not face the *qiblah* during coitus out of deference for the *qiblah.*[88] He should also cover himself and his wife with a garment. The Messenger* of God used to cover his head and lower his voice, saying to the woman, "Remain quiet."[89] A *khabar* says, "If one of you should have intimate relations with his wife, you should not denude yourselves completely like two onagers,"[90] that is, two donkeys.

Let him proceed with gentle words and kisses. The Prophet* said, "Let none of you come upon his wife like an animal, and let there be an emissary between them." He was asked, "What is this emissary, O Messenger of God?" He said, "The kiss and [sweet] words."[91] He* also said, "There are three qualities which are considered deficiencies in a man: one, that he should meet someone whose acquaintance he wishes to make but parts from him before learning his name and lineage; second, that he should be treated kindly and reject the kindnesses done unto him; and third, that he should approach his concubine or wife and have sexual contact with her before exchanging tender words and caresses, consequently, he sleeps with her and fulfills his needs before she fulfills hers."[92]

Intimate relations are undesirable during three nights of the month: the first, the last, and the middle. It is said that the devil is present during copulation on these nights, and it is also said that the devils copulate during these nights. It was related that ᶜAlī, Muᶜāwiyah, and Abū Hurayrah also frowned upon it [during those nights]. Certain ulema recommended intimate relations on Friday and the night before it [Thursday] in fulfillment of one of the two interpretations of the Prophet's* words, "May God bless the one who purifies and performs the ablution, etc."[93]

Once the husband has attained his fulfillment, let him tarry until his wife also attains hers. Her orgasm (*inzāl*)[94] may be delayed, thus exciting her desire; to withdraw quickly is harmful to the woman. Difference in the nature of [their] reaching a climax causes discord whenever the husband ejaculates first. Congruence in attaining a climax is more gratifying to her because the man is not preoccupied with his own pleasure, but rather with hers; for it is likely that the woman might be shy.

It is desirable that he should have intimate relations with her once every four nights; that is more just, for the [maximum] number of wives is four which justifies this span. It is true that intimate relations should be more or less frequent in accordance to her need to remain chaste, for to satisfy her is his duty. If seeking intimate relations [by the woman] is not established, it causes the same difficulty in the same demand and the fulfillment thereof.

He should not approach her during menstruation, immediately after it, or before major ablution (*ghusl*), for that is forbidden according to the decree of the Book.[95] It has been said that it would engender leprosy in the offspring. The husband is entitled to enjoy all parts of her body during menstruation but not to have sodomy; intercourse during menstruation is forbidden (*ḥarām*) because it is harmful, and sodomy will cause permanent harm; for that reason it [sodomy] is more strongly prohibited than intimate relations during menstruation.[96] The words of the Almighty state, "so go to your tilth as ye will" [Kor.

2:223]; that is, "any time you please." He may achieve emission by her hand and can enjoy what is concealed by the loincloth (*izār*) short of coitus. The woman should cover herself with a loincloth from her groin to [a point just] above the knee during the state of menstruation. This is one of the rules of etiquette. He may partake of meals with the woman during her period of menstruation; he may also sleep beside her, etc.[97] He should not avoid her.

If the husband wishes to have intimate relations with one after having had coitus with another, then he should wash his genitals first. If he has nocturnal emission, then he should not have intercourse before washing his genitals or urinating. Sexual intercourse is frowned upon at the beginning of the night for he should not sleep in an impure state. Should he seek sleep or food, then let him perform first the limited ablution (*wuḍū'*), for that is a recommended practice of the sunna. The son of ᶜUmar related, "I said to the Prophet,* 'Should any of us sleep in a state of major ritual impurity (*junub*)?'[98] And he replied, 'Yes, if he has performed the limited ablution (*wuḍū'*).' "[99] However, a dispensation was given in this regard: ᶜĀ'ishah* said, "The Prophet* used to sleep in a state of major ritual impurity having not touched water."[100]

Whenever he returns to his bed, he should wipe the covers or shake them, for he does not know what might have taken place thereon during his absence. He should not shave, trim his fingernails, sharpen the blade [with which he shaves], cause blood to flow, or reveal any part of him while in a state of major ritual impurity; for all parts of his body would be restored to him in the hereafter, and he would thus return to a state of major ritual impurity. It is said that every hair will demand an account for the infraction it committed.

[Coitus Interruptus]

Other etiquettes include refraining from coitus (*ᶜazl*) and not ejaculating except in the place of tilling, which is the womb, for there is not a soul whose existence God has decreed but that will exist.[101] To that effect were the words of the Messenger* of God. As pertains to coitus interruptus, the ulema have split into four groups over whether it is permissible or reprehensible:[102] (a) There are those who consider it unconditionally permissible under all circumstances; (b) there are those who forbid it in all circumstances; (c) there are those who say it is permissible with her consent; evidently those proponents consider the harm [caused to the woman], which is forbidden rather than coitus interruptus itself; (d) there are those who say it is permissible with the bondmaid but not with the free woman.

As far as we are concerned, it is permissible. As to a reprehensible act, it applies to cases where unlawfulness is disregarded, where uprightness is ignored or where virtue is abandoned. It [coitus interruptus] is reprehensible according to the third stipulation; in other words, it involves abandonment of a virtue, as it is said: It is reprehensible for someone in the mosque to sit without being preoccupied with *dhikr* or prayer; and it is reprehensible for someone residing in Mecca not to perform the pilgrimage every year; this reprehensibility applies to the abandonment of what should take precedence and is more convenient, nothing more. This is firmly established in what we have explained concerning the virtue of [having] offspring, and in what has been related concerning the Prophet*: "A man has intimate relations with his wife, and is thus decreed for him the reward of a male offspring who fights for the cause of God and is killed [martyred]."[103] He said so because if such a son is born to him, he would receive the reward of being the cause for his [son's] existence, even though Almighty God is his creator, his sustainer,[104] and the one who strengthens him for jihad. His part in causing [the child] to exist is the act of coitus at the time of ejaculating in the uterus. We have stated that there is no reprehensibility in terms of prohibition and purification, for upholding prohibition is possible only by text[105] or by analogy with a text; there is no text without a basis for analogy. Rather, we have here a basis for analogy—namely, abstaining from marriage altogether, abstaining from intimate relations after marriage, or avoiding emission after penetration; all such abstentions are more preferable, but they do not constitute acts of unlawfulness or disagreement. For the progeny is formed by the sperm being deposited in the uterus, which comes from four causes: marriage, then copulation, then patience until emission takes place after intercourse, then waiting until the sperm is implanted in the uterus. Some of these causes are more closely related than others. [Thus] abstaining from the fourth is like abstaining from the third; likewise, the third is similar to the second, and the second is like the first. All that is not the same as abortion or the burying of girls alive (*wa'd*).[106]

These two things, in effect, constitute a crime against an already existing person; and that also has stages: The first stage of existence is that the sperm should lodge in the uterus, merge with the fluid of the woman, and become thus receptive to life; to interfere with this process constitutes a crime. If it develops into an embryo and becomes attached [a fetus], then the crime becomes more serious. If the spirit is breathed into it and the created being takes form, then the crime [of abortion] becomes more serious still. The crime is most serious after the fetus is born alive [then buried if it is a girl]. We have said that the initial stage of existence is the planting of the sperm in the uterus, not emission from the urethra; for the offspring is not produced by the sperm of the male alone but from the agglutination of the mates, either from both his and her fluid or from his fluid and the blood of menses, and that the blood plays, in relation to it, the same role as milk to its coagulator; the sperm from the man is necessary in coagulating the blood of the menses as the thickening agent (*rawbah*) is for milk since through it the coagulator gels. However that might be, a woman's fluid is a fundamental element in coagulation.

The two fluids are likened unto an offer and related acceptance which result in the consummation of a contract. Whoever makes an offer and goes back on it before it is accepted has breached the contract by rendering it null and void. Whenever an offer and related acceptance take place, rescission becomes a nullification, an annulment, and a severance. As no child can issue forth from a sperm in the vertebra, likewise [a child would not be created] after the expulsion [of the sperm] from the urethra unless it mixes with the fluid or the blood of the woman. This is, therefore, a clear analogy.[107]

Should you say: "But coitus interruptus is not reprehensible on account of opposing the existence of a child, it is likely to be reprehensible on account of the motive behind it; for it cannot be motivated except by a corrupt intention which is blemished by concealed polytheism." I would answer that the motivations for coitus interruptus are five:

The first pertains to concubines who serve to preserve property from the destruction entailed by the right to manumission; the purpose of maintaining property by avoiding manumission and heading off its causes is not prohibited.

The second, preserving the beauty of the woman and her portliness in order to maintain enjoyment, and protect her life against the danger of childbirth (*ṭalq*); and this, too, is not prohibited.

The third, fear of excessive hardship on account of numerous offspring, and guarding against the excessive pursuit of gain and against the need for resorting to evil means. This, too, is not prohibited, because encountering fewer hardships is an aid to religion [faith]. Without doubt, perfection and virtue ensue from dependence on and faith in God's guaranty which is expressed in His words, "No creature is there crawling on the earth, but its provision rests on God" [Kor. 2:6 (Arberry, vol. 1:239)]. Falling short of the apex of perfection, and abandoning what is preferable is not a criminal act. However, we cannot say that taking consequences into account as well as preserving possessions and hoarding them are prohibited, even though they are contrary to dependence [on God].

The fourth, fear of having female children because of the stigma involved in getting them married, as was the custom of the Arabs in burying their female progeny (*fi qatlihim al-'ināth*). This would be an evil intention if marriage or coitus are to be abandoned on its account; a person would be guilty of the intention but not of abstinence from marriage and coitus; so likewise in coitus interruptus. Corruption engendered by belief in disgrace (*ma^carrah*) is stronger in the sunna of the Prophet*. Such would be comparable to the circumstance of a woman who avoids marriage out of disdain for having to lie under a man and thus attempts to emulate them. Undesirability [in this case] is not due to abstinence from marriage per se.

The fifth, that the woman might abstain from having children on account of arrogance, excessive cleanliness, fear of labor pains, childbirth, and nursing. Such was the custom of the Kharijite[108] women in their excessive use of water to the point that they used to perform the prayers during the days of menses and would not enter the bathroom except naked [because] of their excessive cleanliness. This too is an innovation which contradicts the sunna and manifests a corrupt intent. One among them sought permission to see ᶜĀ'ishah* when she came to Basra, but she [ᶜĀ'ishah] did not grant it. Thus it is the intent and not the prevention of having children which is corrupt.

If you should say that the Prophet* said, "Whoever abandons marriage for fear of having dependents is not one of us in the least,"[109] I would say that coitus interruptus is like abstinence from marriage. By "he is not one of us" is meant that he does not concur with our sunna and our Path: Our sunna is the pursuit of the more preferable deed. Should you point out the fact that the Prophet* said regarding coitus interruptus, "That constitutes a secret form of burying children alive" and [also] recited, "and when the girl-child that was buried alive is asked,"[110] which is reported in the *Ṣaḥīḥ* [of Muslim], we would reply [that] in the *Ṣaḥīḥ* are also authentic reports[111] concerning the lawfulness [of coitus interruptus]. His expression "secret form of burying children alive" is like unto his words "secret polytheism," and that is an act which constitutes undesirability but not unlawfulness.

If you should point out the fact that Ibn ᶜAbbās said, "Coitus interruptus constitutes the lesser degree of burying children alive, as conception is prevented (*al-mamnūᶜ wujūduhu bihi*) by coitus interruptus (*al-maw'ūdat al-sughrah*),"[112] then we would reply, "He is equating the prevention of existence to cutting it off, and that is a weak form of analogy." For that reason ᶜAlī* denounced this act upon hearing this saying, "A child is not buried alive until after the seventh, or seven phases have been completed," and he recited the Koranic verse pertaining to the stages of creation [23:12–14]: "Verily We created man from a product of wet earth; then placed him as a drop (of seed) in a safe lodging," up to "and then produced it as another creation";[113] that is to say, we breathed a spirit into him. Then he recited the Almighty's words in [another] verse [81:8]: "And when the girl-child that was buried alive is asked." If you examine what we have already stated concerning analogy and point of view, you will perceive the difference between the method of ᶜAlī* and that of Ibn ᶜAbbās* in seeking hidden meanings and pursuing knowledge.

It appears that the *Ṣaḥīhayn* [of Bukhārī and Muslim] concur in relating what Ibn Jābir had said, "We used to have coitus interruptus in the days of the Prophet* while the Koran was being revealed."[114] In another transmittal: "We used to have coitus interruptus; the Prophet* heard about it, but he did not enjoin us against it."[115] There is also a report that Jābir had said: "A man came to the Prophet* and said, 'I have a bondmaid who is our servant and who brings us water [to drink] during the date-picking season. I do have intimate relations with her, but I am undesirous that she should conceive.' He* replied, 'Have coitus interruptus if you wish; for she shall receive what has been destined for her.' The man was absent for some time, then he came back to him [the Prophet] and said, 'The bondwoman is pregnant.' He replied, 'I told you that she will receive what has been destined for her.'"[116] All this can be found in the *Ṣaḥīhayn* [of Bukhārī and Muslim].

[Etiquette Concerning Having Children]

The eleventh: There are five points concerning the etiquette of having children.

(a) The first, that one should not be overjoyed with the birth of a male child, nor should he be excessively dejected over the birth of a female child, for he does not know in which of the two his blessings lie. Many a man who has a son wishes he did not have him, or wishes that he were a girl. The girls give more tranquility and [divine] remuneration, which are greater.

The Prophet* said, "If a man brings up his daughter well, nourishes her well, and shares with her the gifts which God has bestowed upon him, she will bring him fortune and will facilitate his passage from Hell to Heaven."[117] Ibn ᶜAbbās related that the

Messenger* of God said, "If a man has two daughters and treats them well as long as they remain with him, they will cause him to enter Paradise."[118] Anas said in quoting the Messenger* of God, "If a man has two daughters or two sisters and he treats them well for as long as they remain with him, he and I will be in Paradise like these two [women]."[119] Anas also related that the Messenger* of God declared, "If a man goes to one of the marketplaces of the Muslims, buys something, carries it back to his home, and gives it to the females and not to the males, God will look upon him [with favor], and whomever God looks upon [with favor] He will not torment."[120] Anas also related that the Messenger* of God said, "When a man brings an extraordinary present [*turfah*] from the market to his family, it is like bringing them a charitable gift (*ṣadāqah*) which he places among them. Let him give the females before the males, for whoever brings joy to a female is like crying out of fear of God, and he who cries out of fear of God will be safeguarded by God from the Fire."[121] Abū Hurayrah related that the Prophet* said, "Whoever has three daughters or sisters and tolerates their hardships and ordeals, God will bring him into Paradise for having shown mercy toward them." A man asked, "How about one?" And he said, "Even one."[122]

(b) The second etiquette is that he should chant the prayer (*ādhān*) in the ear of the offspring.[123] Rafi ᶜ related the words of his father: "I saw the Prophet* chanting the *ādhān* in the ear of al-Ḥasan [his grandson] when Fāṭimah* gave birth to him."[124] It was related that the Prophet* said, "When a man has a child and chants the *ādhān* in his right ear and the second call (*iqāma*) in his left ear, he repels epilepsy (*umm al-ṣibyān*) from him."[125] It is desirable that the first words he is taught to speak when he learns to talk be "there is no God but Allah (*la ilāha illa Allāh*)" so that these words may constitute his first utterance. Circumcision on the seventh day is prescribed in a *khabar.*[126]

(c) The third etiquette is that he should be given a good name, for that is the child's right. The Prophet* said, "Should you give a name, let the word *ᶜabd* (*fa ᶜabbidū*) be part of it.[127] He* said, "The names most endearing to God are ᶜAbdullah and ᶜAbd al-Raḥmān." He also said, "Give them my name but not my surname (*kunya*).[128] The ulema said, "That was applicable to his* lifetime"; for he was surnamed ᶜAbd al-Qāsim. Now it is acceptable [to call children by the Prophet's surname]. True, a person should not be called by both the Prophet's name and his surname; for the Prophet said, "Do not give both my name and my surname together."[129] It was said that this, too, was applicable to his lifetime. One person took the name Abū ᶜĪsā, so the Prophet* said, "ᶜĪsā has no father";[130] thus such a name is not desirable.

The miscarried fetus (*al-siqṭ*) must be given a name. ᶜAbd al-Raḥmān b. Yazīd b. Muᶜāwiyah said, "I learned that the miscarried fetus will cry out after its father on the Day of Judgment saying, 'You have destroyed me and left me without a name.' ᶜUmar b. ᶜAbd al-ᶜAzīz said, 'How so, when he might not know whether he is a male or a female?' " ᶜAbd al-Raḥmān replied, "There are names that might apply to both, like Ḥamzah, ᶜAmārah, Ṭalḥah, and ᶜUtbah."

The Prophet* said, "You will be called on the Day of Judgment by your names and the names of your fathers; so let your names be good."[131] Whoever has an undesirable name, it is preferable that it should be changed; the Messenger* of God changed the name al-ᶜĀṣ to ᶜAbdullah.[132] Zaynab's name was Barrah; the Prophet* said, "She purifies her soul," so he called her Zaynab.[133] There has been an injunction against the use of the names Aflaḥ (be lucky), Yasir (well-being), Nāfiᶜ (useful), and Barakah (blessing)[134] for the question is frequently asked, "Is Barakah there?" The answer would be "No."

(d) The fourth is a sacrifice (*ᶜaqīqah*): for the male, two sheep; and for the female, one sheep.[135] But one can be happy with one [sacrifice] be it for male or female.[136] ᶜĀ'ishah recounted that the Messenger* of God ordered that in the case of a lad (*ghulām*), two complementary sheep should be sacrificed and in the case of a girl (*jāriyah*), one sheep.[137] It has been related that one sheep was sacrificed.[138] This makes it permissible to sacrifice only one. The Prophet* said, "For every male, there must be a sacrifice; therefore, shed blood on his behalf and thus remove harm from him."[139]

It is part of the sunna that the weight in gold or silver of the child's hair [cut on the seventh day] be offered to charity. There is a *khabar* to that effect, namely, that "the Prophet* ordered Fāṭimah* on the seventh day of the birth of Ḥusayn to shave his head and to give the weight of his hair in silver to charity.[140] ᶜĀ'ishah said: "None of the bones of the sacrifice should be broken for the newborn."

(3) The fifth is to put in his mouth a masticated date or some other sweet. It was related of Asmā',* the daughter of Abū Bakr,* that she said, "I gave birth to ᶜAbdullah b. al-Zubayr in a tunic; then I brought him to the Messenger* of God and placed the child on his lap. The Prophet called for a date, chewed it, then spat it into the child's mouth."[141] Thus the first thing that entered his stomach was the saliva of the Messenger* of God. Then he chewed a date and rubbed it on his [the child's] palate (*ḥannakuhu*), invoked God's blessing upon him, and gave him his blessings. He was the very first child born in Islam,[142] so they rejoiced over him, for they had been told that the Jews had bewitched them so that they would not be able to have children.

[Divorce]

The twelfth: concerning divorce. Let it be known that it is permissible; but of all permissible things, it is the most detestable to Almighty God. It is permissible only if it involves no harm ensuing from deception; and whenever he divorces her, he brings harm upon her. It is not permissible to bring harm to another unless a crime is committed on her part or out of necessity on his part. Almighty God said, "If they obey you, seek not a way against them" [Kor. 4:34]; that is to say, do not find an excuse for separation.

If his father should loathe her, then he should divorce her. Ibn ᶜUmar* said, "I had a woman I loved, but my father used to loathe her and command me to divorce her, so I consulted the Messenger* of God and he told me, 'O son of ᶜUmar, divorce your wife.' "[143] This indicates that the father's rights take priority, but he must be like ᶜUmar, a father who does not loathe her for an unjust cause.

Whenever she offends her husband or utters foul language against his family, she is guilty; likewise [she is guilty] whenever she is ill-mannered or corrupt in her religion. Ibn Masᶜūd commented on the words of Almighty God, "nor let them go forth unless they commit open immorality" [Kor. 65:1], saying: "Whenever she utters foul language against his family or inflicts harm upon her husband, she has committed a grave act." This comment was made concerning behavior during the prescribed waiting period; nevertheless, it underscores what we mean.

If offense should come from the husband, then she can be redeemed through the payment of a compensation (*khulᶜ*) [divestiture].[144] It is undesirable for the man to take from her more than he has given [as a dowry], for that would constitute injustice against her, unfairness toward her, and a trade [in making profit] on the dowry. Almighty God said, "there is no blame on either of them if she gives something for her freedom" [Kor. 2:229 (ᶜAlī)]; thus returning what she has taken, or less, is appropriate in redeeming herself.

Should she seek divorce for no just reason, she is a sinner. The Prophet* said, "Whichever woman asks her husband to divorce her for no cause will not breathe the aura of Paradise";[145] in other words, Paradise becomes forbidden to her. In still another expression, the Prophet* said, "Women who seek divorce for a compensation are hypocrites."[146]

The husband should observe four matters in divorce: one, that he divorce her during her state of [menstrual] purity (*ṭuhr*), provided he has not had coitus with her. Divorce during menstruation or during a state of purity in which they had coitus, even though it does occur, is an unlawful innovation, as it lengthens the periods of her waiting (*ᶜiddah*).[147] If he should do so, he should take her back. The son of ᶜUmar divorced his wife during menstruation, so the Prophet* told ᶜUmar, "Command him to take her back until she is purified, menstruates, and is purified [again]; after that, he can choose either to divorce or keep her. Such is the period of waiting which God has ordained for divorcing women."[148] He commanded him to wait after taking her back (*ᶜiddat al-rajᶜah*) for two states of purity, lest the intent of taking her back should be divorce only.

The second, that he should restrict himself to one divorce utterance and not pronounce all three at once because the one utterance after a legal period of waiting indicates the intent, and he can benefit from retracting it should remorse develop during the period of waiting in which he can renew the marriage if he wishes after this period. If he pronounces all three divorce utterances [at once], he might regret it and be compelled to have a *muḥallil* marry her and then wait awhile. To contract a *muḥallil* is a denounced act for which the husband would be the cause; besides, his heart [under the circumstances] would be at the mercy of someone else's wife [that is, the wife of the *muḥallil*], and at the mercy of the divorce which he [the *muḥallil*] grants. In addition, this would cause the wife to become disenchanted with him; all these are the fruits of *al-jam*ᶜ (uttering a threefold divorce). Uttering one divorce is sufficient in indicating the intent without danger. I do not mean to say that uttering a threefold divorce is unlawful; rather, it is undesirable for the aforementioned reasons, and by undesirability I mean disregard for himself.

The third, that he should be kind in offering a pretext to divorce her without stern censure and belittlement. He should soothe her heart by way of gratification with a present and cure the wounds inflicted by separation. Almighty God has said, "yet make provision for them" [Kor. 2:236 (Arberry, vol. 1:62)]; and this is a duty whenever it is the case that a dowry had not been specified in the original marriage [contract].

Al-Ḥasan b. ᶜAlī was an unbridled divorcer and marrier. One day he sent one of his companions to divorce two women among his wives and said, "Tell them to prepare for the legal period of waiting." He ordered him to give each one of them 10,000 dirhams. He did; and when he [the companion] returned to him, he [al-Ḥasan] asked him, "What did they do?" he replied, "One of them lowered her head and thus remained, but the other cried and wailed and I heard her say, 'These are very small provisions from a parting loved one.' " Al-Ḥasan bowed his head and invoked blessings on her saying, "Were I to take back a woman after separating from her, I would take her back."

One day al-Ḥasan went to visit ᶜAbd al-Raḥmān b. al-Ḥārith b. Hishām,[149] who was the *faqīh* (jurist) of Medina and its chief, who had no equal in Medina, and whom ᶜĀ'ishah used as an example when she said, "Had I not already traversed this course of mine,[150] I would have preferred to have sixteen males from the Messenger* of God like ᶜAbd al-Raḥmān b. al-Ḥārith b. Hishām." Al-Ḥasan went to see ᶜAbd al-Raḥmān in his house. [ᶜAbd al-Raḥmān] honored him and told him to sit in his place saying, "Would that you had sent for me; I would have come to you." Al-Ḥasan replied, "The need is ours." He [ᶜAbd al-Raḥmān] asked, "What is it?" He told him, "I have come seeking your daughter in marriage." ᶜAbd al-Raḥmān lowered his head, then raised it and said, "By God, there is no one walking upon this earth who is dearer to me than you; but you know that my daughter is flesh of my flesh: what offends her offends me, and what pleases her, pleases me. You are an unbridled divorcer: I fear that you would divorce her. Should you do that, I fear also that my heart would turn away from loving you, and I would be unhappy should my heart be turned away from you, because you are a part of the Messenger's flesh. If you promise not to divorce her, I will give her to you in marriage." Al-Ḥasan was silent, then he arose and left. One of his household heard him saying while walking, "ᶜAbd al-Raḥmān wanted to make his daughter a rope around my neck."

ᶜAlī* used to be impatient with his [al-Ḥasan's] numerous divorces and would apologize on his behalf from the pulpit saying in his sermon (*khuṭbah*),[151] "Ḥasan is very prone to divorce, so do not give him [your daughters] in marriage." A man from Ḥamadān rose and said, "O prince of the faithful, we will give him our daughters in marriage to his heart's satisfaction. If he so wishes he can keep them, and if he so desires he can let them go." That pleased ᶜAlī and he said, "Were I a gatekeeper of Paradise, I would tell Ḥamadān to enter in peace." This is merely an indication that if a man, out of embarrassment, speaks ill of someone dear to him, whether wife or child, it is not necessary that one should agree with him since such an agreement would be undesirable. Rather, it is a rule of etiquette to disagree to the best of one's ability, for that is more pleasing to his heart and in accord with his hidden thought.

The aim of all of this is to show that divorce is permissible. God has promised riches in both separation and in marriage saying, "And marry such of you as are solitary and the pious of your slaves and maidservants. If they be poor, Allah will enrich them of His bounty" [Kor. 24:32]; and also saying, "But if they separate, Allah will compensate each out of His abundance" [4:130].

The fourth, that he should never reveal her secret [private affairs] while divorced or married. Concerning the revealing of women's secrets, an authentic *khabar* transmits great threat.[152] It is related that a virtuous man wanted to divorce his wife and he was asked, "What grievance have you against her?" And he replied, "A wise man does not reveal the secrets of his wife." After divorcing her he was asked, "Why did you divorce her?" And he replied "The affairs of someone else's wife are not my concern." This indicates the husband's obligation.

SECOND PART OF THIS CHAPTER

Examination of the Husband's Rights

The authoritative statement in this context is that marriage constitutes a form of enslavement; thus she is his slave, and she should obey the husband absolutely in everything he demands of her provided such demands do not constitute an act of disobedience. There are many *akhbār* that magnify the rights of the husband.

The Prophet* said, "If a woman dies while her husband is satisfied with her, she will enter Paradise."[153] A man went on a journey and enjoined his wife against descending from the high ground [where they lived] to the low ground where her father lived. He became ill, so the wife sent for the Messenger* of God, asking permission to descend to her father. The Prophet* replied, "Obey your husband." Her father died, and again she sought his [the Prophet's] counsel and he said, "Obey your husband." When her father was buried, the Messenger* of God sent word to her that God has forgiven her father by virtue of her obedience to her husband.[154] The Prophet* said, "If a woman performs her five [daily] prayers, fasts during the month [of Ramadan], preserves her chastity, and obeys her husband, she will enter the Paradise of her Lord."[155] He included obedience to the husband in the basic principles of Islam. The Messenger* of God described women as: "Child-bearers, mothers, nursers who are compassionate toward their children, and those who pray will enter Paradise, provided that they do not commit wrongs against their husbands."[156]

The Prophet* said, "I looked into Hell and found most of the occupants to be women," and we asked him, "Why, O Messenger* of God?" He replied, "Because they curse a lot and enrage their mates";[157] by this he meant the husband with whom they consort. In another *khabar* [the Prophet said], "I looked into Paradise and the minority of its inhabitants were women. So I asked, 'Where are the women?' And I was told, 'They are preoccupied with two red things:[158] gold, and saffron,' "[159] meaning jewelry and dyestuff for clothes.

According to ᶜĀ'ishah*: "A young girl came to the Prophet* and said, 'O Messenger of God, I am a betrothed girl but I detest marriage. What are the husband's rights from the woman?' He replied, 'Were he covered with pus from the tip of his head to the soles of his feet, and were she to lick him, she would not compensate him enough.' Whereupon she said, 'Should I then not get married?' He said, 'Do, for it is good.' "[160]

Ibn ᶜAbbās said, "A woman from Khathᶜam came to the Messenger* of God and said, 'I have no husband and I wish to get married: What is the husband's right?' and he said, 'The rights of the husband incumbent upon a wife are that if he should desire her and seek to have her while she is on the back of a camel, she should not deny him his wish. It is his right that she should not give [away] anything from his household except with his permission; should she do this, the burden is hers and the compensation is his. It is also his right that she should not observe a voluntary fast except with his permission; should she do it, she will suffer hunger and thirst and her fasting will not be acceptable [to God]. If she leaves her house without his permission, the angels will curse her until she returns to his house or repents.' "[161] The Prophet* said, "Were I to command someone to prostrate himself before another, I would command the wife to prostrate herself before her husband on account of the magnitude of her obligation to him."[162] The Prophet* also said, "A woman is nearest to the face of God when she is in the inner sanctum of her house; performing the prayer in the courtyard of her house is better than praying in the mosque, and praying in her house is better than praying in her courtyard, and praying in her bedchamber (*makhda*ᶜ) is better than praying [elsewhere] in her house."[163] The alcove is a quarter within the house; it is a place of shielding. For that reason the Prophet* said, "A woman is deficient; if she goes out, she will please the devil."[164] He also said, "A woman has ten deficient qualities; if she marries, the husband covers one of those qualities, and if she dies, the grave covers all ten."[165]

[EXPOSITION OF THE RIGHTS OF THE HUSBAND]

Thus the husband's rights toward the wife are many, but most important are two: the first is safeguarding and sheltering; the other is to be spared unnecessary demands and the need for having to provide them if they are unlawful. This was the custom of women with the forefathers. When a man went out of his home, his wife or daughter would say to him, "Beware of unlawful gain; we would endure hunger and harm rather than Fire [hellfire]. One of the predecessors was about to go on a journey of which his neighbors disapproved. They said to his wife, "Why do you let him go when he has not left you any provisions?" She said, "Since the day I knew my husband, he has been a consumer and not a provider; but I do have a Lord who provides. The consumer goes, but the Provider remains."

Rābiᶜah [of Syria], the daughter of Ismāᶜīl, asked Aḥmad b. Abū al-Ḥawwārī[166] to marry her. He declined because he was preoccupied with worship and said to her, "My preoccupations are not inclined toward women, because I am too preoccupied with myself." She replied, "I am more preoccupied with myself than you are, and I have no [physical] desire. However, I have inherited much wealth from my husband and I wish you would spend it on your spiritual brothers, and that through you I should come to know the righteous ones, thus finding a path to God, may He be glorified and honored." He replied, "Wait until I seek permission of my master." So he returned to find Abū Sulaymān al-Dārānī, who used to enjoin against his getting married and [who had] said, "None of our companions ever got married without being changed." But when he heard her words, he said, "Marry her, for she is a friend of God. Hers are the words of the righteous." Al-Ḥawwārī said, "I married her; and there was in our house a container made of plaster which had become worn out through use by those who hastily washed their hands and left after meals, not to mention those who had washed with potash." He also said, "I married three wives in addition, but she used to give me the best to eat and used to perfume me. She would say to me, 'Go with energy and strength to your wives.' " Thus Rābi ᶜah of Syria was likened unto Rābi-ᶜah al-ᶜAdawyīah of Basra.[167]

Among the obligations of the woman is that she should not squander his [her husband's] possessions, but rather take great care of them. The Messenger* of God said, "It is not lawful for her to feed anyone from his house without his permission, except from food that would spoil if kept. Should she feed [others] with his blessing, then she would earn the same kind of reward he earns; but if she should feed [them] without his permission, then he would earn the reward and she would bear the burden."[168]

It is the obligation of the parents to train her in the etiquette of cohabitation with her husband. It is related of Asmā', the daughter of Khārijah al-Fazzārī, that she said to her daughter when the latter got married, "You have left a nest in which you grew up and proceeded to a bed which you know not and a mate with whom you have not associated; be an earth for him, and he will be your sky; be a resting place for him, and he will be your pillar; be his bondmaid, and he will be your slave; do not make excessive demands, for he will then desert you; do not become too distant from him, for he will then forget you; should he draw near, then draw close to him; should he become distant, stay away from him. Shield his nose, his hearing and his eye[169] so he will smell nothing from you but that which is sweet, hear nothing but that which is good, and look at nothing but that which is beautiful."

A man said to his wife [in rhyme]:

Seek forgiveness from me, and you will
  earn my constant affection;
Speak not when I am angry;
Do not beat me once as you would beat

the tambourine, for you do not know
what the unknown may hold in store;
Do not complain excessively, for it will
cause love to depart and turn my heart
away from you;
I have seen love in the heart and harm;
if the two should meet, love would
soon disappear.

[ETIQUETTE FOR THE WOMAN]

Without going into lengthy details, a summary of what constitutes etiquette for the woman is the following: She should remain in the inner sanctum of her house and tend to her spinning; she should not enter and exit excessively; she should speak infrequently with her neighbors and visit them only when the situation requires it; she should safeguard her husband in his absence and in his presence;[170] she should seek his pleasure in all affairs and refrain from betraying him through herself or his possessions; she should not leave his home without his permission: if she goes out with his permission, she should conceal herself in worn-out clothes[171] and choose the less-frequented places rather than the main avenues and market places, being careful that no stranger hear her voice or recognize her personally; she should not approach friends of her husband while going about her business, but feign ignorance of those who might recognize her or whom she might recognize; her primary concern should be caring for her own affairs, tending to her house, performing her prayers, and fasting; should a friend of her husband knock at the door when he [the husband] is not present, she should not ask questions or engage in conversation, so as to maintain her self-respect and her husband's; she should be content with the means that God has provided her husband; she should place his rights before hers and before the rights of his relatives; she should always observe the rules of personal hygiene, and be ready at all times for him to enjoy her whenever he wishes; she should be affectionate toward her children, zealous to protect them, refraining from uttering profane words against them and from talking back to her husband.

The Prophet* said, "I and a haggard woman like these two will be in Paradise: a widowed woman who dedicated herself to her daughters until they attained the age of puberty, or [one who has] died."[172] The Prophet* also said, "God has forbidden all the descendants of Adam to enter Paradise before me; but I look and behold on my right a woman [who] has preceded me to the gate of Paradise; so I ask, 'Why does she precede me?' And the answer comes, 'O Muḥammad, this was a fine, beautiful woman who had orphans. She was patient until they attained their present state, so God was pleased with her for that.' "[173]

Other etiquettes governing the woman include the following: that she should not boast to her husband of her beauty, neither should she belittle her husband for his ugliness. It was related that al-Aṣmaʿī[174] said, "I went to the desert and, behold, I saw a woman with a most beautiful face married to a man with the ugliest [face]; so I said to her, 'Woman, are you satisfied to be married to such a man?' She said, 'Be quiet! You have uttered ill words; perhaps he has earned high merits with his Lord and thus I became his reward; or perhaps I have offended my Creator and he thus became my punishment. Should I not then accept what God has seen fit for me?' Thus did she silence me."

Al-Aṣmaʿī also related, "I saw a woman in the desert who was wearing a red garment and carrying a rosary; so I said to her, 'What a discrepancy between the two!' She replied [in rhyme]: 'Part of me belongs to God and I shall not squander it; the other part belongs to folly and idleness.' I learned that she was a virtuous woman who had a husband for whom she adorns herself."

Another decorum of the woman is to be virtuous, and melancholy in the absence of her husband, and to return to her sprightliness and happiness in his presence. She should never harm her husband in any way. Muʿādh b. Jabal related: "The Messenger* of God said, 'Whenever a woman hurts her husband in this world, his houri wife says: "Do not harm him, may God reproach you! For he is a stranger in your house who will soon depart from you to join us."[175]

Her marital obligations include: that she should not mourn over the death of the husband longer than four months and ten days during which time she should avoid perfume and adornment. Zaynab, the daughter of Abī Salāmah, said: "I went to visit Umm Ḥabībah, the wife of the Prophet,* when her father Abū

Sufyān b. Ḥarb died. She asked for perfume containing a yellow tinge (*khalūq*) or something like it. She anointed a female slave with it, then touched both cheeks and said, 'By God, I have no need for perfume; however, I did hear the Messenger* of God say, "It is not lawful for a woman who believes in God and the Day of Judgment to mourn more than three days over the dead unless he be a husband, in which case she should mourn for four months and ten days."[176]

The woman should remain in the house of her marriage until the end of the legally prescribed waiting period, and must not move to her family or leave the house except out of necessity.

Another etiquette is that she should perform every service of which she is capable at home. It was related that Asmā',[177] the daughter of Abū Bakr al-Ṣiddīq,* said: "Zubayr[178] married me when he had on earth neither possessions nor slaves nor anything besides his horse and a [water-carrying] camel (*nāḍiḥ*). I used to feed his horse, give him his provisions, look after him, grind date-stones for his camel, feed him, bring water, string beads to hang on his neck, and knead dough. I used to transport ground date-stones on my head a distance of more than two-thirds of a parasang[179] until Abū Bakr sent me a slave girl, and I was then contented with looking after the horse. It was like being freed.[180] The Messenger* of God came upon me one day with his companions while I was carrying date-stones on my head,[181] and he* said "Akh, akh" to make his she-camel kneel so as to carry me behind him. I was embarrassed to proceed with men and remembered the jealousy of al-Zubayr, for indeed he was the most jealous of men. The Messenger* of God noticed that I was embarrassed; so I came to al-Zubayr and told him what had happened. He said, "By God, it is more painful for me to see you carry ground date-stones on your head than to ride with him."

THE *BOOK OF MARRIAGE* ENDS HERE WITH PRAISE AND THANKS TO GOD
MAY HIS BLESSINGS BE UPON EVERY PURE SERVANT

APPENDIX A

Chronological List of al-Ghazālī's Works

The chronological list of al-Ghazālī's works was derived from a number of bibliographic sources, particularly George F. Hourani's "The Chronology of Ghazālī's Writings" and Caesar E. Farah's manuscript, "A Bibliographical Guide to Islamic Philosophy and Mysticism," which is now being published by Luzac & Co. For a comprehensive study of all of al-Ghazālī's works, where the manuscripts may be found, translations in various languages, reprints in Arabic, and spurious works attributed to him, see ᶜAbd al-Raḥmān Badāwī, *Mu'allafāt al-Ghazālī.* The following list does not include the indeterminable or spurious works. If the student is interested in books attributed to al-Ghazālī, other sources should be consulted.[1] My own translation of most titles and annotations as to content have been incorporated in the list below.

1. "Al-Mankhūl fī Uṣūl al-Fiqh" (The Essentials in the Fundamentals of Canon Law)

 A concise work on law, written during the lifetime of his teacher, Imām al-Ḥaramayn al-Juwaynī, before 478/1085–86.

2. "Shifā' al-ᶜAlīl fī Uṣūl al-Fiqh" (The Curing of the Ill on the Fundamentals of Canon Law)

 The first known manuscript was written in 573/1177 in Egypt. The book, apparently lost, treats questions of fiqh in detail.

3. "Ma'khadh al-Khilāf" (Point of Departure in Disputation)

 On methods of legal debate. Apparently lost.

4. "Lubāb al-Naẓar" (The Essence of Reflection)

On methods of legal debate, or ways of investigation and disputation. No reference to its availability.

5. "Taḥsīn al-Ma'ākhidh" (Refining Points of Departure)

On methods of legal debate. Badāwī states that the book possibly dealt with marriage and divorce. Apparently lost.

6. "Al-Mabādi' wal-ghāyāt" (The Principles and Aims)

On methods of legal debate. Apparently lost.

7. "Khulāṣat al-Mukhtaṣar" (The Essence of the Abridged)

Written in 598/1202, it is a resumé of the "Mukhtaṣar" of Isma^cīl al-Mazānī, who was an early Shafi^cite lawyer (died 877 A.H.). It is the smallest book on selections from jurisprudence (fiqh). Apparently lost.

8. "Al-Basīṭ" (The Simple Work)

In manuscript form, it is an early work on fiqh, summarizing Imām al-Ḥaramayn's "Nihāyat al-maṭlab." The date of the early manuscript was placed at 636/1238.

9. "Al-Wasīṭ" (The Middle Work)

In manuscript, it is a work on fiqh of Ghazālī's earlier life and a summary of "Al-Basīṭ."

10. *Al-Wājiz fī Fiqh al-Imām al-Shāfi^cī* (The Abridged in the Jurisprudence of the Imām al-Shāfi^cī)

Cairo: n.p., 1317/1899–1900.

A summary of Shafi^cite canon law.

11. "Tahdhīb al-Uṣūl" (Organizing the Fundamentals)

A work on fiqh of considerable depth and detail. Apparently lost.

12. *Maqāṣid al-Falāsifah* (Aims of the Philosophers)

(a) Cairo: Sa^cādah Press, 1331/1913.
(b) Edited by M. S. Kurdī. 3 parts. Cairo: n.p., 1355/1936.
(c) German text by George Beer. Leiden: E. J. Brill, 1888.

The book was possibly written as a background to the *Tahāfut* around 484/1091–92.

13. *Tahāfut al-Falāsifah* (The Incoherence of the Philosophers)

(a) In Arabic. Cairo: n.p., 1885.
(b) Texte arabe établi et accompagne d'un sommaire latin, by M. Bouyges in *Bibliotheca Arabic Scholasticorum* II. Beirut: Imprimerie Catholique, 1972.
(c) New edition of Bouyges by Majid Fakhry. Beirut: n.p., 1962.

A treatise in defense of Muhammadan orthodoxy and on logic, written about 487/1094. According to Hourani, Ghazālī stated he "spent 'nearly a year' in critical reflection on philosophy, afterward no less than two years spent in understanding it."

14. *Al-Mustaẓhiri—Faḍā'iḥ al-Bāṭinīyah wa faḍā'il al-Mustaẓhirīyah* (Vices of the Esotericists and Virtues of the Exotericists)

(a) Selections edited by I. Goldziher. *Streitschrift des Gazali gegen die Balinijja-Sekte.* Leiden: E. J. Brill, 1956.
(b) Edited by ^cAbd al-Raḥmān Badāwī. Faḍā'il al-Bāṭinīyah. Cairo: n.p., 1964.

The book is a searching theological critique of Batinism or the *Nizari Isma^cilis* and deals with the holding of office by the ᶜAbbasid caliph al-Muṣtaẓhir, establishing his legitimacy against the opposition of the Bāṭinīyah sect, and also deals with the Fatimid caliph al-Mustanṣir. Rosenthal states that al-Muṣtaẓhir "is generously tempered with political realism and preparedness to make concessions to expediency."[2]

15. "Ḥujjat al-Ḥaqq" (Proof of Truth)

A reply to criticisms made by the Taᶜlīmīs against al-Ghazālī in Baghdad. Apparently lost.

16. *Miᶜyār al-ᶜIlm fī Fann al-Manṭiq* (The Measure of Knowledge in the Art of Logic)

Edited by M. S. Kurdī without the word "Fann." Cairo: n.p., 1329/1911.

A possible appendix to the *Tahāfut* as it explains the technical terms in that work. It is a book on Aristotelian logic.

17. *Miḥakk al-Naẓar fī al-Manṭiq* (Analytical View on Logic)

Edited by Muḥammad Badr al-Dīn al-Naᶜsānī and Muṣṭafā al-Qabbānī. Cairo: n.p., 1925.

A book on Aristotelian logic. This work, along with *Miᶜyār,* was written around 487–488/1094–95.

18. *Al-Iqtiṣād fī al-Iᶜtiqād* (The Mean in Dogmatics)

(a) Cairo: Saᶜādah Press, 1327/1909.

(b) Edited by M. Qabbānī. Cairo: Adabīyah Press, n.d.; reprinted with the same pagination by Tijārīyah Press.

Written about 487/1094–95, it is a "constructive" work on dogmas as opposed to *Qawāᶜid al-ᶜAqā'd,* which is "destructive," as stated by al-Ghazālī; a prosaic piece of *kalām* which he wrote as a Sufi. It is his "chief work of dogmatics."

19. *Mīzān al-ᶜAmal* (Scale of Action)

(a) Edited by M. S. Kurdī and M. S. Nuᶜaymī. Cairo: n.p., 1328/1909–10.

(b) 2d ed. Cairo: ᶜArabīyah Press, 1342/1923.

(c) Translated by Hikmat Hachem. *Critère de l'action.* Preface by L. Massignon. Paris: Librarie orientale et americaine, 1945.

A companion to the *Miᶜyār,* the *Mīzān* gives criteria for sound action: Practice (*ᶜamal*) and knowledge (*ᶜilm*) are required for happiness in this world and the next. This was written about 488/1095.

20. "Al-Risālah al-Qudsīyah" (Jerusalem Treatise)

Possibly written around 489/1096, it is an epistle addressed to the people of Jerusalem and subsequently incorporated into the *Iḥyā'* under the rubric *Qawāᶜid al-ᶜAqā'id* (The Foundations of the Articles of Faith).

21. *Al-Radd al-Jamīl li-Ilāhīyāt ᶜĪsā bi Ṣarīḥ al-Injīl* (The Sweet Response to the Theology of Jesus in the Clarification of the Gospels)

(a) Edited and translated from Arabic into French by R. Chidiac. Preface by L. Massignon. Paris: Leroux, 1939.

(b) Translated into German with comment by F. E. Wilms. *Al-Ghazali's Schrift wider die Gottheit Jesu,* 1966.

A polemic against Christian theology, written about 492/1099.

22. *Iḥyā' ᶜUlūm al-Dīn* (The Revival of the Religious Sciences)

(a) Numerous editions in Arabic. The one used here was ᶜIrāqī's four

volume work. Cairo: Ḥalabī, 1967.
(b) German translation edited by Ernst Friedrich Tscheeuschner. Butersloh: n.p., 1933.

A complete system of Muhammadan moral philosophy in four parts and forty books. Written about 491/1098, it is al-Ghazālī's "greatest work" and a complete guide for the devout Muslim to every aspect of the religious life—worship and devotional practices, conduct in daily life, the purification of the heart, and advance along the mystic way.

23. *Kitāb al-Ḥikmah fī Makhlūqāt Allāh* (Book of Wisdom in God's Creations)
Edited by M. Qabbānī. Cairo: n.p., 1321/1903–4.

The book deals with the wisdom of God. The attribution of this work to Ghazālī was discussed among the historians of Jewish philosophy, and it was said to have been circulated under another name.

24. *Al-Risālah al-Waʿẓīyah,* in *Al-Jawāhir al-Ghawālī min rasā'il al-Imām hujjat al-Islam al-Ghazālī* (The Sermon Epistle Cited in the Precious Jewels of Ghazālī's Epistles)

Hourani states that it was edited in Cairo in 1353/1934. However, Bouyges claims that it was given this title by Ahlwardt, and was edited in Cairo in 1325/1907 under the title *Risālat al-Waʿẓ wa al-Iʿtiqād.*

25. *Marāqī al-Zulfā* (The Degrees of Servile Flattery)

This book probably appeared also under the title *Marāqī al-Zalaf,* according to Badāwī. Apparently lost.

26. "Al-Imlā' fī Ishkālāt al-*Iḥyā*" (Dictations in the Ambiguities of *Iḥyā'*)

Written after 500/1110–17, it is a reaction to criticisms of the *Iḥyā'* and its banning (no reference as to where, possibly Baghdad).

27. *Ayyuhā al-Walad* (O Boy)
(a) Edited by G. H. Scherer. *Ayyuhā al-Walad.* Beirut: American Press, 1933. Translated by E. Lator. Beirut: n.p., 1951.
(b) UNESCO, International Commission for the Translation of the Classics. *O Disciple.* Beirut: Catholic Press, 1951.
(c) Die Beruhmte ethische Abhandlung Ghazali's. Edited by Hammer-Purgstall. *O Kind!* Vienna: Z. Strauss, 1938.
(d) Traduit par Toufic Sabbagh. *O jeune homme.* Beirut: Imprimerie Catholique, 1951, 1969.

Hourani gives no indication as to date except that it came after the *Iḥyā'.* It is suggested by Scherer that this was one of Ghazālī's last works.[3] It is a letter of faith and conduct, consisting of elementary advice in the sphere of ascetic theology and reiterating his conclusions regarding the profound meaning of religion. It was originally compiled in Persian.

28. *Bidāyat al-Hidāyah* (Beginning of Guidance)
(a) Translated by W. Montgomery Watt. *The Faith and Practice of al-Ghazālī.* London: Allen & Unwin, 1953, 1963. (This included *al-Munqidh.*)
(b) J. Heil. *Die Religion des Islam,* vol. 1. Jena: n.p., 1915, 1923.
(c) Edited by Muṣṭafā al-Bābī al-Ḥalabī. Cairo: n.p., 1334/1912.

A collection of pious exhortations leading to salvation, compiled in Persian for the novice.

29. *Al-Maḍnūn Bihi ᶜAlā Ghayr Ahlihi* (Withheld from Outsiders) Cairo: Maymūnīyah Press, 1309/1891–92.

Watt states that this book deals essentially with symbolism, revelation and the interpretation of miracles, and the idea that "God is *bāṭin* (esoteric) because He is so extremely *ẓāhir* (exoteric)." It is an exposition of Ghazālī's own views.

30. *Al-Maqṣid al-Aqṣā fī Maᶜānī Asmā' Allāh al-Husnā* (The Farthest Aim in the Meanings of God's Beautiful Names)

(a) Cairo: Sharafīyah Press, 1328/1910–11.

(b) In a recent edition, the title has been "al-Asnā" rather than "al Aqṣā." Beirut: Dār al-Mashriq, 1971.

An exposition of divine names.

31. *Mishkāt al-Anwār* (The Niche for Lights)

(a) Cairo: n.p., 1353/1934.

(b) A translation with introduction by William Henry Temple Gairdner. London: The Royal Asiatic Society, 1924.

This book contains his developed mystical doctrines and further theological and anti-Bāṭinī essays.

32. *Qawāsim al-Bāṭinīyah* (Divisions of the Esotericists) Arabic and Turkish text, translated by Ahmed Ates. *Ilâhiyat Fakültesi dergisi,* 3(1–2) (1954): 23–54.

Hourani and Badāwī indicated in their listings that it was apparently lost. However, Farah states that there appears to be a translation by Ates. It was mentioned that it referred to Taᶜlīmīs and presumably was listed as "Mawāhim al-Bāṭinīyah" in the *Ṭabaqāt* of Subkī.

33. *Jawāb Mufaṣṣal al-Khilāf* (Answering Details of Disputation)

The *Munqidh* describes it, according to Hourani, as a reply to criticisms made against Ghazālī in Hamadan, and a refutation of the Taᶜlīmīs. Hourani further asserts that "it is not known whether or when Ghazālī was in Hamadan." Apparently lost.

34. *Jawāhir al-Qur'ān* (Jewels from the Koran)

Cairo: Raḥmānīyah Press, 1352/1933.

Bouyges states that al-Ghazālī discloses in this book the Essence, the Attributes, the Acts (of God), and the Return (to God). It is a collection of selected verses.

35. *Al-Arbaᶜīn fī Uṣūl al-Dīn* (The Forty Fundamentals of the Faith)

Cairo: ᶜArabīyah Press, 1344/1926.

It is a short summary of the *Iḥyā'.*

36. *Al-Qiṣṭāṣ al-Muṣtaqim,* in *Al-Jawāhir al-Ghawālī* (The Straight Measure, in The Precious Jewels)

(a) Cairo: n.p., 1353/1934.

(b) Edited by le Père Victor Chelhot. Beirut: Catholic Press, 1959.

The book justifies the use of Aristotelian logic in religious matters; a treatise on ethics.

37. *Fayṣal al-Tafriqah Bayn al-Islām wa al-Zandaqah,* in *Al-Jawāhir al-Ghawālī* (The Points of Separation Between Islam and Apostasy)
(a) Edited by Muṣṭafā al-Qabbānī. Cairo: n.p., 1901.
(b) Cairo: n.p., 1353/1934.
(c) Edited by Hans-Joachim Runge. *Uber Gazali's Faisal al-tafriqa baina 'l-Islam wa 'l-Zandaqa.* Kiel: n.p., 1938.

This is partly directed against the Bāṭinīyah, and is a defense of his own writings against the charge of heresy.

38. "Kitāb al-Darj" (Book of Recording)

As mentioned in *Munqidh,* this book is an answer to "feeble" criticisms by the Taᶜlīmīs against Ghazālī in Ṭūs. Apparently lost.

39. *Kimiyā-Yi Saᶜādat* (Alchemy of Happiness)
(a) In Persian. Bombay: n.p., 1321/1903.
(b) Translated from the Turkish by Henry A. Homes. *The Alchemy of Happiness.* Albany, NY: J. Munsell, 1837. In Persian. *Kimiyā' al-Saᶜādah.* The Alchemy of Bliss; A Treatise on Ethics. Lucknow: n.p., 1865.
(c) Translation into English by C. Field of eight chapters of the Urdu version. *The Alchemy of Happiness.* London: n.p., 1910.

The original is in Persian and was possibly written when al-Ghazālī was at the *zāwiya* (Sufi monastery) in Ṭūs. Hourani states that it is "an abridged popular version of the *Iḥyā'.* The book develops the concept that happiness is knowledge and action, and Ghazālī discusses the attainments of each.

40. *Al-Munqidh min al-Ḍalāl* (Deliverance from Error)
(a) In a collection with *Kitāb ilghām al-ᶜawām; al-maḍnūn bihi ᶜala ghayri ahlihi: al-maḍnūn al-saghīr al-mawsūm bi al-ajwibah al-Ghazzālīyah fī al-masā'il al-ukhrawīyah.* Cairo: Maymūnīyah Press, 1309/1891.
(b) Edited by J. Ṣalība and K. ᶜAyyād. Damascus: n.p., 1358/1891.
(c) Translated by Barbier de Meynard. "Traduction nouvelle du Traite de Ghazzali, intitule *Le Preservatif de l'erreur et Notices sur les extases* (des Soufis)." *Journal Asiatique,* 73 ser., 9 (1877):5–93.
(d) In Dutch. Uit het Arabisch vertaald en toegelicht door, by J. H. Kramers. *De redder uit de dwaling.* Amsterdam: Arbeiderspers, 1951.
(e) Cairo: n.p., 1952.
(f) Edited by F. Jabre. Beirut: n.p., 1959.

The book is an account of the development of his religious opinions and includes his conversion to Sufism. It is equated to the *Confessions* of St. Augustine. Bagley states that it is "also an apology for Sufism."[4]

41. *Al-Mustaṣfa min ᶜIlm al-Uṣūl* (The Condensation of the Science of Fundamentals)
2 vols. Cairo: Tijārīyah Press, 1356/1937.

A treatise on jurisprudence, it embodies also a part of his lectures from three years of teaching at the Niẓāmīyah. It was written possibly around 499/1106.

42. *Al-Tibr al-Masbūk fī Naṣīḥat al-Mulūk* (Counsel for Kings)
(a) In Persian. Edited by Jalal Huma'i. Tehran: n.p., 1317/1899.
(b) Translated by F. R. C. Bagley. *Ghazālī's Book of Counsel for Kings.*

London: Oxford University Press, 1964.

(c) Cairo: n.p., 1317/1899.

(d) Also on margins of *Sirāj al-Mulūk* (Persian text) of Ibn al-Rundakah. 1888.

Hourani states that this is addressed to the Seljuq Sultan Muhammad Ibn Malikshah, whose reign began in 1105.

43. *Iljām al-ᶜAwām ᶜAn ᶜIlm al-Kalām* (Restraining the Masses from Theological Disputation)

(a) First printed in Istanbul in 1278/1861. Cairo: Maymūnīyah Press, 1309/1891–92.

(b) In a collection; see *Al-Munqidh.* Cairo: Maymūnīyah Press, 1309/1891.

Completed in the year of Ghazālī's death, December 18, 1111. It "warns of the dangers in the study of *kalām* for those with little education."

APPENDIX B

Glossary of Selected Arabic Terms

This glossary encompasses only terms used herein that have acquired a technical usage. It mirrors existing standardized definitions as well as adjustments introduced in this work. The terms regarding hadith are used as employed by Guillaume, *The Traditions of Islam.* Other major helpful sources have been Farah, *Islam: Beliefs and Observances;* Schacht, *An Introduction to Islamic Law;* Ibn al-Nadīm, *The Fihrist of al-Nadīm;* Lane, *Arabic-English Lexicon;* and Jabre, *Essai sur le lexique de Ghazali.*

^{c}*abd* Servant of God or slave; used in proper names in combination with Allah

Ahl al-Kitāb People of the Book; in the Koran (5:68–69) the name is used for Christians, Jews, and Sabeans

akhbār (sing. *khabar*) News, reports; the term is applied to traditions traced back, not to the Prophet, but to other authorities such as his companions, well-known jurists, and imams

alim See ulema

^{c}*anat* Fornication or committing a sin

^{c}*aqd* Marriage contract; formalization of the marriage vows

^{c}*aqīqah* Sacrifice; a sheep or goat slaughtered as a sacrifice on the seventh day after the birth of a child

acqra^{c} To cast or draw lots, or practice sortilege among women

^{c}*Āshūrā'* Name of a voluntary fast day, the tenth day of Muḥarram

^{c}*aṣr* Period of sunset, time of one of the ritual prayers *āthār* (sing. *athar*) Traces; applied to traditions relating the deeds and utterances of Muhammad and his companions

baqā' Subsistence in God; an ultimate Sufi state

bāṭin Internal, hidden or inner meaning; esoteric

ḍaʿīf Not fulfilling the required conditions for transmittal

dhikr Remembrance or recollection of God; an exercise by Sufis to induce ecstasy

fanā Annihilation, or passing away of oneself in God; the mystical union of the soul with God

faqīh Islamic jurist or jurisprudent

farāgh Emptying or purifying the heart; a Sufi tenet

farḍ Canonically imposed duty or obligation of faith

fiqh The corpus of Islamic jurisprudence

fiṭrah Natural disposition of the heart to know God

gharīb Authentic, but resting on the authority of only one companion

ghusl Major or full ablution ceremony involving the entire body; see also *wuḍū'*

hadith Traditions of the Prophet; collection of sayings and precedents of the Prophet, handed down by his associates and followers

ḥajj A canonically prescribed pilgrimage to Mecca

ḥarām Canonically forbidden; a sin

ḥasan Of fair authority, with a slight fault; approved form of transmittal

ḥasan gharīb Authentic, of fair authority

ḥasan ṣaḥīḥ Genuine, of fair authority

ḥayḍ Menstruation; important in connection with determining the time of conception and responsibility for fatherhood, as well as significant for ritual purification

ḥikmah Exercise of judicial authority, a rule, a decree; an edict or a prescript

ḥirāthah Tilth; intercourse for the purpose of having offspring

ḥulūl Ecstasy; union with God through mystical practices

ibdāl Substitution (when certain righteous people die, God substitutes others for them)

ʿiddah Legally prescribed waiting period of a woman before remarriage

^{c}*iddat baynūnah* Legally prescribed waiting period for final divorce; woman cannot remarry her husband

^{c}*iddat al-ray*^{c}*ah* Legally prescribed waiting period pending remarriage with one's divorced wife

iḍṭibā^{c} Cloaking oneself over the left shoulder during the pilgrimage to Mecca

ijmā^{c} Consensus; interpretation of the law according to the opinions of the leading jurists

^{c}*ilal* Defects, causes

imam Used here for leading religious personalities; it also has a number of other significations

iqāmah Call to prayer repeated at the beginning of the prayer ritual

irādah Desire; the aspiration to do only God's will; in a Sufi context, a willful determination to undertake the rigors of the Path

^{c}*ishā'* Evening meal and time of the fourth ritual prayer

isnād Literally means "leaning upon"; the chain of authority which precedes and introduces the text of hadith

izār Seamless white cloth wrapped around loins to knee level by the pilgrim performing the *ḥajj*

jam^{c} Uttering a threefold divorce

jayyid Good, reliable form of transmittal

jihad Striving on behalf of the faith; Holy War of the Muslims against the infidels

junub Major ritual impurity; signifies a man under obligation of performing a total ablution, by reason of sexual intercourse and discharge of the semen

Kaaba The shrine at Mecca sacred to the Muslims

karāhīyah Abomination or reprehensible

kasaba To earn; Koranic usage connotes the performance of an act for which one merits reward or punishment on the Day of Judgment

khabar See *akhbār*

khul^{c} Divorce requested by the wife, who must pay a compensation (*khul*^{c}*ah*)

khuṭbah An exhortation or admonition recited, generally in rhyming prose, during the noon service of the mosque on Friday by an orator (*khaṭīb*)

kitābīyah See Ahl al-Kitāb
*li*ᶜ*ān* Oath of condemnation; in Islamic Law, can also be a sworn allegation of adultery committed by either husband or wife
*ma*ᶜ*ād* Return journey; the ultimate state of existence in the world to come
madhhab (plur. *madhāhib*) Juridical rite to which a Sunni Muslim may adhere
maghrib Sunset; time of one of the ritual prayers
mahr A dowry or a nuptial gift given to the bride in a contract of marriage
makrūh A reprehensible or an evil act, but not a forbidden one
manzil (plur. *manāzil*) Stages; a Sufi tenet
maqāmāt (sing. *maqām*) The stations of the faith; a Sufi tenet
*ma*ᶜ*rifah* Knowledge, learning; the knowledge of Allah, the experience of ecstasy, and the gnosis of the mystics
martabah A Sufi rank or station
*ma*ᶜ*rūf* Weak tradition, yet known because it is confirmed by another
maw'ūdah: al-maw'ūdat al-sughrah Coitus interruptus; significance similar to that of burying a girl child alive
*Mi*ᶜ*raj* Muhammad's nocturnal journey to the Seventh Heaven
mubāḥ Permissible; a deed neither recommended nor prohibited
mubham Obscure; a tradition derived from a person about whom nothing is known save his name
mufti The legal authority in Islam who gives expert decisions by which the courts are guided
muḥallil A man who marries a divorced (three pronouncements of formula) woman on condition that he divorce her after consummation of the marriage so she may lawfully remarry her former husband
*mukhtali*ᶜ*āh* Women who incite, urge, or induce their husbands to divorce them for a gift or a compensation (*khul*ᶜ*ah*) without any injurious conduct from the latter
mukhtalif A tradition which apparently contradicts another, but which can be reconciled to it
munkar A tradition of weak authority contradicted by a weaker one

munqaṭi^{c} An *isnād* from which a name has disappeared
murīd A novice, a disciple of a *murshid* (teacher of a Sufi order)
mursal A text without *isnād*, or one with an incomplete *isnād*
murū'ah Manliness; a pre-Islamic Arab concept which comprises all knightly virtues and the ideal of manhood
musnad Authorities by whom a hadith is passed down
mut^{c}*a* The contracting of temporary marriage; legalized by the Shi^{c}i law
muṭṭafaq ^{c}*alayhi* A tradition that is agreed upon and received by Bukhārī and Muslim
muttaṣil A tradition with an uninterrupted *isnād*
nafaqah In Islamic Law, it signifies adequate support for a wife or expenditure
nafs Self, soul, ego
naqīb A surety for the people, leader
nāsikh Abrogating; refers to the chain of authority and is used by Muslim theologians in reference to a verse or sentence of the Koran which cancels or abrogates a previous one
qiblah The south, or the direction to be faced in prayer
rak^{c}*ah* Bow, prostration; a bending of the torso from an upright position, followed by two prostrations with each standing for a full prayer cycle
ramal Trotting while performing the circuit around the Kaaba
Razzāq Provider; one of the ninety-nine attributes of God
ṣadāqah Voluntary, nonstatutory alms rendered for the sake of acquiring merit with God; in Islamic Law, legally prescribed alms tax (*ṣadaq*)
saḥḥaḥ Transmittal made genuine
ṣaḥīḥ Genuine; fulfilling all conditions
Shari^{c}a The Muslim law derived from the Koran, the hadith, and the processes of jurisprudence
shirk Polytheism; associating other deities or "partners" with Allah
shukr Thankfulness; it is one of the stations of the mystic
siqṭ Miscarried fetus
sunna (plur. *sunan*) The theory and practice of conventional Muslims, based on the Koran and the hadith
ta^{c}*biyah ilāhīyah* Divine fulfillment
tahlīl Exaltation (of God)

takbīr To glorify, praise, to exclaim *"allahu akhbār"*
ṭalāq Divorce; three "I divorce thee" utterances either at separate intervals or at one time for finalization
tawbah Repentance; the first station on the Sufi path
thayyib A woman who is deflowered or married; a divorcee or a widow
thiqah A trustworthy transmittal
ṭuhr The days of a woman's state of purity from the menstrual discharge
ulema (sing. alim) Scholars who are knowledgeable in Islamic beliefs and dogmas
ᶜumrah Lesser pilgrimage to Mecca
uṣūl (sing. *aṣl*) Ascendants, fundamentals; also meaning roots, origins, principles
ᶜutul One who has a harsh tongue and who is cruel toward his family
waḥy Revelation
walīy Legal guardian; also refers to the believer as "friend of God"
wiṭr A form of prayer, in which an odd number of prostrations is performed, after the night prayer
wuḍū' Limited ablution for or preparatory to prayer; see also *ghusl*
zindīq Freethinker; in the ninth and tenth centuries, the term was applied as a rule to the partisans of Zoroastrians and Manichaeans who were feared as rebels
zuhd Asceticism; a way of life which included renunciation of worldly things, fasting, prayer, studying the Koran, and similar religious observances and practices
ẓuhr Noon; time for the third daily prayer incumbent upon Muslims

Notes

As in the text, all references to the Koran are from Pickthall's *The Glorious Koran* unless otherwise noted.

PREFACE

1. For more details see Badāwī, *Mu'allafāt al-Ghazālī,* 118–22; Farah, "Bibliographical Guide," 38–50.

Part I. INTRODUCTION

1. al-Ghazālī, *Confessions,* 10.
2. I use the spelling "al-Ghazālī" throughout this study, but I have not changed alternative spellings quoted from other works. For standard biographical accounts see al-Ghazālī, *Faith and Practice;* Jabre, *Le Lexique de Ghazali;* and Badāwī, *Mu'allafat al-Ghazālī.*
3. al-Ghazālī, *Counsel for Kings,* xxxiii.
4. Nawab ᶜAlī, *Moral and Religious Teachings,* viii. The word *Ḥujjat,* an honorific title, may also be translated "argument for," or "demonstration of."
5. Nicholson, *Eastern Poetry and Prose,* 8.
6. *Life and Works of Jāḥiẓ*, 258. His full name was Abū ᶜUthmān ᶜAmr b. Bahr al-Kināni al-Fuqaimi al-Baṣri, a leading expository writer of Islam. He was born in Basra and lived from 160/776–77 to 255/868–69. He was of African origin and his ancestors were slaves. "Al-Jāḥiẓ" is a nickname given him because of his protruding eyes and physical grotesqueness.
7. Fyzee, *Muhammadan Law,* 111.
8. This period is three months from the date of the declaration of divorce or, if the woman is pregnant, until delivery (see Fyzee, *Muhammadan Law,* 114–50; Kor. 2:228, 231–32, 234–35; Kor. 33:49; Kor. 65:46–47).
9. Shukri, *Law of Marriage and Divorce,* 21
10. Ibn al-Jawzī, *Zād al-Masīr fī ᶜIlm al-Tafsīr,* 52–53. See also al-Bukhārī, *Ṣaḥīḥ,* 7:16.
11. The legal and social implications are extremely important since this entitlement changed the woman from an object of sale to an individual human being; she became a legal person capable of entering into a contractual

relationship with her husband, the document being equally binding on both parties.

12. The legal term, *thayyib,* refers to a woman who lost "her virginity lawfully in wedlock; or who is by a conclusive presumption of the law held to have done so, on the grounds that she has resided in her husband's house twelve months, she being then above puberty"; however, defloration by illicit relations will not render a woman *"thayyib"* (Russell and Suhrawardy, *Muslim Jurisprudence,* 4).

13. Bint al-Shāṭi', *Nisā' al-Nabī,* 2.

14. al-Bukhārī, *Ṣaḥīḥ,* 3:64.

15. al-Suhrawardy, *Sayings of Muhammad,* 52.

16. Schacht, *Islamic Law,* 21.

17. See Wensinck, *Handbook,* 221–22.

18. Schacht, *Muhammadan Jurisprudence,* 181. For frequency of pre-Islamic divorces, see W. R. Smith, *Kinship and Marriage,* 83.

19. This list expands on al-Ghazālī's brief analysis of divorce in chapter 3, but he also refers to some of these forms of divorce in other sections. The list also embraces the legal aspects as set forth by Fyzee (*Muhammadan Law,* 139–79) and Schacht (*Islamic Law,* 163–66).

20. Fyzee, *Muhammadan Law,* 146.

21. de St. Elie ("La Femme du desert," 187) emphasizes the point that divorce is less frequent among the nomads than among the seminomads or agriculturists.

22. de St. Elie (Ibid.) described this method as most common in pre-Islam, which contradicts Fyzee's view that "prior to Islam the wife had practically no right to ask for divorce" (*Muhammadan Law,* 155). Pickthall cites the utterance in a footnote that refers to the sura 33:4. See also Stern, *Marriage in Early Islam,* 127.

23. Ibn Sīnā takes an identical position on divorce, which he allows as a last resort. See his *Aqsām al-ᶜUlūm* in *Rasā'il Ibn Sīnā,* 235–43.

24. Gibb, *Civilization of Islam,* 28.

25. al-Ghazālī, *Confessions,* 4.

26. al-Ghazālī, *Counsel for Kings,* xxxix.

27. Watt, "Study of al-Ghazali," 121.

28. al-Ghazālī, *Iḥyā'* (Tijārīyah edition), 5.

29. Arberry, *Sufism,* 82.

30. Nawab ᶜAlī, *Moral and Religious Teachings,* ix.

31. For the origin and position of this school, as well as those of Abū Ḥanīfa, Mālik b. Anas, and Ibn Ḥanbal, see Macdonald, *Muslim Theology, Jurisprudence and Constitutional Theology*; Fyzee, *Muhammadan Law*; and Schacht, *Islamic Law.*

32. Farah, *Islam,* 174.

33. Farīd al-Dīn ᶜAṭṭār, *Muslim Saints and Mystics,* 51.

34. Massignon, *La Passion d'al-Hallaj,* 518.

35. Watt, *Muslim Intellectual,* 176–77.

36. Guillaume, *Traditions of Islam,* 145.

37. Andrae, *Mohammad,* 255–56

38. Abū Dā'ūd, *Sunan,* 1:173.

39. M. Smith, *Rābiᶜa the Mystic,* 165. For a similar tradition see Lane, *Arabian Society,* 221.

40. Margoliouth, *Early Development of Mohammedanism,* 141; Macdonald, *Muslim Theology, Jurisprudence and Constitutional Theory,* 89.

41. al-Ḥujwīrī, *Kashf al-Maḥjūb,* 361.

42. al-Makkī, *Kitāb Qūt al-Qulūb,* 1:153.

43. This is expounded upon in al-Ghazālī's twenty-third book of the *Iḥyā'* (3:131). See also M. Smith, *Rābiᶜa the Mystic,* 11; and Bercher, "Extrait du livre XXIII," 313–31.

44. M. Smith, *Rābiᶜa the Mystic,* 13; Farīd al-Dīn ᶜAṭṭār, *Muslim Saints and Mystics,* 46.

45. al-Suhrawardī, *ᶜAwārif al-Maᶜārif,* 77.

46. Ibid., 81.

47. Ibid., 76. See also Bercher, "Extrait du livre XXIII," 318; and al-Ghazālī, *Iḥyā',* 3:128.

48. al-Qushayrī, *Risālah,* 368. In al-Qushayrī (Ibid., 365–74) is a complete discussion of sayings and arguments given by Sufis for solitude and asceticism.

49. al-Suhrawardī, *ᶜAwārif al-Maᶜārif,* 78.

50. Ibid.

51. al–Makkī, *Kitāb Qūt al-Qulūb,* 2:239.

52. M. Smith, *Studies in Early Mysticism,* 62.

53. al-Ḥujwīrī, *Kashf al-Maḥjūb,* 95–96.

54. al-Ghazālī, *Iḥyā',* 3:130.

55. Ibid. Only four "inconveniences" are listed; the fifth, a psychological one, is then treated in more detail.

56. al-Suhrawardy, *Sayings of Muhammad,* 116.

57. Lane, *Arabian Society,* 227.

58. Ibid.

59. M. Smith, *Studies in Early Mysticism,* 246.

60. al-Ḥujwīrī, *Kashf al-Maḥjūb,* 364.

61. Bousquet, *L'Ethique sexuelle,* 185.

62. Ibn Mājah, *Sunan,* 1:217.

63. Ibid.

64. This is referring to fornication by the eye, which is an abomination. Ibn Sīnā argues that the lawful gratification of human passions purifies the heart and balances the mind. He considers biological needs to be means to an end and not ends in themselves (see his *Aqsām al-ᶜUlūm* in *Rasā'il Ibn Sīnā,* 235–43).

65. See al-Shāfiᶜī, *Risālah,* 568.

66. Ibid., 354–55, 566–67.

67. Menstruation is considered to be from one to fifteen days (al-Tirmidhī, *Sunan,* 1:156–57).

68. al-Shāfiᶜī, *Risālah,* 118–19.

69. al-Tirmidhī, *Sunan,* 3:313.

70. Ibid., 165, 167. (See *ṣadāqah* in Glossary.)

71. Ibid., 165.

72. al-Bukhārī, *Ṣaḥīḥ,* 1:83.

73. Ibid., 6:21.

74. al-Tirmidhī, *Sunan,* 4:102–3. See also Ibn Mājah, *Sunan,* 1:620.

75. al-Tirmidhī, *Sunan*, 4:103-4. See also al-Bukhārī, *Ṣaḥīḥ*, 7:42.

76. As defined in *Munjid*, 17.

77. al-Tirmidhī, *Sunan,* 4:102–3.
78. Ibn Mājah, *Sunan,* 1:620.
79. al-Tirmidhī, *Sunan,* 4:104.
80. Bousquet, *L'Ethique sexuelle,* 69.
81. The reference here is clearly to sodomy as he uses the word *lūṭ*. However, one usually associates incest with Lot and his daughters; but since they belonged to the Sodomites, the other context (sodomy) herein referred to becomes applicable. See the articles on Sodom and Lot in *Interpreter's Dictionary of the Bible,* 4:395–97.
82. al-Tirmidhī, *Sunan,* 1:152.
83. al-Bukhārī, *Ṣaḥīḥ,* 1:83.
84. Ibid., 153.
85. Ibn Mājah, *Sunan,* 1:856.
86. Ibid.
87. Ibn Ḥanbal, *Musnad,* 4:134.
88. Ibid.
89. Ibid., 3:356, 389, 395.
90. Ibn Ṭufayl, *Ḥayy b. Yakẓān,* 69–72.
91. This is the traditional conception of man, for as Nasr continues: "[It is] the *corpus, anima* and *spiritus* of Hermeticism and other sapiential doctrines . . . and not the erroneous and truncated concept of man as a creature formed only of body and mind, a concept that is due more than anything else to Cartesian dualism along with a misunderstanding of certain tenets of scholasticism" (*Sufi Essays,* 68).
92. al-Ghazālī, *Counsel for Kings,* 170 (with mistakes corrected).
93. al-Ghazālī, *Faith and Practice,* 88.

Part II. BOOK ON THE ETIQUETTE OF MARRIAGE

AL-GHAZĀLĪ'S INTRODUCTION

1. See al-Bukhārī, *Ṣaḥīḥ,* 7:9.
2. "Tillage," frequently used by al-Ghazālī, is interpreted by Watt to mean "a development of the primitive metaphor which compares sexual intercourse with the sowing of seed, and speaks of children as the fruit of the womb" (*Companion to the Qu'rān,* 41).
3. The Ḥalabī edition indicated *bil-nuṭaf.* It is difficult to ascertain the meaning with the preposition as an antecedent.
4. I translated *al-indhār* from the Azharīyah edition as a "warning," while the Ḥalabī edition indicates *bil-indhār,* "with warning."

Chapter 1. ADVANTAGES AND DISADVANTAGES OF MARRIAGE

1. In Arabic: *ʿulamā'* (sing. *ʿālim,* literally "learned man"). They are the scholars who are learned in Islamic law, beliefs and dogmas (Hughes, *Dictionary of Islam,* 650).
2. It is possible that al-Ghazālī is idealizing the past here as no other source has been found to substantiate his remarks. Von Grunebaum reinforces this belief when he states, "The Muslim hates change. The best Islam was in the beginning. . . . By clinging to the ways of the forebears, by upholding and reliving the tradition of the ancients, by eschewing innovation, the standing of his betters who preceded him would be preserved one instant longer" (*Medieval Islam,* 240).

3. *Akhbār* (sing. *khabar,* literally "news, report") is applied to traditions traced back, not to the Prophet, but to other authorities such as his companions, well-known jurists, imams, etc.

4. *Āthār* (sing. *athar*, literally "trace") is applied to traditions relating the deeds and utterances of Muhammad and his companions.

5. Watt states that this injunction is "usually taken to mean that the relatives should not oppose remarriage to the former husband, but might refer to opposition by the former husband to another husband" (*Companion to the Qur'ān,* 42).

6. Hereafter, invocations after saints, prophets, companions and those who have passed away will be deleted; an asterisk will indicate the deletions. The invocation after a saint or a prophet is, "May the prayer and peace of God be upon him"; after companions, "God be satisfied with him"; and others, "May God have mercy upon him."

7. See discussion in note 110, this chapter. Actually, "whoever likes my religion which I practice."

8. This hadith was related by Abū Yaᶜla in his *Musnad* with an introduction and conclusion from the hadith of Ibn ᶜAbbās on the authority of Ḥasan (ᶜIrāqī).

9. This hadith was related by Abū Bakr Ibn Murdawayyah in his commentary from the hadith of Ibn ᶜUmar without his including "even if you should fall." His transmission is weak, and this addition was also mentioned by al-Bayhaqī through his knowledge of al-Shāfiᶜī who he claimed had informed him of it (ᶜIrāqī).

10. First part conforms with the hadith of Anas: "Whoever refrains from my sunna, he is not of me"; and the rest was preceded by hadith (ᶜIrāqī). See also ᶜAbd al-Bāqī, *Lu'lu' wa al-Marjān,* 3:100.

11. Abū Manṣūr al-Daylamī related this hadith in his *Musnad al-Firdaws* from Abī Saᶜīd's hadith in a weak transmission and in the *Musnad* of al-Darāmī and in the *Muᶜjam* of al-Baghawī and in the *Marāsīl* as related from the sayings of Abū Najīh, "whoever is able to marry and does not marry, he is not of us," and Abū Najīh dissented in his friendship (ᶜIrāqī).

12. Ibn Mājah related this hadith from the hadith of ᶜĀ'ishah in a weak (*ḍaᶜīf*) transmission (ᶜIrāqī).

13. Reference is to lustfulness.

14. This hadith is agreed upon by the sayings taken from the hadith of Ibn Masᶜūd (ᶜIrāqī). See also ᶜAbd al-Bāqī, *Lu'lu' wa al-Marjān,* 3:99; and al-Bukhārī, *Ṣaḥīḥ,* 7:3. The term used here, *wijā'un,* literally means "bruising of the veins of the testicles until they break, so that it is like gelding" (Lane, *Arabic-English Lexicon,* 292).

15. Arousal of sensuous desire through eyeing the opposite sex.

16. Implies satisfaction of sexual urges.

17. al-Tirmidhī made this transmittal known from the hadith of Abū Hurayrah (ᶜIrāqī).

18. In Sufi lexicography, the term is also used to signify sainthood or "friendship of God" (Jabre, *Le Lexique de Ghazali,* 278).

19. Aḥmad related this hadith in a weak transmission from the hadith of Muᶜādh Anas (ᶜIrāqī).

20. Ibn al-Jawzī related this hadith in the *ᶜIlal* from the hadith of Anas in a weak transmission (ᶜIrāqī).

21. Implies desire for sex. According to Ibn Manẓūr the term applies

to sexual organs of both male and female (*Lisān al-ᶜArab,* 3:166). Hans Wehr mentions only "vulva" under *farj* (*Dictionary,* 702).

22. Implies desire for food.

23. Muslim relates this hadith from Abū Hurayrah (ᶜIrāqī).

24. ᶜUmar b. al-Khaṭṭāb, second caliph, is one of the greatest figures of early Islam and founder of the Arab empire. The West has given him the epithet of "St. Paul of Islam." He is also referred to as *amīr al-mu'minīn,* in a sense renewing the theocratic regime of the time of the Prophet; it ceased with ᶜUmar, but the transmission of prophetic powers was revived later by the Shiᶜa. He was the father-in-law of the Prophet, who married his daughter, Ḥafṣah. He died 23/644 (*Encyclopaedia of Islam,* supplement, new ed., s.v. "āthār").

25. *Fujūr* also means to act immorally, sin, live licentiously, lead a dissolute life, indulge in debauchery" (Wehr, *Dictionary,* 697).

26. Ibn ᶜAbbās ᶜAbd al-Muṭṭalib, died 68/687, was a companion and an uncle of the Prophet (*Encyclopaedia of Islam,* new ed., s.v. "ᶜAbbās"; see also Ibn al-Nadīm, *Fihrist,* 932).

27. *Farāgh,* emptying the heart, is a Sufi tenet. It means that by ridding himself of selfish desires, man is able to receive God's graces and become tranquil (Lane, *Arabic-English Lexicon,* 2382).

28. Abū ᶜAbd Allāh b. ᶜAbd Allāh ᶜAkramah, a slave of berber origin attached to the governor of al-Baṣrah, became an authority on the Koran and hadith. He died in 107–8/725–26 (Ibn al-Nadīm, *Fihrist,* 75, 82, 1012).

Muḥammad b. al-ᶜAlā' b. Kurayb al-Hamdānī Abū Kurayb, from al-Kufāh, was an authority on hadith. Al-Ṭabarī, a jurist of his age, acquired knowledge of the hadith from him. He died in 244/858 (Ibn al-Nadīm, *Fihrist,* 563, 1033).

29. Ibn Masᶜūd, who died in 32–33/653–54, was a companion of the Prophet and was one of the first converts. He is a traditionist and an authority on the Koran and the sunna. To him is attributed 848 traditions, which are collected in *Musnad Aḥmad* (*Encyclopaedia of Islam,* new ed., s.v. "al-Masᶜūdī").

30. Muᶜādh Ibn Jabal Ibn Aws was appointed by the Prophet as judge of al-Yaman, and helped to collect revelations of the Koran. He died about 18/639 (Ibn al-Nadīm, *Fihrist,* 62, 1045).

31. *Baᶜd* is translated "one" rather than "some"; the referent is singular (Wehr, *Dictionary,* 67).

32. The term used, *baniyy,* stands for a descendant or a member of a family, clan or tribe.

33. Aḥmad related this hadith from Rābiᶜah al-Aslamī in a lengthy narration. The transmission is of fair authority (ḥasan) (ᶜIrāqī).

34. Reference is to early ascetics who did not marry, but felt if they did, a wife would distract them from their devotion to the One; consequently, their material needs were the bare essentials. Al-Suhrawardī reiterates this in his commentary in the margins of the Azharīyah edition (*ᶜAwārif al-Maᶜārif,* 78).

35. Bishr b. al-Ḥārith, or Abū Nasr Bishr b. al-Ḥāfi, was born near Merv ca. 150/767 and died in Baghdad in 227/841. Bishr, who studied traditions in Baghdad, abandoned formal learning for the "life of a mendicant, destitute, starving and barefoot," hence the name "al-Ḥāfi." He was admired and respected by Aḥmad b. Ḥanbal and Caliph al-Ma'mūn (Farīd al-Dīn ᶜAṭṭār, *Muslim Saints and Mystics,* 80).

36. Aḥmad b. Muḥammad b. Ḥanbal, known as Ibn Ḥanbal, died at Baghdad in 241/855. He was an adherent to the *Ahl al-Hadith,* or the old traditional views. Where possible, he "derives every law from traditional sources. This compels him to be very indulgent to the hadith and sometimes to admit very feeble traditions as the basis of his decision." He was a founder of one of the the four *madhāhib* (juridical rites) in Islam, the Ḥanbali school. He did not establish a fiqh (jurisprudence) system of his own but did answer pupils' questions pertaining specifically to legal matters. His son, ᶜAbdullah, collected the traditions and lectures in the *Musnad* (*Encyclopaedia of Islam,* new ed., s.v. "hadith").

37. That is, he was in an unenviable position.

38. Al-Qushayrī uses *martabah* and *maqām* in the same context. He discusses twenty stations along the mystic's path, the first of which is repentance (*tawbah*), (*Risālah,* 253–408; see also Ḥujwīrī, *Kashf al-Maḥjūb,* 294; and Arberry, *Sufism,* 75–79).

39. *Talqānī* (you encounter me) was translated instead of *yalqānī* (he encounters me), as in the Azharīyah edition, to agree with the subject.

40. Ibrāhīm Ibn Adham, or Abū Isḥāq Ibrāhīm b. Adham, was born in Balkh of pure Arab descent—a prince who renounced his kingdom somewhat after the fashion of the Buddha. His conversion is a classic in Sufi legend. He left his kingdom and family to become an itinerant dervish, living an ascetic life, then gathered a following. He died ca. 165/782 in Syria (Farīd al-Dīn ᶜAṭṭār, *Muslim Saints and Mystics,* 62).

41. Farīd al-Dīn ᶜAṭṭār maintains that Ibn Adham was married (*Muslim Saints and Mystics,* 68).

42. *Mujāhid* is one who "fought against unbelievers and the like in the way of God, that is, in the cause of religion" (Lane, *Arabic-English Lexicon,* 473).

43. *Rakᶜah* literally means "a bending of the torso from an upright position, followed by two prostrations [in Muslim prayer rituals]" (Wehr, *Dictionary,* 358).

44. Reference is probably to the Arabicized Muslim whereby the "Arabic civilization becomes Muslim civilization, and it is the spontaneous collaboration of the best minds of all the Empire's nationalities that accounts for the stupendous rise of this civilization in those two hundred years, from 750 to 950, so breathlessly crowded of human accomplishment" (Von Grunebaum, *Medieval Islam,* 201).

45. Abū Yaᶜla relates this hadith from Ḥadhīfah, and al-Khiṭābī in *al-ᶜUzlah* from his own hadith and the hadith of Abūi Amāmah; both weak transmittals (ᶜIrāqī).

46. Al-Khiṭābī related this hadith in *al-ᶜUzlah* from the hadith of Ibn Masᶜūd who was guided by al-Bayhaqī in *al-Zahū,* who was guided by the hadith of Abū Hurayrah; all weak transmittals (ᶜIrāqī).

47. Al-Qaḍāᶜī related this hadith in the *Musnad* of al-Shihāb [followed by other references and transmittals]; both transmittal lines are weak (ᶜIrāqī).

48. Abū Sulaymān al-Dārānī, a mystic of the ninth century, died in Syria in 215/830. To him is attributed the first delineations of the doctrine of *maqāmāt* (stations) of the Sufi path (Jāmī, *Nafaḥāt al-Uns,* 39).

49. See al-Suhrawardī, *ᶜAwārif al-Maᶜārif,* 76.

50. Al-Ghazālī is apparently voicing his discontent toward the writers of hadith in emulation of Muhammad, who said to those writing hadith, "Do

you not know that nothing but the writing of books besides the book of God led astray the peoples that were before you?" (Guillaume, *Traditions of Islam,* 16).

51. Abū al-Ḥasan Aḥmad b. al-Ḥawwārī was from Damascus, and was a scholar and a mystic. He died in 230–31/844–45 (Ibn al-Nadīm, *Fihrist,* 456, 1002).

52. In the Ḥalabī edition *yussabbib* is used to imply that producing children is the primary aim of coitus; in the Azharīyah edition *bisabab* is used when a child is the accidental result of coitus.

53. The term used is *walad,* which connotes a male or female offspring.

54. That is, increase the ranks of the faithful (Muslims).

55. That is, after the father has passed away.

56. Although the verse, Kor. 2:48 (ᶜAlī), rules out intercession in Islam, many Muslims believe in it: "And fear the day when no soul shall serve as a substitute for another soul at all, nor shall intercession be accepted for it; nor shall ransom be taken from it; nor shall they be helped."

57. This is a reference to the reports that in the Jāhilīyah (pre-Islam) period Arabs buried their daughters alive. W. R. Smith asserts that the reason for this was twofold: fear by the parents that they could not provide for all their offspring and fear that their daughters might be taken captive and thus bring disgrace on their kin (*Kinship and Marriage,* 291–96; see also Fyzee, *Muhammadan Law,* 5).

58. Al-Ghazālī expounds further on this subject from a slightly different position in chapter 3. In the hadith, there are transmittals both allowing and disapproving coitus interruptus. See Wensinck, *Handbook,* 112.

59. Watt explains "lend" as "contributing to God's causes" (*Companion to the Qur'an,* 43).

60. His use of such terms as *fanā'* and *baqā'* may be conscious allusions to Sufi significations since both constitute final states in the Sufi's search for communion with God; *fanā'* is the annihilation or passing away of the self, but is not equivalent to the cessation of the individual consciousness as in Nirvana; and *baqā'* is the "subsistence or remaining" in God (Jabre, *Le Lexique de Ghazali,* 265; see also Ḥujwīrī, *Kashf al-Maḥjūb,* 243; and *Encyclopaedia of Islam,* new ed., s.v. "*fanā'*").

61. The hadith states that "God says." It is related by al-Bukhārī from the hadith of Abū Hurayrah that Mukhlid al-Qatawānī is the only one who quoted it (ᶜIrāqī).

62. The complete verse is: "Who hath created life and death that He may try you" (Kor. 67:2).

63. The Azharīyah edition adds: *wa yaḥṣul al-wiqāᶜ*—that is, "and coitus results as a consequence of desire."

64. *Al-ramal* (trotting) and *al-iḍṭibāᶜ* (cloaking) are performed in imitation of the Prophet and his companions who did these things so that the people of Mecca might know that there was strength in them (Lane, *Arabic-English Lexicon,* 1159).

65. The text is *al-iftidā'* (ransom, sacrifice, redeem), but *al-iqtidā'* of the Azharīyah edition was translated to mean "emulation."

66. Abū ᶜUmar al-Tawqānī indicates this hadith in his book *Maᶜāshirat al-Ahlayn,* basing it on the transmittal of ᶜUmar b. al-Khaṭṭāb, but this cannot be supported or justified (ᶜIrāqī).

67. Al-Bayhaqī reveals this hadith from the hadith of Ibn Abī ᶜAdiyah al-Ṣadafī as genuine (*ṣaḥīḥ*) and based on Saᶜīd b. Yasār as the ultimate source (ᶜIrāqī).

68. Ibn Ḥabbān relates it in his *Ḍuᶜafā'* (book of weak transmittals) as related by Bahaz b. Ḥakīm, who quoted his father, who quoted his grandfather; weak transmittals (ᶜIrāqī).

69. Ibn Mājah relates the hadith from ᶜAlī and says "miscarried fetus" rather than "child"; weak transmittal (ᶜIrāqī).

70. Muslim relates the hadith from Abū Hurayrah (ᶜIrāqī).

71. Ibn Ḥabbān first related this hadith in the *Ḍuᶜafā'* from the transmittals of Bahaz b. Ḥakīm, who related it from his father, who related it from his grandfather: It is not genuine. However, al-Nisā'ī related it from the hadith of Abū Hurayrah in a good (*jayyid*) transmittal. He states that "it was said to them to enter paradise; they would say, 'Not until our parents enter,' then it would be said, 'Enter paradise, you and your parents' " (ᶜIrāqī).

72. The hadith in its entirety does not have a reliable source (ᶜIrāqī).

73. Al-Bazzār and al-Ṭabarānī related the hadith from Zuhayr b. Abī ᶜAlqamah; and by Muslim from the hadith of Abū Hurayrah (ᶜIrāqī).

74. Al-Bukhārī relates the hadith from Anas without mentioning "even two"; Aḥmad related this addition from the hadith of Muᶜādh which is agreed upon (*muttafaq ᶜalayhi*) (ᶜIrāqī).

75. The word is *wildān* (sing. *walīd*), that is, "newborn children, young infants"; a child who dies in early infancy, or who is prematurely born, is in paradise (Lane, *Arabic-English Lexicon,* 2966).

76. Lane quotes this whole hadith from *Nuzhat al-Mutaammil* (*Arabian Society,* 197–98).

77. In the Azharīyah edition, it is *al-taghbīyah* which would be translated as "divine concealment."

78. The Sufis are referred to as those who are knowledgeable in the esoteric, hidden or inner meanings (Jabre, *Le Lexique de Ghazali,* 39).

79. The line before Kor. 8:73, which lends meaning to the quotation, is: "And those who disbelieve are protectors one of another—If ye do not so. . . ."

80. The term literally means "the members, or limbs, of a man, with which things are gained or earned, or with which one works" (Lane, *Arabic-English Lexicon,* 405).

81. Al-Ghazālī uses *murīd,* which is a Sufi term for a novice or disciple of a *murshid* or teacher of a Sufi order who is on the Path to attain the knowledge of the One (al-Qushayrī, *Risālah,* 731, 746–50; see also Palacios, *La Espiritualidad de Algazel,* 4:90).

82. The concept of the heart and its purification is a main tenet of the Sufis in attaining their goal (al-Qushayrī, *Risālah,* 566).

83. al-Suhrawardī, *ᶜAwārif al-Maᶜārif,* 84).

84. Possibly ᶜIrāqī Qatādah (d. 117/735), one of the companions of the Prophet and a transmitter of hadith (Goldziher, *Muslim Studies,* 2:23; see also a reference to him as a transmitter in Ibn Kathīr's *Tafsīr al-Qur'ān,* 491).

85. Watt refers to this verse (Kor. 2:286) as "charges . . . to its capacity"; that is, "requires of no one more than he is able to perform" (*Companion to the Qur'an,* 45).

86. See note 28, this chapter, for identity of ᶜAkramah.

87. This is possibly Abū al-Ḥajjāj Mujāhid b. Jabr, of Mecca, who lived from 21/642 to 104/722 and was a disciple of Ibn ᶜAbbās and an authority for reading and commentary on the Koran (Ibn al-Nadīm, *Fihrist,* 1061).

88. "Darkness: sometimes said to mean an eclipse of the moon," as interpreted by Watt (*Companion to the Qur'an,* 333).

89. Muslim relates the hadith from Ibn ᶜUmar, which is confirmed by the hadith of Abī Saᶜīd. However, Muslim was unable to affirm its utterance (ᶜIrāqī).

90. Al-Bayhaqī related it in the *Invocations* (*al-Duᶜawāt*) from the hadith of Umm Salamah in a transmission which contained weaknesses (ᶜIrāqī).

91. Hadith; as set forth in the *Invocations* (ᶜIrāqī).

92. Literally, the text states that he "became stationary between His hands" (Wehr, *Dictionary,* 1091–92).

93. Aḥmad related it from the hadith of Abī Kabshah al-ᶜAmmārī—its chain of authority is reliable (*jayyid*) (ᶜIrāqī).

94. This is also related by Ibn Ḥanbal, *Musnad,* 3:348, 395.

95. This is the hadith of Jābir. It was related by Muslim and al-Tirmidhī —it is of fair authority (ᶜIrāqī).

96. *Al-mughayyibāt* (absentee) was translated because of the context, rather than *al-maghabāt* (outcome, consequence), in the Azharīyah edition.

97. Al-Tirmidhī related it from the hadith of Jābir; it is authentic (*gharīb*) (ᶜIrāqī).

98. From the hadith of Ibn ᶜAbbās. It was stated by the Prophet and related by al-Bukhārī (ᶜIrāqī).

99. A son born of a concubine automatically becomes a slave as was the custom in the pre-Islamic period. On the other hand, a distinction was made also between the sons of a foreign woman and those of a freeborn tribeswoman (W. R. Smith, *Kinship and Marriage,* 89).

100. See 2 Peter 3:8: "But, beloved, be not ignorant of this one thing, that one day is with the Lord as a thousand years, and a thousand years as one day."

101. The Arabic term *ᶜālim* (literally, "a learned man"; a scholar knowledgeable in Islamic beliefs) is not used as frequently as the plural form *ᶜulamāʾ* (ulema).

102. Hadith. It was so stated to Ḥasan b. ᶜAlī. This utterance was said to Jaᶜfar b. Abī Ṭālib and agreed upon by the hadith of al-Barrāʾ. However, Ḥasan also resembled the Prophet . . . which is agreed upon in the hadith of Jaḥīfah; al-Tirmidhī corrected it. Ibn Ḥabbān relates it from the hadith of Anas who said, "No one resembles the Prophet more than Ḥasan" (ᶜIrāqī).

103. Aḥmad related it from the hadith of al-Miqdād b. Maᶜadyakrab in a chain of authority which is considered reliable (ᶜIrāqī).

104. Mughīrah Ibn Shuᶜbah, a companion and martyr, died ca. 48 or 51/668–671. He holds in tradition a record for marriages and divorces which varies: 300, 700, 1,000. Among the public offices he held was the governorship of Kūfa. His slave, Abū Lu'lu'ah, assassinated Caliph ᶜUmar (*Encyclopaedia of Islam,* new ed., s.v. "al-Mughīra b. Shuᶜba").

105. Ibn Ḥabbān related it from the hadith of Abī Dharr in a lengthy tradition from the scriptures of Abraham (ᶜIrāqī).

106. The Azharīyah rendition of *ṭāmiᶜan* (desirous) was used, and not *ẓāᶜinan* (journeying) which appears in the Ḥalabī edition.

107. This is in reference to the verse, "Take thou provisions from the present world, i.e., make thou provision in it, for the world to come" (Lane, *Arabic-English Lexicon,* 1267).

108. Same transmittal and narration as in note 105, this chapter.

109. In a Sufi context, *irādah* connotes a willful determination to undertake the rigors of the Path, that is, to have the "desire" to seek nothing but what God desires (Arberry, *Sufism,* 77).

110. A similar tradition with a different connotation and spelling (*faṭrah*) given by Lane states, "Verily there is an eagerness [*shirrah*] for this Kur-an: then men have a weariness [*faṭrah*] of it" (*Arabic-English Lexicon,* 1525; see also Jabre, who refers to it as a "natural disposition" that exists in the heart to know God [*Le Lexique de Ghazali,* 222–23]).

111. Aḥmad and al-Ṭabarānī related it from the hadith of ᶜAbdallah b. ᶜUmar; and al-Tirmidhī related something similar from the hadith of Abū Hurayrah. The tradition is genuine (*ṣaḥīḥ*) (ᶜIrāqī).

112. This is related by Ibn ᶜAdiyy, Ibn ᶜAbbās, al-ᶜAqīlī, Ibn Ḥabbān, and al-Azadī; all weak transmittals (ᶜIrāqī). *Harīsah* is a dish of cooked meat and bulgur (al-Jāḥiẓ, *Le Livre des avares de Ǧāḥiẓ,* 310).

113. Al-Nisā'ī and al-Ḥakīm related it from the hadith of Anas in a good transmittal. However, al-ᶜAqīlī weakened it (ᶜIrāqī).

114. Literally, *dhikr* means "mentioning Allah," enjoined upon Muslims in the Koran; or in a Sufi context, "the glorifying of Allah with certain fixed phrases, repeated in a ritual order, either aloud or in the mind, with peculiar breathings and physical movements" (*Encyclopaedia of Islam,* new ed., s.v. "dhikr"; see also al-Qushayrī, *Risālah,* 464–71).

115. Al-Tirmidhī related it and improved it; it was also related by Ibn Mājah; there is a break in the chain of authority (ᶜIrāqī).

116. The terms he uses here are *dhikr* (remembrances) and *shukr* (thanksgiving), both mystic terms (al-Qushayrī, *Risālah,* 383–89; see also note 114).

117. Possible reference to his wives as a unit. His devil is not as was defined earlier—i.e., when a woman approaches, she approaches in the form of a devil—but is used here in a metaphorical sense. In this instance, she abetted his fulfillment of Muslim obligations, hence equating the two devil-Muslims.

118. Al-Khaṭīb related it in the history [of Baghdad] from the hadith of Ibn ᶜUmar. This was also related by Muslim from the hadith of Ibn Masᶜūd (ᶜIrāqī).

119. There are three suras (Kor. 22:53, Kor. 75:2, and Kor. 89:27–30) that deal with the physical, moral, and spiritual levels of "self." Al-Ghazālī comments on the first two. See also Jabre, *Le Lexique de Ghazali,* 263–65.

120. *Ahl* connotes "wives" here since all the verbs in the sentence are in the feminine plural and, therefore, do not have the general meaning of "family, relative," etc.

121. Al-Ṭabarānī and al-Bayhaqī related it from the hadith of Ibn ᶜAbbās; it was preceded by the words "sixty years." It is agreed upon by the hadith of Ibn ᶜUmar (ᶜIrāqī).

122. Al-Ghazālī fails here to give the other two counts.

123. In Islamic law, *ṣadāqah* is a legally prescribed alms tax (Wehr, *Dictionary,* 509).

124. Agreed upon from the hadith of Ibn Mas^cūd and others in which *fī* [literally, "mouth"] is included (^cIrāqī). The Azharīyah edition gives *yarfa^cuha ila fī imra'atihi,* while the translated text excludes *fī.* Another interpretation could be to "offer it to the mouth" of his wife.

125. This refers to "The Substitutes, or Lieutenants, that is, certain righteous persons, of whom the world is never destitute; when one dies, God substituting another in his place." According to some, the assertion refers to seventy men, while according to others, to seven (Lane, *Arabic-English Lexicon,* 168).

126. Abū Ya^cla relates it from the hadith of Abī Sa^cīd al-Khuḍarī in a weak transmittal (^cIrāqī). The "two women" he refers to are not identified.

127. Ibn Mājah relates it from the hadith of ^cUmrān b. Ḥusayn. The transmittal is weak (^cIrāqī).

128. Aḥmad relates it from the hadith of ^cĀ'ishah. However, he stated *bil-huzn* [in sadness, grief] while Layth b. Abī Salīm does not agree (^cIrāqī). As was expressed in the beginning of the fifth advantage, through tolerance and exercise of just protection of the family and children, a man can gain "salvation," or atone for his sins.

129. Al-Ṭabarānī relates it in *al-Awsaṭ* and Abū Nu^caym [al-Isfahānī] in *Ḥulyat* [*al-Awliyā'*] and al-Khaṭīb in *al-Talkhīṣ* which resembles the hadith of Abū Hurayrah. The transmittal is weak (*ḍa^cīf*) (^cIrāqī).

130. Al-Kharā'iṭī relates it in *Makārim al-Akhlāq* in a weak transmission but differs from the relater, Ibn ^cAbbās. This hadith is also related by Abī Dā'ūd and al-Tirmidhī who have worthy transmitters, but there is still controversy over its transmittal (^cIrāqī).

131. See *gharīb* in the Glossary.

132. The text uses *jawāriḥ* to imply extraneous or physical acts. See note 80, this chapter.

133. That is, because he has sufficiently subdued his passions.

134. This contradicts his statement in the Conclusions (this chapter), wherein he states it as a condition and not as an absolute: ". . . to earn gain in an improper way is unlawful. Seeking gain takes place continually and in it lies his [ultimate] ruin and the ruin of his family."

135. The scales are those on which the deeds will be weighed on the day of judgment (see Kor. 4:59, Kor. 5:9 [^cAlī]).

136. ^cIrāqī stated that he could not find a basis for the origin of this hadith.

137. The author of the *Firdaws* mentioned it from the hadith of Abī Sa^cīd. However, the son of Abū Manṣūr could not find it in his *Musnad* (^cIraqī).

138. *Yafa* (redeem) instead of *baqa* (remain) was translated from the Azharīyah edition.

139. Abū Dā'ūd and al-Nisā'ī related it by stating "whom he abandons," rather than "for whom he provides." Muslim had still a third version (^cIrāqī).

140. The author of the statement apparently is referring to the emptying of the heart, a station on the path of union with God which is an arduous process. Hence the novice can barely take care of himself much less be occupied with and care for another being. See also note 143, this chapter.

141. See note 40, this chapter.

142. Watt translated it (Kor. 2:228) as: "Women have such honourable rights as obligations." Literally, he states that women " 'have rights similar to their duties according to what is honourable (or reputable) or customary.' This is sometimes said to mean that both parties should keep the way open for reconciliation" (*Companion to the Qur'ān,* 41).

143. That is, he is afraid even to raise a chicken lest he leave it on the road and become a butcher. Al-Suhrawardī restates this and the need for a Sufi to be preoccupied with his own needs (*ʿAwārif al-Maʿārif,* 78).

144. Meaning a master over his place of abode.

145. Al-Bukhārī related it from the hadith of Anas who also related "they are eleven" (ʿIrāqī). One tradition states that the Prophet had nine wives, among whom were "ʿĀ'isha, daughter of Abū Bakr; Ḥafṣa, daughter of ʿUmar; Umm Ḥabība, daughter of Abū Sufyān; Umm Salama, daughter of Abū Umayya b. al-Mughīra; Sauda, daughter of Zamʿa b. Qays; Zaynab, daughter of Ḥuyay b. Akhṭab" (see al-Bukhārī, *Ṣaḥīḥ,* 7:4, and ʿAbd al-Bāqī, *Lu'lu',* 1:74). Another tradition states that he married thirteen women, among whom is Khadīja (daughter of Khuwaylid) who was his first wife (Guillaume, *Life of Muhammad,* 792). Ibn al-Jawzī refers to fourteen wives (*Talbīs Iblīs,* 330).

146. Al-Bukhārī related it from the hadith of Anas which also contains the statement that the Prophet received revelations while he was in the bed of ʿĀ'ishah and not the others (ʿIrāqī).

147. Ibn ʿAbbās has a similar allegory: "L'eau, c'est la science; et les ruisseaux, les coeurs" (Massignon, *Les Origines du lexique technique,* 139–40).

Chapter 2. AS CONCERNS MARRIAGE: CONDITIONS OF THE WOMAN AND STIPULATIONS OF THE MARRIAGE CONTRACT

1. The text has "sultan," but the term actually implies ultimate authority holder.

2. This hadith is from Ibn ʿUmar who states: "Does not engage his brother's fiancee until the engaged man leaves her, or permission is taken for him" (ʿIrāqī). See also al-Shāfiʿī, *Risālah,* 307.

3. He is referred to as ʿUmar II, who ruled from A.D. 717 to 720. He was renowned for his piety and asceticism and was considered the only pious member of the Umayyad Caliphate (Hitti, *History of the Arabs,* 219–22).

4. The term *al-zubadu bil-nirsiyān* is used here to describe an ideal combination; it is misspelled in the Ḥalabī edition, where *tirsiyān* (shield, disk of the sun) is given.

5. Name of the tenth month of the Muslim year.

6. The Prophet contracted the marriage to ʿĀ'ishah when she was seven and lived with her in Medina when she was nine or ten. She was the only virgin that he married. Her father, Abū Bakr, married her to him (Guillaume, *Life of Muhammad,* 792).

7. Muslim related it from the hadith of ʿĀ'ishah (ʿIrāqī).

8. This list is al-Ghazālī's compilation of divergent views. However, for an elaboration of these views and practices observed by the four juridical rites—Hanafi, Hanbali, Shafiʿi, Maliki—as well as Sunni versus Shiʿi concepts, see Hughes, who expounds upon nine prohibitions (*Dictionary of Islam,* 314–18), and Fyzee (*Muhammadan Law,* 92–96, 106–8).

9. Muhammad decreed that Muslims cannot marry a Magian except under certain circumstances. Magians were a religious sect in Persia that was reformed by Zoroaster in the sixth century before Christ (Hughes, *Dictionary of Islam,* 310).

10. The term *kitābīyah* refers to a female of the *Ahl al-Kitāb* (or those who possess an inspired Book, i.e., Jews, Christians, or Sabeans) (Hughes, *Dictionary of Islam,* 280). According to the Shiᶜites, the term can also extend to Samaritans, Sabeans, and Zoroastrians (Fyzee, *Muhammadan Law,* 94).

11. The Azharīyah edition states, "does not fear fornication."

12. When two unrelated people are nursed by the same woman, they are considered to be blood brothers or sisters (Hughes, *Dictionary of Islam,* 314).

13. The Ḥalabī edition indicates "grandmother." However, the Azharīyah word was translated here meaning "granddaughter."

14. For a further explanation, see al-Shāfiᶜī, *Risālah,* 205–6.

15. *ᶜIddat baynūnah* is final divorce whereby the woman cannot remarry the husband, contrary to *ᶜiddat al-rajᶜah,* whereby she can (Lane, *Arabic-English Lexicon,* 285–86, 1040).

16. The concept of *ḥall* (literally, "untying" or "resolving") is that after a man divorces his wife, she has to become the wife of another man, the *muḥallil,* before he can remarry her; *muḥallil* literally means one who "unties or resolves" the problem, making her lawful to remarry her husband (Lane, *Arabic-English Lexicon,* 619–20).

17. *Liᶜān* is the oath of condemnation; it can also be, in Islamic law, a "sworn allegation of adultery committed by either husband or wife" (Wehr, *Dictionary,* 870).

18. Al-Ghazālī uses the term *thayyīban ṣaghīrah* for "deflowered young woman."

19. Literally, the term *farjihā* means "to safeguard her sexual organ." See chapter 1, note 21.

20. This hadith was related by Abū Dā'ūd and al-Nisā'ī, which was related from the hadith of Ibn ᶜAbbās. Al-Nisā'ī stated that this hadith was not agreed upon, while Aḥmad stated it was of weak authority (*munkar*). Also al-Jawzī mentioned it in *Al-Mawḍuᶜāt* (ᶜIrāqī).

21. Agreed upon; from the hadith of Abū Hurayrah (ᶜIrāqī). *Taribat yadāk* is a form of imprecation meaning, "May thine arm, or thy hands, cleave to the dust, or earth, by reason of poverty" (Lane, *Arabic-English Lexicon, 300).*

22. Al-Ṭabarānī related this hadith in *al-Awsaṭ* from the hadith of Anas. Another version of this hadith was related by Ibn Ḥabbān in *al-Duᶜafa'* (a collection of weak transmittals) (ᶜIrāqī).

23. Ibn Mājah related it from the hadith of ᶜAbdallah b. ᶜUmar in a weak transmittal (ᶜIrāqī).

24. See chapter 1, note 27.

25. Al-Tirmidhī related and refined this transmittal from the hadith of Jābir stating that God said, "I detest and shall keep away on the Day of Resurrection the prattler, the braggart, and the long-winded." This transmittal was also related and refined by al-Tirmidhī and Abū Dā'ūd from the hadith of ᶜAbdallah b. ᶜUmar (ᶜIrāqī).

26. *Sā'ih,* the term used here, denotes an itinerant dervish as well.

27. In Islamic law, a compensation (*khulʿah*) must be paid by the wife when a divorce is sought by her (Hughes, *Dictionary of Islam,* 274). This law is laid down in Kor. 2:229: "And if ye fear that they may not be able to keep the limits of Allah, in that case it is no sin for either of them if the woman ransom herself."

28. *Nashaz* is the noun derived from the same root as *nāshiz.* In Islamic law, *nushūz* means "violation of marital duties on the part of either husband or wife, specifically, recalcitrance of the woman toward her husband, and brutal treatment of the wife by the husband" (Wehr, *Dictionary,* 966).

29. Shariʿa is the Muslim law derived from the Koran, the hadith, and the processes of jurisprudence (Ibn al-Nadīm, *Fihrist,* 923).

30. Ibn Mājah related this hadith in a weak transmittal from the hadith of b. Maslamah. It was also related by al-Tirmidhī and al-Nisā'ī with slight variations.

31. The Anṣār, or Medinans, were followers of Muhammad and early converts who granted him refuge after the Hegira (Hughes, *Dictionary of Islam,* 16).

32. Muslim related it from the hadith of Abū Hurayrah (ʿIrāqī).

33. Abū Bakr Sulaymān al-Aʿmash, a traditionist, died in Rufa in 148/765. He received traditions from al-Zuhrī and Mālik b. Anas. He was also a great admirer of ʿAlī (*Encyclopaedia of Islam,* new ed., s.v. "al-Aʿmash").

34. The words "to Bilāl" were left out of this text, but they do occur in previous editions. Bilāl, an Abyssinian Negro who was freed by the Prophet, became the first muezzin in Islam. Muhammad honored and distinguished him as the "first fruits of Abyssinia" (Hughes, *Dictionary of Islam,* 42).

35. Mālik b. Dinār al-Sāmi, who died at the age of ninety in 131/748 at Basra, is mentioned as a reliable traditionist, transmitting from such authorities as Mālik b. Anas and Ibn Sirīn. He was the son of a Persian slave from Sujistān (or Kabul) who became a disciple of Ḥasan of Basra (a mystic) (Ḥujwīrī, *Kashf al-Mahjūb,* 89; Ibn al-Nadīm, *Fihrist,* 1037).

36. A houri is a white-skinned, black-eyed woman who is referred to as a virgin of paradise, or a nymph of the Islamic paradise. *Al-ḥawar* and the Arabic word for houri (sing. *ḥūr*; pl. *ḥūrīyah*) are derived from the same root. See Kor. 55:56–78 for a complete description of the women of paradise.

37. Al-Nisā'ī related this hadith from the hadith of Abū Hurayrah in a genuine transmittal. Aḥmad and Abū Dā'ūd related this hadith from Ibn ʿAbbās in a genuine transmittal (ʿIrāqī).

38. Related by Ibn Ḥabbān from the hadith of Ibn ʿAbbās. This was also related by ʿĀ'ishah and by Abū ʿUmar al-Tawqānī in the book *Maʿāshirat al-Ahlayn* who enhanced it (ʿIrāqī).

39. It was related by the transmitters of the sunna and extending to ʿUmar; al-Tirmidhī enhanced it (ʿIrāqī).

40. "Dirham" may be used for money or for a silver coin (Ibn al-Nadīm, *Fihrist,* 910).

41. Related by Abū Dā'ūd al-Ṭayālsī and al-Bazzār from the hadith of Anas; by al-Ṭabarānī in *al-Awsaṭ* from the hadith of Abī Saʿīd; and by Aḥmad from the hadith of ʿAlī; and by al-Ḥakīm who made its transmittal reliable (ʿIrāqī).

42. *ʿIliyy* comes from the term *ʿilliyān* and is translated here to mean a "stone, sometimes placed upon two other stones, upon which is put to dry

the preparation of curd; also used for other purposes" (Lane, *Arabic-English Lexicon,* 2146). It is difficult to ascertain any other referent here. The word was deleted from the Azharīyah edition.

43. *Mudd,* a dry measure. "It is a quarter of a *ṣāᶜ*; the *ṣāᶜ* being five pints and one third; such was the *mudd* of the Prophet" (Lane, *Arabic-English Lexicon,* 2697).

44. Al-Bukhārī related this hadith from the hadith of ᶜĀ'ishah (ᶜIrāqī).

45. Related by al-Arbaᶜah from the hadith of Anas and also by Muslim (ᶜIrāqī). *Sawīq* is a kind of mush made of wheat or barley. It can also be made with sugar and dates (Lane, *Arabic-English Lexicon,* 1472).

46. Related by al-Arbaᶜah from the hadith of ᶜUmar. Al-Tirmidhī stated that it was genuine and of fair authority (*ḥasan ṣaḥīḥ*) (ᶜIrāqī).

47. This is from the hadith of Anas stating that ᶜAbd al-Raḥmān b. ᶜAwf got married for five dirhams. It was related by al-Bayhaqī (ᶜIrāqī).

48. Compare what al-Ghazālī states here with his statement on page 158 in *Counsel for Kings.*

49. Aḥmad and al-Bayhaqī related it from the hadith of ᶜĀ'ishah. Its chain of authority is reliable (ᶜIrāqī).

50. This is related by Abū ᶜUmar al-Tawqānī from the hadith of ᶜĀ'ishah and by Aḥmad and al-Bayhaqī. Its transmission is reliable (ᶜIrāqī).

51. Sufyān al-Thawrī, or Abū ᶜAbd Allāh Sufyān Ibn Saᶜīd al-Thawrī, was claimed by the Sufis as a saint. He was an ascetic who founded a school of jurisprudence which survived for about two centuries. However, he opposed the authorities and was compelled to go into hiding in Mecca. He was born in Kufa in 97/715 and died at Basra in 161/778 (Farīd al-Dīn Aṭṭar, *Muslim Saints and Mystics,* 129).

52. This is related by al-Bukhārī in the book *al-Adab al-Mufrad* and by al-Bayhaqī from the hadith of Abū Hurayrah in a reliable chain of authority (ᶜIrāqī).

53. Abū Dā'ūd and al-Nisā'ī related it from the hadith of Muᶜqal b. Yasār. Its chain of authority is genuine (ᶜIrāqī).

54. This transmittal is agreed upon from the hadith of Jābir (ᶜIrāqī).

55. The Azharīyah edition uses the comparative form *aakad* (surest) while the Ḥalabī edition uses *akad* (to assure, convince).

56. This was related in a tradition as follows: "Avoid ye the beautiful woman that is of 'bad origin'; she is thus likened to the herbage that grows in the *diman* (dung), that appears to be in a flourishing condition, but is unwholesome as food, and of stinking origin" (Lane, *Arabic-English Lexicon,* 916).

57. Al-Dāraquṭni related this hadith in *al-Afrād* and stated that al-Waqīdī repeated it but made it weak (ᶜIrāqī).

58. *Al-ᶜirqu nazzāᶜun* means "the radical, or ancestral, or hereditary, quality is wont to return to its usual possessor; or it may mean, is wont to draw" (Lane, *Arabic-English Lexicon,* 916).

59. Ibn al-Ṣalāḥ stated that he could find no basis for this hadith (ᶜIrāqī).

60. Related by Abū ᶜUmar al-Tawqānī in *Maᶜāsharat al-Ahlayn.* This is supported by the hadith of ᶜĀ'ishah and Asmā', daughters of Abū Bakr. The transmittal is genuine (ᶜIrāqī).

61. Grandson of the Prophet, ᶜAlī's son.

Chapter 3. ETIQUETTE OF COHABITATION, WHAT SHOULD TAKE PLACE DURING THE MARRIAGE, AND THE OBLIGATIONS OF HUSBAND AND WIFE

1. This is from the hadith of Anas—agreed upon (ʿIrāqī).

2. Muhammad consummated his marriage with Ṣafiyyah b. Ḥuyayy, who was a captive and was married without a dowry, on his return from Khaibar (Stern, *Marriage in Early Islam,* 86).

3. This was related from the hadith of Anas by the four transmitters of hadith (ʿIrāqī). See chapter 2, note 45, for description of *sawīq.*

4. This hadith is attributed to al-Tirmidhī who related it from the hadith of Ibn Masʿūd, and who made the transmission weak.

5. *Gharīb* means "authentic, but resting on the authority of only one companion" (Guillaume, *Traditions of Islam,* 181).

6. Hadith of Abū Hurayrah as related by Abū Dā'ūd and al-Tirmidhī; Ibn Mājah perfected and introduced it in the *Invocations* (ʿIrāqī).

7. It was related and enhanced by al-Tirmidhī, and by Ibn Mājah from the hadith of Muḥammad b. Ḥaṭīb (ʿIrāqī). The term *sawt* (voice) is used to imply singing.

8. This was related by al-Tirmidhī from the hadith of ʿĀ'ishah; however, al-Bayhaqī enhanced it and made it weak (ʿIrāqī).

9. Hadith of al-Rubayyiʿ, daughter of Muʿawwidh, as was related by al-Bukhārī with a slight change (ʿIrāqī).

10. ʿAlī interprets it to mean "anything that has no civil rights. It includes captives or slaves, people in your power" (*Holy Qur'ān,* 191, n.553).

11. Book 15 of al-Ghazālī's *Iḥyā'* deals with prayer.

12. Al-Nisā'ī brought it forth in *al-Kubrā,* and Ibn Mājah from the hadith of Umm Salamah. The Prophet never ceased to stress "prayers and what your right hand (possesses)." In reference to the care of women, he stressed this in the last pilgrimage which was related by Muslim from the hadith of Jābir al-Ṭawīl (ʿIrāqī).

13. This refers to "a recompense, or reward, from God to a man, for righteous conduct" (Lane, *Arabic-English Lexicon,* 24).

14. ʿIrāqī could not find any basis for this hadith. However, see Kor. 28:9 in support of this statement.

15. This is related from the hadith of ʿUmar as stated in the hadith of al-Ṭawīl—agreed upon (ʿIrāqī).

16. The earlier hadith did not contain "O foolish woman," and "he is better than you" (ʿIrāqī).

17. Ḥafṣah was the daughter of Caliph ʿUmar and the second wife of the Prophet (Guillaume, *Life of Muhammad,* 792).

18. See Kor. 66:1–3. Abū Bakr was ʿĀ'ishah's father.

19. No basis can be found for this transmittal (ʿIrāqī).

20. Al-Tirānī transmitted it in *al-Awsaṭ* as did al-Khaṭīb in *al-Tarīkh.* Both transmittals are weak and come from the hadith of ʿĀ'ishah (ʿIrāqī).

21. Abū Yaʿla brought it forth in his *Musnad* and Abū al-Shaykh in *Kitāb al-Amthāl* from the hadith of ʿĀ'ishah, which was also transmitted by Ibn Isḥāq (ʿIrāqī).

22. Related from the hadith of ᶜĀ'ishah—agreed upon (ᶜIrāqī).

23. This was first related by the two *shaykh*s from the hadith of ᶜUmar and Ibn al-ᶜĀṣ; then Ibn al-Jawzī shaped it and related it in *al-Mawḍuᶜāt* from the hadith of Anas; . . . however, his love for Khadīja is well known and documented in the hadith (ᶜIrāqī).

24. From the hadith of ᶜĀ'ishah—agreed upon without exception. It was related with the addition by al-Zubayr b. Bakkār and al-Khaṭīb (ᶜIrāqī).

25. Al-Bukhārī related it from the hadith of ᶜĀ'ishah (ᶜIrāqī).

26. Hadith Anas. However, Muslim related, "I have never seen anyone kinder than the Prophet with women," but ᶜAlī b. ᶜAbd al-ᶜAzīz and al-Baghawī added "and children" (ᶜIrāqī).

27. Abū Dā'ūd and al-Nisā'ī related it in *al–Kubrā,* and Ibn Mājah from the hadith of ᶜĀ'ishah—the transmittal is genuine (ᶜIrāqī).

28. Al-Ḥasan b. Sufyān related it in his *Musnad* from the hadith of Anas without his saying "with his wives"; it was also related by al-Bazzār and al-Ṭabarānī in *al-Ṣaghīr* and *al-Awsaṭ* by stating "with his children," which was supported by Ibn Lahīᶜah (ᶜIrāqī).

29. *ᶜĀshūrā'* is the name of the voluntary fast day. It is held the tenth day of Muharram on the anniversary of Ḥusayn's martyrdom at Kerbela (60 A.H.). It is a day of mourning sacred to the Shiᶜites (Wehr, *Dictionary,* 614).

30. The hadith is agreed upon with few exceptions; "a holy day" rather than the day of *ᶜAshūrā'* was mentioned; while al-Nisā'ī stated in his *Kubrā* that ᶜĀ'ishah said, "Don't rush," rather than, "Be quiet"; and that the Prophet said, "O she-ass!" The chain of authority is genuine (ᶜIrāqī).

31. It is a trustworthy transmittal (*thiqah*) which is related by the two *shaykh*s: al-Tirmidhī and al-Nisā'ī (ᶜIrāqī).

32. Al-Tirmidhī brought it forth and authenticated it from the hadith of Abū Hurayrah without saying, "and I am the best among you toward my wives"; and from the hadith of ᶜĀ'ishah, "people" was replaced by "wives" (ᶜIrāqī). Note, however, that "wife" is one of many meanings of the word *ahl* (Wehr, *Dictionary,* 33).

33. *Ahl* is translated here to mean "family."

34. "Found a man," that is, act like a man or be firm.

35. Abū Bakr b. Lāl related it in *Makārim al-Akhlāq* from the hadith of Abū Hurayrah in a weak transmittal. It is also stated in the two *Ṣaḥīḥ*s from the hadith of Jāriyah b. Wahab al-Khazāᶜī and Abū Dā'ūd (ᶜIrāqī).

36. Agreed upon from the hadith of Ẓāhir (ᶜIrāqī).

37. *Murū'ah* also means "abstinence from things unlawful, or in chastity of manners, and the having some art or trade" (Lane, *Arabic-English Lexicon,* 2702).

38. No basis was found for this statement. However, al-Bukhārī related it from the hadith of Abū Hurayrah as, "Miserable is he who is a servant of the dinar and the dirham" (ᶜIrāqī).

39. Compare Kor. 14:34.

40. A *fitr* is the "space between the end of the thumb and the end of the index finger when extended" (Wehr, *Dictionary,* 694).

41. A cubit in Iraq and Syria is 0.68m, in Egypt it is 0.58m (Wehr, *Dictionary,* 309).

42. The Nabataeans were a tribal group who lived in Arabia as early as the seventh century B.C. During the Muslim period, the Arabs called those

inhabitants of Syria and Iraq who were neither shepherds nor soldiers, "Nabataeans"—a term used in "a contemptuous tone to the Aramaic-speaking peasants" (*Encyclopaedia of Islam,* new ed., s.v. "Nabataeans").

43. For further details, see Kor. 12:28–31.

44. Al-Ṭabarānī related it from the hadith of Abī Imāmah in a weak transmittal; and Aḥmad from the hadith of ᶜUmar and b. al-ᶜĀṣ. However, al-Nisā'ī related in his *Kubrā* that the Prophet stated: "If among all the crows, there is a white-footed crow with a red beak, then no woman shall enter Paradise except one like this crow." This transmittal is genuine (ᶜIrāqī).

45. Abū Manṣūr al-Daylamī related it in the *Musnad al-Firdaws* from the hadith of Abū Hurayrah in a weak transmittal. However, . . . a slight transmittal . . . states the "three poverties, one of which is: 'If you come to her, she will hurt you, and if you are away from her, she will be unfaithful to you.' " This was related by al-Ṭabarānī from the hadith of Faḍālah b. ᶜUbayd as of fair authority (ᶜIrāqī).

46. From the hadith of ᶜĀ'ishah—agreed upon (ᶜIrāqī). It is interesting to note here that all the good transmittals concerning women were transmitted by women, especially by ᶜĀ'ishah.

47. See Kor. 66:3.

48. The translation given by Watt is, "If you two [Ḥafṣah and ᶜĀ'ishah] repent to God"; that is, "If you repent, good and well" (*Companion to the Qur'ān,* 271).

49. This is agreed upon from the hadith of ᶜUmar, and the two women are ᶜĀ'ishah and Ḥafṣah (ᶜIrāqī).

50. Al-Bakhārī related it from the hadith of Abī Bakrah (ᶜIrāqī).

51. This is related by al-Ṭabarānī in *al-Awsaṭ* from the hadith of Jābir. Muslim states that the Prophet "forbade the man to enter upon his wife at night for he betrays them or seeks their faults." However, al-Bukhārī does not mention the prohibition of entering at night (ᶜIrāqī).

52. Aḥmad related it from the hadith of Ibn ᶜUmar. The transmittal is reliable (ᶜIrāqī).

53. Agreed upon from the hadith of Abū Hurayrah (ᶜIrāqī). See al-Bukhārī, *Ṣaḥīḥ,* 7:33–34. Ibn Ḥanbal quotes Abū Hurayrah differently: "Women were created from a rib which was not straightened at creation; if you straighten it . . ." (*Musnad,* 2:497).

54. Abū Dā'ūd, al-Nisā'ī, and Ibn Ḥabbān related it from the hadith of Jābir b. ᶜAtīk (ᶜIrāqī).

55. From the hadith of Abū Hurayrah; al-Bukhārī deleted "and the believer is jealous." This is agreed upon (ᶜIrāqī).

56. Possibly refers to Saᶜd, who was in love with Asmā'. He was the subject of poetry and perhaps was himself a poet. There is a book entitled *Saᶜd and Asmā'* whose traditions are transmitted among the "Names of the Passionate Lovers during the Pre-Islamic Period, and the Period of Islam" (Ibn al-Nadīm, *Fihrist,* 710, 1086).

57. From the hadith of al-Mughīrah b. Shaᶜbah—agreed upon (ᶜIrāqī).

58. From the hadith of Jābir who deleted "The night I was taken through Paradise" and "maid"—agreed upon; he mentioned "maid" in another transmittal from the hadith of Abū Hurayrah—also agreed upon (ᶜIrāqī).

59. Abū Dā'ūd, al-Nisā'ī, and Ibn Ḥabbān related it from the hadith of Jābir b. ᶜAtīk, but it was also related in four other hadiths (ᶜIrāqī).

60. The first part of the statement was related first, while the second part was related by Abū ᶜUmar al-Tawqānī in the book, *Muᶜāsharat al-Ahlayn,* from the narrative of ᶜAbdullah b. Muḥammad; and it appears that ᶜAbdullah b. al-Ḥanafiyah is the transmitter (ᶜIrāqī).

61. Al-Bazzār and al-Dāraquṭnī related it in *al-Afrād* from the hadith of ᶜAlī. The transmittal is weak (ᶜIrāqī).

62. This is agreed upon from the hadith of Ibn ᶜUmar, who stated, "The women were permitted to go to the mosques at night" (ᶜIrāqī).

63. From the hadith of ᶜĀ'ishah—agreed upon. However, al-Bukhārī related instead, "he would have prevented them from the mosques" (ᶜIrāqī).

64. Hadith of Ibn ᶜUmar which is agreed upon (ᶜIrāqī).

65. From the hadith of Umm ᶜAṭayyah—agreed upon (ᶜIrāqī).

66. Literally, that it is "safe" to "sit" or remain at home.

67. Watt translates "keep not thy hand chained" as meaning "do not be niggardly" (*Companion to the Qur'ān,* 135).

68. From the hadith of ᶜĀ'ishah—brought forth and made genuine (*saḥḥaḥ*) by al-Tirmidhī (ᶜIrāqī).

69. Muslim related it from the hadith of Abū Hurayrah (ᶜIrāqī). Al-Tirmidhī states it differently in a genuine hadith: "The dinar which earns you the greatest reward is the one spent on your wife, your riding animal (*dābbah*) and your companions in the way of God" (*Sunan,* 6:193).

70. Precepts as spelled out in codes based on the Shariᶜa.

71. Book 2 of the *Iḥyā'* deals further with menstruation and prayer.

72. Reference is to the time element, because more than one *rakᶜah* is usually involved; hence she could not fully perform these *rakᶜah*s within the prescribed period. For further details see Book 2 of the *Iḥyā'.*

73. Presumably this is a reference to a Sufi ritual. See chapter 1, note 114.

74. From the hadith of ᶜĀ'ishah—agreed upon (ᶜIrāqī). A preferable translation, found in Lane, is that "he ordered, or commanded, them to cast, or draw lots, or to practice sortilege [among themselves]" (*Arabic-English Lexicon,* 2987).

75. This was related by the authors of the *Sunan* and Ibn Ḥabbān, from the hadith of Abū Hurayrah [with slight variations] by Abū Dā'ūd, Ibn Ḥabbān, and al-Tirmidhī stating, "He does not deal equitably between them" (ᶜIrāqī).

76. Ḥabbān and the authors of the *Sunan* related it from the hadith of ᶜĀ'ishah (ᶜIrāqī).

77. From the hadith of ᶜUmar and b. al-ᶜĀṣ—agreed upon—who related that when the Prophet was asked, "Whom do you love the most among your women?" he replied, "ᶜĀ'ishah" (ᶜIrāqī).

78. This hadith was related by Ibn Saᶜd in *al-Tabaqāt,* and by al-Bukhārī from the hadith of ᶜĀ'ishah, and in the *Ṣaḥīḥayn* [of Bukhārī and Muslim] (ᶜIrāqī). ᶜAbd al-Bāqī stated that the Prophet remained with ᶜĀ'ishah until his death (*Lu'lu',* 3:185).

79. Abū Dā'ūd related it from the hadith of ᶜĀ'ishah; also related by al-Ṭabarānī, al-Bukhārī, and al-Bayhaqī with slight variations (ᶜIrāqī).

80. This was related from the hadith of ᶜĀ'ishah (ᶜIrāqī).

81. This is from the hadith of Anas. Ibn ᶜĀdī related it in *al-Kāmil.* This was related by al-Bukhārī who also stated that the Prophet had nine wives (ᶜIrāqī). See chapter 1, note 145.

82. See chapter 2, note 28.

83. Abū Dā'ūd and al-Nisā'ī related it in *al-Kubrā* and Ibn Mājah from a narration of Muᶜāwiyah Ibn Ḥaydah—the transmittal is good and reliable (ᶜIrāqī).

84. Ibn al-Jawzī related it in *al-Wafā'* without any support. This was also mentioned in the *Ṣaḥīḥayn* [of Bukhārī and Muslim] from the hadith of ᶜUmar as well as in a story from the hadith of Jābir (ᶜIrāqī).

85. Reference is made to the utterance of the formula, *lā ilāha illa Allah* (There is no God but Allah).

86. From the hadith of Ibn ᶜAbbās—agreed upon (ᶜIrāqī).

87. This latter phrase, "and made thereof relatives and in-laws, for thy Lord is omnipotent," did not occur in the Azharīyah edition (ᶜIrāqī). The Koran's version (25:54) is: "And He it is Who hath created man from water, and hath appointed for him kindred by blood and kindred by marriage; for thy Lord is ever Powerful."

88. *Qiblah* is the direction to which Muslims turn in praying (toward the Kaaba) or a prayer niche which is a recess in a mosque indicating the direction of the Kaaba (Wehr, *Dictionary,* 740).

89. Al-Khaṭīb related it from the hadith of Umm Salamah in a weak transmittal (ᶜIrāqī).

90. Ibn Mājah first related it from the hadith of ᶜAtabah b. ᶜAbd in a weak transmittal (ᶜIrāqī).

91. Abū Manṣūr al-Daylamī related it in the *Musnad al-Firdaws* from the hadith of Anas—it is of weak authority (ᶜIrāqī).

92. Abū Manṣūr al-Daylamī related it from a much shortened hadith, and this is some of the hadith with which he agrees (ᶜIrāqī).

93. This hadith was forwarded in the fifth chapter of the book of prayer (ᶜIrāqī).

94. Arabic has one term, *inzāl,* which is here translated as "orgasm," "climax," "ejaculation," or "emission," since it would be difficult to use one English term for the referent.

95. See the complete reference in Kor. 2:222.

96. Everything that can happen to man, everything that he can do, falls into five categories in Islam: *farḍ, sunna, mubāḥ, makrūh,* and *ḥarām.* "*Farḍ* is that which is commanded, that which is unavoidable in order to find favour in the eyes of God, as giving of alms. *Sunna* is doing good, meritorious acts in the sight of God. But it is not a sin to omit such acts. . . . *Mubāḥ* are the deeds which are indifferent to both God and man. Their number is not large and they bring neither reward nor punishment. *Makrūh* is the evil, but not the forbidden. One can commit it without fear of God's punishment. But the pious will omit it. *Ḥarām* . . . is sin, express violations of God's commands. Whoever commits *ḥarām* may be sure of God's punishment" (Essad, *Mohammed,* 355–56).

97. See al-Tirmidhī, *Sunan,* 1:159–62.

98. *Junub,* translated here as major ritual impurity, signifies a man "under the obligation of performing a total ablution, by reason of sexual intercourse and discharge of the semen" (Lane, *Arabic-English Lexicon,* 466).

99. From the hadith of Ibn ᶜUmar as the one who posed the question —agreed upon (ᶜIrāqī).

100. From the hadith of ᶜĀ'ishah, as related by Abū Dā'ūd, al-Tirmidhī, and Ibn Mājah (ᶜIrāqī).

101. From the hadith of Abī Saᶜīd—agreed upon (ᶜIrāqī). See also al-Tirmidhī, *Sunan,* 4:103.

102. ᶜIrāqī found no basis for the following hadith. However, al-Ghazālī's deductions are correct as he summarized existing views on coitus interruptus. See al-Tirmidhī, *Sunan,* 4:102–5.

103. No basis was found for this hadith (ᶜIrāqī).

104. In the Azharīyah edition, literally *muḥyihi,* or "keeping him alive," was translated rather than *muḥibbīhi* (his attachment, affection) of the Ḥalabī edition.

105. Reference is made here to an evidence or a proof made manifest by a text of the Koran or of the sunna used as an authority in an argument for proof of an assertion.

106. *Wa'd* refers to a daughter buried alive. "It was customary for a man in the time of paganism, when a daughter was born to him, to bury her alive when her mother brought her forth, from fear of reproach and want: but this is forbidden in the Koran, XVII, XXXIII; and some of them used to bury their children alive in times of famine; the tribe of Kindeh used to bury their daughters alive" (Lane, *Arabic-English Lexicon,* 2913; see also W. R. Smith, *Kinship and Marriage,* 153–55, 291–96).

107. The views of al-Ghazālī on the matter of coitus interruptus appear to be ambivalent, tending toward a contradiction of the view expounded in chapter 1 on the advantages of marriage.

108. The Khawārij (sing. Khārijite), or seceders, constitute the earliest religiopolitical sect in Islam. Once supporters of ᶜAlī, they became his deadly opponents (Hitti, *History of the Arabs,* 246–47).

109. This hadith was previously introduced at the beginning of the chapter on marriage (*al-nikāḥ*) (ᶜIrāqī). See chapter 1, note 11.

110. Muslim related it from the hadith of Jadhdhāmah, daughter of Wahab (ᶜIrāqī).

111. There are numerous transmittals regarding the disclosed averting of conception by coitus interruptus: Muslim from the hadith of Abī Saᶜīd, al-Nisā'ī from the hadith of Abī Sarma, the two *shaykh*s from the hadith of Jābir, and al-Nisā'ī from the hadith of Abū Hurayrah (ᶜIrāqī).

112. Although this "resembles that of burying a child alive, and is done with the same motive," the words also refer to coitus interruptus (Lane, *Arabic-English Lexicon,* 2913).

113. Watt elucidates this point by saying, "a new creature" (*Companion to the Qur'ān,* 158).

114. See al-Bukhārī, *Ṣaḥīḥ,* 7:42–43.

115. From the hadith of Jābir—which is agreed upon—in the *Ṣaḥīḥayn* [of Bukhārī and Muslim]. However, the clause "but he did not enjoin us against it" is unique to Muslim (ᶜIrāqī).

116. Hadith of Jābir. Al-Muṣnaf mentioned that it was in the *Ṣaḥīḥayn* [of Bukhārī and Muslim], which is not true; only Muslim related it (ᶜIrāqī).

117. Al-Ṭabarānī first related it in *al-Kabīr* and al-Kharā'iṭī in *Makārim al-Akhlāq* from the hadith of Ibn Masᶜūd. The transmittal is weak (ᶜIrāqī).

118. Hadith of Ibn ᶜAbbās. It was related by Ibn Mājah and al-Ḥākim. The transmittal is genuine (ᶜIrāqī).

119. Hadith of Anas; al-Kharā'iṭī related it in *Makārim Akhlāq* in a weak transmittal (ᶜIrāqī).

120. Hadith of Anas, which was related by al-Kharā'iṭī in a weak transmittal (ᶜIrāqī).

121. Ibid.

122. Hadith Abū Hurayrah as related by al-Kharā'iṭī and al-Ḥākim, but it did not say "or sisters." The transmittal is genuine (ᶜIrāqī).

123. *Adhdhana* (noun *ādhān*) is "to call to prayer." It is customary in Islam that a newborn baby should first hear the call to prayer, which always begins with *allāhu akbar* (God is the Greatest).

124. Hadith Abī Rāfiᶜ. Aḥmad, Abū Dā'ūd, and al-Tirmidhī related it and made it genuine. However, the transmittal of Ibn al-Qaṭṭān is weak (ᶜIrāqī).

125. Related by Abū Yaᶜlā al-Mawsilī, Ibn al-Sinna in *al-Yawn wa-Layla* and al-Bayhaqī in *al-Shaᶜb al-Imān* from the hadith of al-Ḥusayn b. ᶜAlī in a weak transmittal (ᶜIrāqī).

126. Al-Ṭabarānī related it in *al-Ṣaghīr* from the hadith of Jābir in a weak transmittal (ᶜIrāqī). Circumcision among the Jews, a practice dating from the time of Abraham, generally takes place on the eighth day (Genesis 14:10–12). In Islam, circumcision is founded upon the customs of the Prophet, as it is not once alluded to in the Koran. Circumcision is "recommended to be performed upon a boy between the ages of seven and twelve, but it is lawful to circumcise a child seven days after his birth" (Hughes, *Dictionary of Islam,* 57). Lane stated that circumcision on the seventh day is not approved, and that it is generally performed at the age of five or six (*Arabian Society,* 192).

127. Al-Ṭabarānī related this transmittal from the hadith of ᶜAbd al-Mālik b. Abī Zuhayr, who in turn related it from his father, Muᶜādh. Its transmittal is genuine; al-Bayhaqī related it from the hadith of ᶜĀ'ishah (ᶜIrāqī). The word *ᶜabd* refers to one of God's qualities; the literal meaning is "servant of."

128. From the hadith of Jābir which is agreed upon when beginning with the verb *tusammū* [is named] rather than *sammū* [name, command] (ᶜIrāqī).

129. Aḥmad and Ibn Ḥabbān related it from the hadith of Abū Hurayrah; also related by Abū Dā'ūd and al-Tirmidhī; and by Ibn Ḥabbān from the hadith of Jābir: "Whoever gives my first name, should not give my surname; and whoever gives my surname, should not give my first name." The transmittal is genuine (ᶜIrāqī).

130. Abū ᶜUmar al-Tawqānī related it in *Muᶜāsharat al-Ahlayn* from the hadith of Ibn ᶜUmar in a weak transmittal; and Abū Dā'ūd related that ᶜUmar pointed out a child named Abū ᶜĪsā; and Mughīrah b. Shaᶜbah disapproved of using the name Abū ᶜĪsā and stated that the Messenger of God said, "Name after me"—its transmittal is genuine (ᶜIrāqī).

131. Abū Dā'ūd related it from the hadith of Abī al-Dardā'. Al-Nawawī said that its transmittal is reliable, and al-Bayhaqī said that its transmittal was incomplete (*mursal*) (ᶜIrāqī).

132. Al-Bayhaqī related it from the hadith of ᶜAbdullah b. al-Ḥārith b. Jiz' al-Zubaydī. The transmittal is genuine (ᶜIrāqī). (See also ᶜAbd al-Bāqī, *Lu'lu', 2:60.)*

133. From the hadith of Abū Hurayrah, which is agreed upon (ᶜIrāqī).

134. Muslim related it from the hadith of Samrah b. Jandab. This was also related from the hadith of Jābir (ᶜIrāqī).

135. Ibn Ḥanbal regards this sacrifice on the seventh day as absolutely obligatory: "If a father sacrifice not for his son, and he [the son] die, that son will not intercede for him on the day of judgment" (Lane, *Arabian Society,* 191). However, the founders of the other three principal rites regard it in different and less important lights. It is obvious here that al-Ghazālī is resorting to the practices at the time of the Prophet. These practices not only include the animal sacrifice on the seventh day, but circumcision and shaving the hair of the child and giving its weight in silver or gold to the poor as well. According to Lane, these religious ceremonies can be performed not only on the seventh day, but on multiples of seven—fourteenth, twenty-first, twenty-eighth, or thirty-fifth—after the birth of the child as well (Ibid. See also al-Bukhārī, *Ṣaḥīḥ,* 7:108–10; and al-Tirmidhī, *Sunan,* 5:237–40).

136. This appears in the Azharīyah edition and completes the thought.

137. Hadith of ᶜĀ'ishah, which was brought forth and made genuine (ᶜIrāqī).

138. Al-Tirmidhī related it from the hadith of ᶜAlī, stating that its transmittal is not uninterrupted, while al-Ḥakīm made it uninterrupted (*muttaṣil*). Abū Dā'ūd related it from the hadith of Ibn ᶜAbbās, except that he said "a ram" [rather than a sheep] (ᶜIrāqī).

139. Al-Bukhārī related it from the hadith of Salmān b. ᶜĀmir al-Ḍabbī (ᶜIrāqī). (See al-Bukhārī, *Ṣaḥīḥ,* 7:109.)

140. Al-Ḥakīm [al-Tirmidhī] related and clarified it from the hadith of ᶜAlī; al-Tirmidhī's transmittal is cut off, up to the word *Ḥasan,* while its transmittal is not uninterrupted (ᶜIrāqī). Al-Tirmidhī stated that Ḥasan's hair weighed a dirham or so (*Sunan,* 5:234).

141. Hadith Asmā', which is agreed upon (ᶜIrāqī). (See also ᶜAbd al-Bāqī, *Lu'lu',* 2:62.)

142. ᶜAbd al-Bāqī notes that the hadith ends here, excluding the rest of the phrase. He also explains "Islam" as meaning "Medina" (*Lu'lu',* 2:82). (See also al-Bukhārī, *Ṣaḥīḥ,* 7:108.)

143. Hadith Ibn ᶜUmar. It was related by the companions of the *Sunan.* Al-Tirmidhī stated that it was genuine and of fair authority (ᶜIrāqī).

144. This occurs in exceptional cases as explained by ᶜAlī: "If there is any fear that in safeguarding her economic rights, her very freedom of person may suffer, the husband refusing the dissolution of marriage, and perhaps treating her with cruelty, then . . . it is permissible to give some material consideration to the husband, but the need and equity of this should be submitted to the judgment of impartial judges, i.e., properly constituted courts. A divorce of this kind is called *khulᶜ*" (*Holy Qur'ān* 91, n.258; cf. W. R. Smith, *Kinship and Marriage,* 122).

145. This tradition with the additional words, "and Paradise will be forbidden unto her," was related by Abū Dā'ūd and al-Tirmidhī, who made it better; and by Ibn Mājah and Ibn Ḥabbān from the hadith of Thawban (ᶜIrāqī).

146. Al-Nisā'ī related it from the hadith of Abū Hurayrah, and al-Ṭabarānī related it from the hadith of ᶜAqba b. ᶜĀmir in a weak transmittal (ᶜIrāqī).

147. There are two concepts here: having had coitus with her automatically nullifies the *ᶜiddah*; and the lengthening of the *ᶜiddah* stems from the necessity to make sure that she has not conceived (see "Divorce" in the Introduction).

148. From the hadith of Ibn ᶜUmar, which is agreed upon (ᶜIrāqī). (See also ᶜAbd al-Bāqī, *Lu'lu',* 2:125.)

149. He died in 43/663 and was one of the people who "helped to transcribe the official canon" of the Koran (Ibn al-Nadīm, *Fihrist,* 48, 377).

150. Past the time of childbearing from the Prophet.

151. A *khuṭbah* may encompass exhortation or admonition, recited by a *khaṭīb* (orator) from the pulpit during the noon service of the congregational mosque on Friday, and generally delivered in rhyming prose (Lane, *Arabic-English Lexicon,* 763).

152. Muslim related it from the hadith of Abū Saᶜīd, reiterating the words of the Prophet: "The greatest betrayal in the opinion of God on the Day of Judgment is for the man to reveal [everything] to the woman and vice versa, then reveal her secret" (ᶜIrāqī).

153. Al-Tirmidhī first related it, but the transmittal is authentic of fair authority (*ḥasan gharīb*); Ibn Mājah related it from the hadith of Umm Salamah (ᶜIrāqī).

154. Al-Ṭabarānī first related it in *al-Awsaṭ* from the hadith of Anas, excluding "by virtue. . . ." The transmittal is weak (ᶜIrāqī).

155. Ibn Ḥabbān related it from the hadith of Abū Hurayrah (ᶜIrāqī).

156. This hadith was first related by Ibn Mājah and al-Ḥakīm, who made it genuine from the hadith of Abī Amāmah, excluding "nursers." This is related by al-Ṭabarānī in *al-Ṣaghīr* (ᶜIrāqī).

157. From the hadith of Ibn ᶜAbbās, which is agreed upon (ᶜIrāqī).

158. Aḥmad related it from the hadith of Abū Amāmah in a weak transmittal, stating "silk" instead of "saffron"; and Muslim from the hadith of ᶜIzzat al-Ashjaᶜīya—its transmittal is also weak (ᶜIrāqī). *Al-aḥmarān* means flesh-meat and wine, which are said to destroy men; it also refers to gold and saffron, which are said to destroy women, that is, the love of ornaments and perfumes, also called *al-aṣfarān* [two yellow things] (Lane, *Arabic-English Lexicon,* 642).

159. Hadith ᶜĀ'ishah; al-Ḥakīm [al-Tirmidhī] first related it and made genuine its transmittal from the hadith of Abū Hurayrah (ᶜIrāqī).

160. Hadith ᶜĀ'ishah; al-Ḥakīm [al-Tirmidhī] first related it and made genuine its transmittal from the hadith of Abū Hurayrah (ᶜIrāqī).

161. Hadith Ibn ᶜAbbās. Al-Bayhaqī first related it in a shortened version, and related it *in toto* from the hadith of Ibn ᶜUmar, but it is weak (ᶜIrāqī).

162. Al-Tirmidhī and Ibn Ḥabbān related it from the hadith of Abū Hurayrah. Also related by Abū Dā'ūd from the hadith of Qays b. Saᶜd, by Ibn Mājah from the hadith of ᶜĀ'ishah, and by Ibn Ḥabbān from the hadith of Ibn Abī Awfā (ᶜIrāqī).

163. Ibn Ḥabbān related only the first part of the hadith of Ibn Masᶜūd; the latter part was related (abridged) by Abū Dā'ūd from his own hadith without mentioning "inner sanctum of the house." Al-Bayhaqī related it from the hadith of ᶜĀ'ishah: "It is better to pray in the house than in the mosque"—its transmittal is of fair authority; and by Ibn Ḥabbān from the hadith of Umm Ḥamīd (ᶜIrāqī).

164. It is related by al-Tirmidhī as genuine, and by Ibn Ḥabbān from the hadith of Ibn Masᶜūd (ᶜIrāqī).

165. This was related by al-Ḥāfiz Abū Bakr Muḥammad b. ᶜUmar al-Jiᶜābī in the *Tārīkh al-Ṭālibīn* from the hadith of ᶜAlī in a weak transmittal; and by al-Ṭabarānī in *al-Ṣaghīr* from the hadith of Ibn ᶜAbbās (ᶜIrāqī).

166. See chapter 1, note 51.

167. Rābiᶜah al-ᶜAdawīyah, orphaned at an early age, was sold into slavery as a child. She later settled in Basra where she was well known as a saint and a preacher and where she was highly esteemed by her pious contemporaries. To her is attributed the theme of divine love in Islamic mysticism. She was a celibate; is often confused with Rābiᶜah of Syria who was married. She is entombed near Jerusalem. Her death date is given variously as 135/752 and 185/801 (cf. Farīd al-Dīn ᶜAṭṭār, *Muslim Saints and Mystics,* 39–51, and M. Smith, *Rābiᶜa the Mystic,* 5–6, 45, 140–43).

168. Abū Dā'ūd al-Ṭayālsī and al-Bayhaqī related it from the hadith of Ibn ᶜUmar; it was also related by Abū Dā'ūd from the hadith of Saᶜd; and by Muslim from the hadith of ᶜĀ'ishah; al-Dāraquṭnī made it genuine in his *al-ᶜIlal.* All had slight variations in their transmittals (ᶜIrāqī).

169. That is, cater to his senses.

170. The word "presence" is missing in this text but appears in the Azharīyah edition.

171. So as not to attract attention. She should not satisfy her own vanity, but be humble and meek.

172. Related by Abū Dā'ūd from the hadith of Abī Mālik al-Ashjaᶜī in a weak transmittal (ᶜIrāqī).

173. Al-Kharā'iṭī related it in *Makārim al-Akhlāq* from the hadith of Abū Hurayrah in a weak transmittal (ᶜIrāqī).

174. This is possibly ᶜAbd al-Mālik b. Qurayb al-Aṣmaᶜī, who was the famous philologist and grammarian at the court of Harūn al Rashīd. He studied the language of the Arabs of the desert, which is considered to be a "pure" model for linguistics. He died in Basra in 213/828 (Ibn al-Nadīm, *Fihrist,* 963).

175. Hadith Muᶜādh which was related by al-Tirmidhī, who said it was authentic and of fair authority; it was related by Ibn Mājah (ᶜIrāqī).

176. Hadith Umm Ḥabībah, agreed upon (ᶜIrāqī).

177. Asmā' was the daughter of Kutayla, Abū Bakr's first wife. She was the elder half-sister of ᶜĀ'ishah and one of the early converts to Islam in Mecca. She was married to al-Zubayr b. al-ᶜAwwām, and their son, ᶜAbdullah, was "reputedly the first child born in the Muslim community" at Medina. She died in Mecca in 73/693 (*Encyclopaedia of Islam,* new ed., s.v. "Asmā' ").

178. Zubayr b. al-ᶜAwwām, cousin and companion of the Prophet, was killed at the Battle of the Camel in 36/656. He was a member of the council to choose the third caliph. He was also referred to as *al-Ḥawāri,* a term that refers to the earliest missionaries of Islam. There were twelve *Ḥawāri*s, "who are said to have been appointed *naqīb*s of the Medinans" by Muhammad (or by those present) as "surety for their people just as the apostles were sureties for ᶜĪsā b. Maryam" (Ibn al-Nadīm, *Fihrist,* 292–93, 1133).

179. A parasang is a Persian measure of length, anciently of about thirty stadia (2.8 to 4.2 miles).

180. Hadith of Asmā', agreed upon (ᶜIrāqī).

181. The Azharīyah edition indicates that she came upon the Prophet.

APPENDIX A

1. Massignon, *Recueil de textes inédits;* repeated by Brockelmann, *Geschichte der arabischen Literatur*; Palacios, *La Espiritualidad de Algazel*; Watt, "Authenticity of the Works Attributed to al-Ghazali"; Jabre, *La Notion de certitude*

selon Ghazali; Macdonald, "Life of al-Ghazzali"; *Shorter Encyclopaedia of Islam,* 111–14; Bouyges, *Essai de chronologie des oeuvres de al-Ghazali,* 9–11.

2. Rosenthal, *Political Thought in Medieval Islam,* 38.
3. Scherer, "Introduction."
4. al-Ghazālī, *Counsel for Kings,* xxxvi.

Bibliography

Abbott, Nabia. "Women and the State in Early Islam." *Journal of Near Eastern Studies* 1 (1942):106–26, 341–68.

ʿAbd al-Bāqī, Muḥammad Fuʾād. *Al-Muʿjam al-Mufahras li-'Alfāẓ al-Qurʾān al-Karīm.* Cairo: ʿĪsā al-Bābī al-Ḥalabī, 1968.

——————. *Al-Luʾluʾ wa al-Marjān.* 3 vols. Cairo: ʿĪsā al-Bābī al-Ḥalabī, 1949.

Abū Dāʾūd. *Al-Sunan.* 2 vols. Cairo: Muṣṭafā al-Bābī al-Ḥalabī, 1952.

Abū al-Faraj al-Iṣbahānī. *Kitāb al-Aghānī.* 23 vols. Beirut: Dār al-Thaqafah, 1957–61.

Abū al-Nūr, Muḥammad al-Aḥmadī. *Manhaj al-Sunnah fī al-Zawāj.* Egypt, 1972.

ʿAfīfī, Ṭāhā ʿAbd Allāh. *Ḥaqq al-Zawj ʿalā zawjatihi wa ḥaqq al-Zawjah ʿalā Zawjihā.* Egypt, 1980.

ʿAlī, A. Y. *The Holy Qurʾān: Arabic Text with English Translation and Commentary.* Lahore: Aḥmadīyah Anjuman Ishāʿ at Islam, 1951.

Ali, Ameer. *The Spirit of Islam.* London: Christophers, 1955.

Ali, Muhammad. *Maulana. A Manual of Hadith.* Lahore: Ahmadiyya Anjuman Ishaat Islam, 1944, 1951.

Allman, James, ed. *Women's Status and Fertility in the Muslim World.* New York and London: Praeger Publishers, 1978.

Alwaye, Mohiaddin. "The Status of Woman in Islam." *Majlis al-Azhar* 47, no. 4 (1975):1–5.

ʿAmārah, Muṣṭafā Muḥammad. *Jawāhir al-Bukhārī.* Cairo: Al-Maktabah al-Tijārīyah al-Kubrā, 1922.

Amiruddin, Begum Sultan Mir. "Woman's Status in Islam." *Muslim World* 28 (1939):153–63.

Anawati, G. C., and Louis Gardet. *Mystique musulmane.* Paris: J. Vrin, 1961.

——————. *Introduction à la théologie musulmane.* Paris: Etudes de Philosophie médiévale, 1948.

Andrae, Tor. *Mohammed: The Man and His Faith.* New York: Charles Scribner's Sons, 1936.

Arberry, A. J. *Classical Persian Literature.* London: Unwin Brothers, 1958.

———. *Sufism: An Account of the Mystics of Islam.* London: Allen & Unwin, 1950.

———. *Religion in the Middle East: Three Religions in Concord and Conflict.* Vol. 2, *Islam.* Cambridge: Cambridge University Press, 1969.

———. *The Holy Koran: An Introduction with Selections.* London: Allen & Unwin, 1953.

———. *The Koran Interpreted: A Translation.* 2 vols. Toronto: Macmillan; London: Allen & Unwin, 1955.

Arnold, Sir Thomas, and Alfred Guillaume. *The Legacy of Islam.* London: Oxford University Press, 1960.

al-Aṣbahānī, Aḥmad b. ᶜAbdallah. *Hulliyyat al-Awliyā',* vol. 1. Cairo: Al-Khānji and al-Saᶜādah, 1351/1932–33.

ᶜAzzam, ᶜAbd al-Rahman. *The Eternal Message of Muhammad.* Translated by Caesar E. Farah. New York: Devin-Adair Co., 1964.

Badāwī, ᶜAbd al-Raḥmān. *Mu'allafāt al-Ghazālī.* Cairo: Al-Majlis al-Aᶜlā li Riᶜāyat al-Funūn wa al-Ādāb wa al-ᶜUlūm al-Ijtimāᶜīyah, 1961.

Bashir, Zakaria. *Muslim Women in the Midst of Change.* Leicester: Islamic Foundation, 1980.

Basyūnī, Ibrāhīm. *Nash'at al-Taṣawwuf al-Islāmī.* Cairo: Dār al-Maᶜārif, 1969.

Beck, Lois, and Nikki Keddie, eds. *Women in the Muslim World.* Cambridge: Harvard University Press, 1978.

Bercher, Leon. "Extrait du Livre XXIII du *Kitāb Iḥyā' ᶜUlūm al-Dīn* d'al-Gazālī." *Hesperis* 40 (1953):313–31.

Berque, J. "Sociologies de ou sur l'Islam?" *Archives de Sociologie de religions* 46 (1978):193.

Bint al-Shāṭi'. *Nisā' al-Nabī.* Egypt, 1965.

Bousquet, Georges Henri. *L'Authentique tradition musulmane: Choix de h'adiths par el Bokhari.* Paris: Fasquelle, 1964.

———. *L'Ethique sexuelle de l'Islam.* Paris: Maisonneuve et Larose, 1966.

Bouyges, Maurice. *Essai de chronologie des oeuvres de al-Ghazzali.* Édité et mis à jour par Michel Allard. Beirut: Imprimerie Catholique, 1959.

Brockelmann, C. *Geschichte der arabischen Literatur.* Supplementband I. Leiden: E. J. Brill, 1937.

Brown, John P. *The Dervishes.* London: Trubner & Co., 1869.

Browne, Edward G. *A Literary History of Persia.* 4 vols. Cambridge: Cambridge University Press, 1969.

al-Bukhārī, Abū ᶜAbdallah. *The Translation of the Meanings of Ṣaḥīḥ al-Bukhārī.* Arabic-English by Dr. Muhammad Muhsin Khan. 3 vols. Chicago: Kazi Publications, 1977–79.

———. *Ṣaḥīḥ al-Bukhārī.* 9 vols. Cairo: M. A. Ṣabīḥ, n.d.

Bukhsh, S. Khuda. *Marriage and Family Life Among the Arabs.* West Pakistan: Sh. Muhammad Ashraf, 1953.

Bultājī, Muḥammad. *Dirāsāt fī aḥkām al-usrah.* Egypt, 1974.

Burckhardt, Titus. *An Introduction to Sufi Doctrine.* Lahore: Sh. Muhammad Ashraf, 1959.

Carpenter, Edward. *Intermediate Types Among Primitive Folk.* New York: Arno Press, 1975.

Castagen, J. *Le Mouvement d'emancipation de la femme musulmane en Orient.* Paris: Librarie Orientaliste Paul Geuthner, 1929.

de St. Elie, Anastase Marie. "La Femme du desert autrefois et aujourd'hui." *Anthropos* 3 (1908):53–67, 181–92.

DeVaux, Baron Carra. *Les Penseurs de l'Islam.* Paris: Librairie Orientaliste Paul Geuthner, 1923.

Donaldson, D. M. "Temporary Marriage in Iran." *Muslim World* 26 (1936): 358–64.

Encyclopaedia of Islam. 4 vols. and supplement. New ed. Leiden: E. J. Brill, 1965.

Essad, Bey. *Mohammed: A Biography.* Translated by Helmut L. Ripperger. New York: Longmans, Green & Co., 1936.

Fadel, Mustapha. *Islamic Law and Modern Life.* Ministry of Foreign Cultural Relations. Cairo: Al-Shaᶜb Printing House, 1966(?).

Farah, Caesar E. *Islam: Beliefs and Observances.* New York: Barron's Educational Series, 1968.

————. "A Bibliographical Guide to Islamic Philosophy and Mysticism." Unpublished ms.

Farīd al-Dīn ᶜAṭṭār. *Muslim Saints and Mystics: Episodes from the Tadhkirat al-Auliya'.* Translated by A. J. Arberry. Chicago: University of Chicago Press, 1966.

Fawqi, Lamia. "Women's Rights and the Muslim Women." *Islam and the Modern Age* 32 (1972):76–99.

Fyzee, Asaf A. A. *Outlines of Muhammadan Law.* 3d ed. London: Oxford University Press, 1964.

al-Ghandūr, Aḥmad. *Al-Ṭalāq fī al-sharīᶜah al-Islāmīyah wa al-qānūn.* Egypt, 1967.

al-Ghazālī, Abū Ḥāmid. *The Confessions of al-Ghazali.* Translated by Claud Field. Lahore: Ashraf, n.d.

————. *The Faith and Practice of al-Ghazali.* Translated by W. Montgomery Watt. London: Allen & Unwin, 1953, 1963.

————. *Ghazali's Book of Counsel for Kings (Naṣīhat al-Mulūk).* Translated by F. R. C. Bagley. London: Oxford University Press, 1964.

————. *Iḥ'ya ᶜouloûm el-din; ou Vivification des sciences de la foi.* Analyse et index par G. H. Bousquet. Paris: M. Besson, 1955.

————. *Iḥyā' ᶜUlūm al-Dīn.* 4 vols. Cairo: Al-Maṭbaᶜath al-Azharīyah al-Misrīyah, 1302/1884–85.

————. *Iḥyā' ᶜUlūm al-Dīn.* Cairo: Al-Maktabah al-Tijārīyah al-Kubrā, n.d.

__________. *Iḥyā' ᶜUlūm al-Dīn.* 2d ed. 4 vols. Cairo: Al-Ḥalabī, 1967.

__________. *The Mysteries of Almsgiving.* Translated by Nabih Amin Faris from al-Ghazali's Iḥyā' ᶜUlūm al-Dīn. Beirut: Centennial Publications, 1966.

__________. *The Mysteries of Purity.* Translated by Nabih Amin Faris from al-Ghazali's Iḥyā' ᶜUlūm al-Dīn. Lahore: Ashraf, 1966.

__________. *O jeune homme.* Translated by Toufic Sabbagh. Beirut: Imprimerie Catholique, 1951, 1969.

al-Ghulāmī, Muḥammad Ra'īf. *Aṣḥāb Badr.* Baghdad: n.p., 1966.

Gibb, H. A. R. *Studies on the Civilization of Islam.* Edited by Stanford J. Shaw and William R. Polk. Boston: Beacon Press, 1962.

__________. *Arabic Literature.* London: Oxford University Press, 1963.

__________. *Mohammedanism.* London: Oxford University Press, 1957.

Goldziher, Ignác. *A Short History of Classical Arabic Literature.* Translated, revised, and enlarged by Joseph Desmogyi. Hildesheim: George Olms, 1966.

__________. *Muslim Studies.* Edited by S. M. Stern. 2 vols. London: Allen & Unwin, 1971.

Guillaume, A. *The Life of Muhammad.* A translation of Isḥāq's *Sīrat Rasūl Allāh.* London: Oxford University Press, 1955.

__________. *The Traditions of Islam.* Oxford: Clarendon Press, 1924.

al-Ḥakīm, Muḥammad Taqī. *Al-Zawāj al-muwaqqat.* Beirut: n.p., n.d.

Happold, F. C. *Mysticism: A Study and an Anthology.* New York: Penguin Books, 1967.

Hastings, J., ed. *Encyclopaedia of Religions and Ethics.* 13 vols. New York: Scribner's, 1908–26.

Hitti, Philip K. *History of the Arabs.* London: Macmillan & Co., 1960.

Hourani, George F. "The Chronology of Ghazali's Writings." *American Oriental Series Journal* 79 (1959):225–33.

Hughes, T. P. *A Dictionary of Islam.* London: W. H. Allen & Co., 1885.

al-Ḥujwīrī, ᶜAlī b. ᶜUthmān. *Kashf al-Maḥjūb of Ḥujwīrī.* Translated by R. A. Nicholson. E. S. W. Gibb Memorial, vol. 17. Leiden: E. J. Brill, 1911.

Ibn Ḥajar al-ᶜAsqalānī, Aḥmad ibn ᶜAlī. *Iṣābah fī Tamyīz al-Ṣaḥābah.* 4 vols. Cairo: Maṭbaᶜath M. Muḥammad, 1939.

__________. *Kitāb Tahdhīb al-Tahdhīb.* Hyderabad: Majlas dā'irat al-Maᶜārif, 1325/1907–8.

Ibn Ḥanbal, Aḥmad b. Muḥammad. *Musnad al-Imām Aḥmad b. Ḥanbal.* 6 vols. Beirut: Al-Maktab al-Islāmī, 1969.

Ibn Iskandar, Kaykāvūs. *Qābūs Nāmah.* Milli, Iran, 1963.

Ibn al-Jawzī, Abū al-Faraj ᶜAbd al-Raḥmān b. ᶜAlī. *Talbīs Iblīs.* Beirut: Dār al-Waᶜy al-Arabī, n.d.

__________. *Zād al-Masīr fī ᶜIlm al-Tafsīr.* Beirut: n.p., 1965.

Ibn Kallikān. *Wafayāt al-Aᶜyān.* Cairo: Maktabah al-Wahḍah al-Miṣrīyah, 1957.

Ibn Kathīr, Ismāʿīl b. ʿUmar. *Tafsīr al-Qur'ān.* Cairo: Maṭbaʿath al-Istiqamah, 1954.

Ibn Mājah, Muḥammad b. Yazīd. *Sunan b. Mājah.* 2 vols. Cairo: ʿĪsā al-Bābī al-Ḥalabī, 1952.

Ibn Manẓūr, Jamāl al-Dīn Muḥammad b. Mukarram al-Anṣārī. *Lisān al-ʿArab.* 20 vols. Cairo: Maṭbaʿath al-Amirīah, 1882–89.

Ibn al-Nadīm. *The Fihrist of al-Nadīm.* Edited and translated by Bayard Dodge. New York and London: Columbia University Press, 1970.

Ibn al-Sharīf, Maḥmūd. *Al-Islām wal-ḥayāt al-jinsīyyah.* Egypt, 1960.

Ibn Sīnā. *Rasā'il Ibn Sīnā.* Cairo: n.p., 1910.

Ibn Ṭufayl. *Ḥayy b. Yakẓān.* Damascus: Damascus Press, 1962.

Index Islamicas. Cambridge: W. Heffer & Co., 1958, 1956–60. Supplement, published 1962.

The Interpreter's Dictionary of the Bible. 4 vols. New York: Abingdon Press, 1962.

Jabre, Farid. *Essai sur le lexique de Ghazali.* Beirut: Publications de l'Université Libanaise, 1970.

———. *La Notion de certitude selon Ghazali: Dans ses origines psychologiques et historiques.* Paris: J. Vrin, 1958.

al-Jāḥiẓ. *The Life and Works of Jāḥiẓ.* Translations of selected texts by Charles Pellat; translated from the French by D. M. Hawke. London: Routledge & Kegan Paul, 1969.

———. *Le Livre des avares de Ǧāḥiẓ.* Traduction française avec une introd. et des notes par Charles Pellat. Paris: Maisonneuve, 1951.

Jāmī, ʿAbd al-Raḥmān b. Aḥmad. *Nafaḥāt al-Uns.* Tehran: Kitab Firushi Mahmudi, 1337/1918.

Jilānī, Ḥazrat Shaikh Muḥyiddīn Abdul Qādir. *Futūḥ al-Ghaib: Or, the Revelations of the Unseen.* 2d ed. Translated by Maulavi Aftab-ud-Din Ahmad. Lahore: Maktaba Nawa-i-Waqt, 1958.

al-Junayd ibn Muḥammad, Abū al-Qāsim. *The Life, Personality and Writings of al-Junayd.* Translated by Ali Hassan Abdel-Kader. E. J. W. Gibb Memorial, New Series, vol. 22. London: Luzac & Co., 1962.

Kalābādhī, Abū Bakr Muḥammad. *The Doctrine of the Sufis (Kitāb al-Taʿarruf li-Madhhab ahl al-Taṣawwuf).* Translated by A. J. Arberry. Cambridge: Cambridge University Press, 1935.

Keddie, Nikki R. "Problems in the Study of Middle East Women." *International Journal of Middle East Studies* 10 (1979):225–40.

Kennedy, Pringle. *Arabian Society at the Time of Muhammad.* Calcutta: Thacker, Spink & Co., 1933.

Kettani, M. Ali. *The Muslim Minorities.* Leicester: Islamic Foundation, 1979.

Lammens, H. *Islam: Beliefs and Institutions.* Translated from the French by Sir E. Denison Ross. New York: Dutton & Co., 1926.

———. *L'Islam: Croyances et institutions.* Beirut: Imprimerie Catholique, 1943.

Lane, Edward William. *Arabian Society in the Middle Ages.* Edited by Stanley Lane-Poole. New York: Barnes & Noble, 1873.

———. *Arabic-English Lexicon,* Book I, 8 parts. Edited by Stanley Lane-Poole. New York: Frederick Ungar, 1955.

al-Laythī, Ḥasan Muḥammad. *Al-Taṣawwuf fī al-Islām.* Cairo: Dār al-Fikr al-Ḥadīth, n.d.

Levy, Reuben. *The Social Structure of Islam.* Cambridge: Cambridge University Press, 1957.

Macdonald, Duncan B. *Development of Muslim Theology, Jurisprudence and Constitutional Theory.* Beirut: Khayyāts, 1965.

———. "The Life of al-Ghazzali." *American Oriental Series Journal* 20 (1899):71–132.

Mahmood, Tahir. *Family Planning: The Muslim Viewpoint.* New Delhi: Vikas, 1977.

al-Maqdisī, Jūrj. *Ibn ᶜAqīl et la résurgence de l'Islam traditionaliste. . . .* Damas: Institut français de Damas, 1963.

al-Makkī, Abū Ṭālib Muḥammad b. ᶜAlī. *Kitāb Qūt al-Qulūb.* 2 vols. Cairo: Maymunīyah, 1306/1888–89.

Mālik b. Anas. *Al-Muwaṭṭa'.* 2 vols. Cairo: Al-Majlis al-Aᶜlā lil Shu'ūn al-Islāmīyah, 1951.

Margoliouth, D. S. *The Early Development of Mohammedanism.* London: Williams and Norgate, 1914.

Massignon, Louis. *Essai sur les origines du lexique technique de la mystique musulmane.* Paris: J. Vrin, 1954.

———. *La Passion d'al-Hallaj, martyr mystique de l'Islam.* Paris: n.p., 1922.

———. *Receuils de textes inédits concernant l'histoire de la mystique en pays d'Islam.* Paris: Librairie orientaliste Paul Geuthner, 1929.

Massignon, Louis, and Paul Kraus. *Akhbar al-Hallaj.* Arabic-French text. Paris: Imprimerie "Au Calame," 1936.

Mole, Marijan. *Les Mystiques musulmans.* Paris: Presses Universitaires de France, 1965.

Al-Munjid. 20th ed. Beirut: Dār al-Mashriq, 1969.

Muslim b. al-Ḥajjāj al-Qushayrī. *Kitāb Ṣaḥīḥ al-Imām al-Ḥafiẓ Abī al-Ḥusayn Muslim.* Cairo: Maṭbaᶜath al-Saᶜādah, 1327/1909.

Nader, Albert Nasri. *Les Principales sectes musulmanes.* Beirut: Imprimerie Catholique, 1958.

———. *Al-Taṣawwuf al-Islāmī.* Beirut: Catholic Publications, 1960.

Nasr, Seyyed Hossein. *Sufi Essays.* London: Allen & Unwin, 1972.

———. "The Sufi Master as Exemplified in Persian Sufi Literature." *Iran* 5 (1967):35–40.

Nawab ᶜAlī, Sayed. *Some Moral and Religious Teachings of al-Ghazzali: Translation of Extracts from his* Iḥyā' *and* Minhāj-ul-Ābidīn. Lahore: Ashraf, 1944.

Nelson, C. "Social Change and Sexual Identity in Contemporary Egypt." In *Responses to Change*, ed. G. A. DeVos, pp. 323–41. New York: Van Nostrand Reinhold, 1976.

Nicholson, Reynold A. *The Idea of Personality in Sufism.* Lahore: Ashraf, 1964.

———. *A Literary History of the Arabs.* Cambridge: Cambridge University Press, 1953.

———. *The Mystics of Islam.* London: Bell & Sons, 1914.

———. *Studies in Islamic Mysticism.* Cambridge: Cambridge University Press, 1921.

———. *Translations of Eastern Poetry and Prose.* Cambridge: Cambridge University Press, 1922.

Palacios, Asin. *La Esperitualidad de Algazel y sus Sentidos Cristiano,* vol. 4. Madrid-Granada: Crestomatia Algazeliana, 1941.

Patai, Raphael. *Society, Culture and Change in the Middle East.* 3d ed. Philadelphia: University of Pennsylvania Press, 1971.

Pennings, Gerrit J. "The Moslem Convert and Polygamy." *Muslim World* 28 (1939):164–79.

Pickthall, Muhammed Marmaduke. *The Glorious Koran.* New York: New American Library, 1954.

al-Qushayrī, Abū al-Qāsim. *Al-Risālah al-Qushayrīyah.* Cairo: Saᶜādah, 1954.

el-Rashidi, Galal. *The Arabs and the World of the Seventies.* New Delhi: Vikas, 1977.

Rosenthal, Erwin I. J. *Political Thought in Medieval Islam.* Cambridge (England): Cambridge University Press, 1962.

Russell, Alexander David, and Abdullah al-Ma'mun Suhrawardy. *First Steps in Muslim Jurisprudence.* London: Luzac & Co., 1963.

al-Saᶜdāwī, Nawāl. *The Hidden Face of Eve: Women in the Arab World.* Translated and edited by Sherif Hetata. London: Zed Press, 1980.

al-Sarrāj, Abū Naṣr. *The Kitāb al-Lumaᶜ. . . .* Edited by R. A. Nicholson. E. J. W. Gibb Memorial, vol. 22. Leiden: E. J. Brill, 1914.

Schacht, Joseph. *An Introduction to Islamic Law.* Oxford: Clarendon Press, 1964.

———. *The Origins of Muhammadan Jurisprudence.* Oxford: Clarendon Press, 1959.

Schaya, Leo. *La Doctrine soufique de l'Unité.* Paris: Adrien-Maisonneuve, 1962.

Scherer, G. H. "Introduction" in *Ayyuhā al-Walad* by al-Ghazālī. Translated by Toufic Sabbagh. Beirut: n.p., 1951.

al-Shāfiᶜī, Muḥammad b. Idrīs. *Al-Risālah.* Cairo: Muṣṭafā al-Bābī al-Ḥalabī, 1940.

Shafqat, C. M. *The Muslim Marriage, Dower and Divorce.* Lahore: n.p.,1955.

Shahristānī, Imām Abū al-Fāth Muḥammad b. ᶜAbd al-Karīm. *Al-Milal wa-al-Niḥal.* 3 vols. Cairo: Maṭbaᶜath Ḥijāzī, 1948.

al-Shintināwī, Aḥmad. *Taṭawwur al-ᶜAlāqāt al-Jinsīyyah.* Egypt, 1969.

Shorter Encyclopedia of Islam. Leiden: E. J. Brill, 1953.

Shukri, Aḥmed. *Muhammedan Law of Marriage and Divorce.* New York: AMS Press, 1966.

Siddiqui, Muhammad M. *Women in Islam.* Lahore: Institute of Islamic Culture, 1952.

Smith, Jane I. *Women in Contemporary Muslim Societies.* London: Association of University Presses, 1980.

Smith, Margaret. *Rabiʿa the Mystic and Her Fellow-Saints in Islam.* Cambridge: Cambridge University Press, 1928.

__________. *Al-Ghazzali, the Mystic.* London: Luzac & Co., 1944.

__________. *Studies in Early Mysticism in the Near and Middle East.* London: Sheldon Press, 1931.

Smith, W. Robertson. *Kinship and Marriage in Early Arabia.* Boston: Beacon Press, 1903.

Stern, Gertrude H. *Marriage in Early Islam.* London: The Royal Asiatic Society, 1939.

__________. "Muhammad's Bond with the Women." *British Society of Oriental and Asiatic Studies* 10 (1940–42):185–97.

al-Suhrawardī, Imām. *ʿAwārif al-Maʿārif.* (Written in margin of al-Ghazālī's *Iḥyā',* vol. 2.) Cairo: Al-Maṭbaʿath al-Azharīyah al-Misrīyah, 1302/1884–85.

al-Suhrawardy, Allama Sir Abdullah al-Mamun. *The Sayings of Muhammad.* Foreword by Mahatma Gandhi. London: Bitler & Tanner, 1945.

al-Tirmidhī, Muḥammad b. ʿĪsā. *Sunan al-Tirmidhī.* 10 vols. Homs: Fajr, 1967.

Unat, Faik Resit. *Hicri Tarihleri Miladi Tarihe Cevirme Kilavuzu.* Ankara: Turk Tarih Kurumu Basimevi, 1959.

Von Grunebaum, Gustave E. *Medieval Islam: A Study in Cultural Orientation.* 2d ed. Chicago: University of Chicago Press, 1953.

Watt, W. Montgomery. "The Authenticity of the Works Attributed to al-Ghazali." *Journal of the Royal Asiatic Society,* 1952: 24–45.

__________. *Companion to the Qur'ān.* London: Allen & Unwin, 1967.

__________. *Islam and the Integration of Society.* London: Routledge & Kegan Paul, 1961.

__________. *Islamic Philosophy and Theology.* Edinburgh: University Press, 1962.

__________. *Muslim Intellectual: A Study of al-Ghazali.* Chicago: Aldine Publishing Co., 1963.

__________. "The Study of al-Ghazālī." *Oriens* 13–14 (1961):121–31.

__________. *Truth in the Religions.* Edinburgh: University Press, n.d.

Wehr, Hans. *A Dictionary of Modern Written Arabic.* Edited by J. Milton Cowan. New York: Cornell University Press, 1966.

Wensinck, A. J. *Concordance et indices de la tradition musulmane: Les Six livres le Musnad d'al-Darimi, le Muwatt' de Malik, le Musnad de Ahmad ibn Hanbal.* Leiden: E. J. Brill, 1936–69.

———. *A Handbook of Early Muhammadan Traditions.* Leiden: E. J. Brill, 1927.

———. *La Pensée de Ghazzali.* Paris: Adrien-Maisonneuve, 1940.

Woodsmall, Ruth Frances. *Moslem Women Enter a New World.* New York: Round Table Press, 1936.

———. *Women and the New East.* Washington, D.C.: The Middle East Institute, 1960.

Index